brothers

brothers

from childhood to oasis
the real story

Paul Gallagher
& Terry Christian

Virgin

First published in Great Britain in 1996 by
Virgin Books
an imprint of Virgin Publishing Ltd
332 Ladbroke Grove
LONDON W10 5AH

A catalogue record for this book is available from the
British Library.

ISBN 1 85227 671 1

Type design by Roger Kohn
Picture sections designed by Eric Drewery
Typeset by TW Typesetting, Plymouth, Devon
Printed and bound by
Mackays of Chatham, Lordswood, Kent

This book is dedicated to my mother and two brothers, Noel and Liam. Also to my grandmother, Margaret, without whom this book wouldn't have been possible.

Paul Gallagher, 1996

Contents

Acknowledgements

Thanks to everyone at MPC Entertainment, particularly Michael Cohen and Nigel Forsyth, and everyone at Virgin Publishing, particularly Rob Shreeve, Hannah MacDonald and Mal Peachey. Thanks also to all my friends for their support. You know who you are. Thanks to Alan McGee for believing in me.

Paul Gallagher

Thanks to everyone at Red Alert for all their patience, Paul Bardsley, The Burnage Boys, Tony Meehan, my brother Kevin for sorting my computer's strange personality out, and all the editors at Virgin Publishing, especially Rob Shreeve, Mal Peachey, Hannah MacDonald and Ben Dunn, for their patience, insight and valuable help. Thanks also to Penny Anderson and Steve Colwell for being there first, Noel Gallagher for all the great songs, Louise Jones, Peggy Gallagher for being a diamond, everyone in Ireland for the warm welcome on our travels, especially in Ballina, Longford and Charlestown, everyone at MPC, especially Nigel Forsyth and Michael Cohen, Vinny Davies for being so reliable, and Mick Middles and Sarah Champion for the inspiration. Finally, thanks to my long-suffering girlfriend and all my family and friends who thought I'd turned into a hermit – get the beers in!

Terry Christian

Sources

Manchester Evening News; Uptown; City Life; NME; Melody Maker; Vox; Select; Smash Hits; The Times; Observer; Guardian; Herb Garden (fanzine); *News of the World; Daily Mirror; Daily Star; Daily Mail; Irish Sun; Dublin Herald; USA Today; LA Times; New York Times; Spin; TV Hits; Just Seventeen.*

Introduction

I always wanted to achieve something in life, but generally, as you'll see from this story, most of my expectations were low. I dreamed my way through school and work, sometimes with the aid of artificial stimulants, but with the exception of Manchester City Football Club, never really had a love or a passion I could express or share.

I love my mother and both my brothers, but it's not a comfortable love. It's locked inside somewhere and gets mixed up with other emotions. I grew up with Noel and Liam. We were just brothers and on the outside we appeared the same as anybody else, if a bit more argumentative and disagreeable. Then one day they both showed a staggering talent for music and a surge of confidence that led them to achieve. It left me questioning my life. I shared the same genetic material, was of the same blood, I even had the same kind of burning desire to prove myself, but I felt like a failure. Suddenly their lives changed and so did mine and I'm still scrambling around in my head trying to work out whether it was for the better. Contentment to me was working in a job that paid more than £120 a week, Manchester City winning a game (which wasn't happening often), and thinking that my mother would always be there. I wondered why I couldn't feel any real love for anyone outside of my family or express it for anyone inside.

My two younger brothers went on to become celebrities. They are adored by fans and receive accolades from all sorts of strangers – and usually accept them gracefully. People crowd in on them, squeezing me out. I wanted to tell them that I was proud and happy for them too, but somewhere inside it got stuck with the submerged junk of my life's experiences. When strangers pressed around my brothers telling them how fantastic and talented they were, I realised I was in awe of them, too. It hit me like a rocket; I couldn't be myself with my

BROTHERS

own brothers, because I didn't know who I was; I never did. I was frightened. Those feelings were hard to understand.

It wasn't solely a case of jealousy, although there was a little; there always has been among the three of us. The paradox was that we were never really comfortable with each other, and the way I felt was in danger of driving us even further apart. Every accolade and award they achieved became another reminder of how different our lives were and of how unfulfilled I felt. What was wrong with me? Then I began to think of the times when we were kids, and I realised that all the feelings I had and especially the ones I didn't have, were buried there – the feelings of low self-esteem, the constant seeking of approval from others, not wanting to be left out, the immature way I acted, the lack of understanding of my own emotions that would suddenly erupt like a volcano, and the deep and profound sadness I sometimes felt within.

It came to me one day. The thoughts that crept up on me at night when I was alone and the hurt that seemed such a normal part of me, was something I'd shared with Noel and Liam. It wasn't pop music or stardom that had driven us apart; it was that they could express that hurt through music. They could put it across through their concerts and their records, and the answers were in those songs for me, too.

So then there was this book. This is my personal catharsis, for what it's worth. It's not a sad story, despite the tragic and sometimes comic contents. It's a story of what made and shaped what to me is the best rock and roll band in the world today. So to all the people who see this book and think, Oh look, Mr Paul Anthony Gallagher is cashing in on his brothers' fame, yes you are right, and I'm spending every penny to buy myself some self-esteem and understanding of how all our lives have changed. I'm confident that not even my mam has got that catalogue.

xii

Foreword: In the beginning . . .

They invite strangers to their banquets, and only after the meal do they ask who they are and of what they stand in need. At dinner they are wont to be moved by chance remarks to wordy disputes and, after a challenge, to fight in single combat, regarding their lives as naught . . . they frequently exaggerate with the aim of extolling themselves and diminishing the status of others. They are boasters and threateners and given to bombastic self-dramatisation, and yet they are quick of mind and with good natural ability for learning. They also have lyric poets whom they call 'Bards'. They sing to the accompaniment of instruments resembling lyres, sometimes a eulogy, and sometimes a satire. They have also certain philosophers and theologians who are treated with special honour, whom they call 'Druids'. The whole race is madly fond of war, high-spirited and quick to battle, but otherwise straightforward and not of evil character. To the frankness and high spiritedness of their temperament must be added traits of childish boastfulness and love of decoration. They wear ornaments of gold, torques on their necks, and bracelets on their arms and wrists, while people of high rank wear dyed garments besprinkled with gold. It is this vanity which makes them so unbearable in victory and so utterly downcast in defeat. They let their hair grow long and wear baggy trousers; instead of the ordinary tunics they wear divided tunics with sleeves, reaching down as far as their private parts and the buttocks.

Posidonius writing about the Celts, 160 BC

How apt that the ancient Celts should share the same personality traits and fashion sense as half the Manchester bands over the past ten years. I've always been of the opinion that culturally Manchester owes a huge debt to the Irish. Many of its famous musical sons and daughters have been of Irish descent, from Peter Noone of Herman's Hermits fame in the sixties via John Maher and Steve Garvey of the Buzzcocks, most of the Fall, to all the members of the Smiths (Stephen Patrick Morrissey, Johnny Marr, Andy Rourke and Mike Joyce) – Manchester Irish, immigrant white folk trying to make their way in an Anglo-Saxon society, never quite fitting in. Most people of Celtic ancestry will recognise in themselves many of the traits described above by a Roman historian over 2000 years ago – with fire in the blood and folk in the soul. With a love of stories, argument, music, parties and over-indulgence, the ancient Celts were born to rock.

This book is about Manchester's most famous sons of the 'Gael', a story both private and true. Hype and fiction are no strangers to rock and roll, but any stories fabricated for press consumption have no place here – the truth is laid bare. The real story is fascinating and builds a more complex picture of the lads from Manchester than any scally-type mythologies currently in circulation. Everyone who knows Noel Gallagher will tell you he is a brilliant storyteller and that he's great company down the pub (a rare talent in itself), but it's the passion and honesty in his music that blows everything else away. It's a talent that eclipses any egotistical rantings. Noel's own bragging and, at times, graceless vituperation of his musical peers, doesn't describe the music within him, and if he sometimes despairs and thinks someone an idiot for not appreciating his musical achievements, I'd say given the evidence he's perfectly justified. Noel Gallagher possesses an ingenious grasp of what makes a great song, and if pop means popular, then he's pop music's number one writer. It's alienating for any human being to be described as a genius. There's no doubting that in the maelstrom of overnight rock and roll fame, what the music business calls 'the Mindfuck' sets in. Noel's doubts cause him to wrestle with self-realisation.

Liam Gallagher is as complex in his own way as Noel. Liam has taken on the mantle of the ultimate scally. The latest edition of the *Oxford English Dictionary* defines a scally as a rogue or a chancer from Liverpool or Manchester, but it's much more than that. Scally is the expression of the aspiring working classes in the new technological age. The phenomenon will be explored in the course of this book. Liam is different from Noel; being perhaps more indulged in his youth, he is no stranger to his own share of the limelight. That was important in helping to forge the type of self-belief which carried the band to the very top.

As for Oasis, I was first made aware of them in the spring of 1992. At that time I was writing 'The Word' column in the *Manchester Evening News*; a whole page dedicated to covering up-and-coming pop talent from the northwest of England. Culturally Manchester is very much a second city to London, in the same way that Barcelona is to Madrid. The city has the largest student population in western Europe and a very cosmopolitan outlook. Musically, it's got a healthy tradition of rock and roll going all the way back to the Hollies, the Bee Gees and Herman's Hermits in the sixties; through to 10cc, the Buzzcocks and Joy Division in the seventies; until it really exploded in the eighties with New Order, Simply Red, the Smiths, the Stone Roses and some of the best clubs and dance music in Europe.

In Manchester at any one time there are literally hundreds of bands rehearsing and trying to find a gig. It's the classic way out of the inner city, the school kid's dream, a passport to a different if not better life. The money and the fame obviously have their appeal on the surface, but it's the burning desire to get out there and say 'I'm someone' that really drives these musicians on. If this is lacking, they rarely get past first base in this city. Following the local music scene isn't a proto student thing in Manchester, despite the sheer numbers in and around the city centre. Almost everyone in Manchester knows somebody directly or indirectly who's in a band. Gigs are often attended out of curiosity and because it's a big mates and extended family night out. The music in the early stages is almost peripheral to the get-together. It's the working classes who follow the scene and give critical acclaim or verbal damnation to any new group starting out. Word of mouth is everything and it's a long and frustrating process for would-be pop stars playing to an audience of mates and cynics. Audiences made up of friends and family aren't going to be kind, not in a place as unforgiving as Manchester. Just like a football crowd they'll jeer and poke fun if a gig's a flop or the band are ropy, but if you're getting out there and doing the business they'll get behind you. Once a group from Manchester start headlining, the buzz goes out, and that audience really wants their money's worth, even the ones on the mammoth guest lists. It's not enough to be merely good; you have to sparkle with originality, show some panache and serious attitude. People in Manchester want to see the home side go all the way and play the beautiful game at the same time.

In 1992 it seemed that outside mainstream pop, the doors of the national music press were firmly shut to bands from Manchester; but Manchester had a self-sustaining scene. There were plenty of outlets locally for bands from the area. Back in 1990, ex-indie pirate station KFM in Stockport became Britain's first and, to date, only indie music station geared to playing at least one third of its music by artists from within a 30 mile radius of Manchester. There was little or no support from the national music press who were more concerned with gaining a licence for XFM in London than giving a breath of publicity to a station already covering south Manchester and north Cheshire. KFM was groundbreaking in many ways. The entire evening output concentrated on sessions and interviews with local bands. Its DJ line-up included Craig Cash who now writes for *The Mrs Merton Show* and Paul Whitehouse's *Fast Show*; journalist, broadcaster and one-time manager of the Man From Delmonte, Jon Ronson; Caroline Ahearne, also known as Caroline Hook, now even better known to millions of TV viewers as award-winning comedienne Mrs Merton; and myself, fresh from being sacked by Piccadilly Key 103 FM for playing too much 'obscure' music (which was how a new programme controller referred to the Happy Mondays, Stone

Roses, 808 State, A Guy Called Gerald and the Inspiral Carpets back in October 1989).

Manchester was buzzing. Ian Brown of the Stone Roses had said in early 1989 that the only way Manchester could be better was if it had a beach. Bands in Manchester could more or less survive and prosper just by being big in their home area, because there was nothing odd about bands selling as many as 6000 singles in Manchester alone and playing to over 1500 people. This scenario didn't go down too well with journalists based in London who liked to be able to say that they had discovered an artist or band and then lie back to bathe in the reflected glory. I don't believe talent is discovered – it's recognised, and if it's top quality then the fact that you are paid as a DJ or journalist to cover it should be reward enough. It's difficult to 'discover' Manchester bands, as the majority of regular gig-goers in the city would be well aware of any half-decent band long before they ever set foot in London to play third on the bill.

Manchester is a working-class city with a strong cultural identity of its own. There's a friendliness in the people albeit hard-boiled. The humour's dry, acerbic, cuttingly sarcastic and like those Celts of old, there's a rebel heart that beats beneath it all. Mancunians are mainly sons, daughters and grandchildren of immigrants. The traditional textile jobs have gone and the heavy engineering factories have shut down. Two world wars and a technological revolution have not managed to break down the class system in Britain, but a few bands from Manchester out for a party have celebrated and brought pride to that living-on-the-edge, ducking and diving character that is the scally; the ultimate outsider who, though downtrodden, refuses to be beaten and just keeps waiting for the next opportunity. While the educated middle classes and switched-on working classes in the southeast were yuppifying in the Thatcherite boom years of the eighties, the northwest scallies were preparing for the birth of their own enterprising culture. The rave scene created plenty of opportunities – gig promotions, nightclubs, flyposting, street fashions, and merchandising and selling the new quick-profit designer drug, ecstasy. It was easy to score 100 ecstasy tablets for £700, sell them on for £15–£20 each at a rave or a club and make a nice profit. Drug money and territory became the new focus in Manchester, selling crack and cocaine Thatcher's new enterprise culture. Inexorably, Madchester became Gunchester. Clubs closed down or had to change their music policies to avoid attracting 'the wrong crowd'. It wasn't the music press who destroyed that whole Madchester scene, it was too many guns and drugs on the street.

Meanwhile normal young Mancunians would try to get by, more often than not doing some low-paid, part-time job for cash in hand and signing on at the same time. It was survival and it was socially significant. Nobody was ashamed of their lack of employment or of signing on; good times were here and now, not around the next corner, and any notions of lingering inadequacy were pushed to the back of the psyche.

It was into this arena of crossfire and lost opportunities that Oasis stepped boldly. The Stone Roses were embroiled in court cases with their record company and manager; the Happy Mondays blew the whole gaff by getting strung out and drugged up in the West Indies; Factory Records went belly up and the city went into one of its bleak periods. The focus had shifted from Manchester and so the city turned in on itself. Yes, there were successes. The In The City international music seminars tried to get things kick-started and succeeded to a degree; M People took off and several rave dance groups from the area stormed the charts in both Britain and Europe, not forgetting Take That who became a squeaky-clean phenomenon. But those pop kids in Manchester who loved guitars and liked to see their mates in bands still hankered for the heady delights of '88, '89 and '90. It would take just one band to set Manchester buzzing again, one group of snotty ne'er-do-wells we could pour scorn on and champion at the same time, representing all our aspirations. Finally, it happened. When over 80,000 fans frugged about in the cool night air at Maine Road on 27 and 28 April 1996, singing along to every single song played by Oasis on that stage, it was like a communion all over again. Everyone seemed to know someone who knew someone in Oasis. We knew they represented us, the Druid bards leading their congregation, a scally festival which, despite the hordes of liggers up from London was, for we Mancunians, triumphantly private.

And so to the story in this book. Paul Gallagher is the older brother of Noel and Liam. As his brothers have become world famous and notoriously infamous, he has borne the strain of living in the shadow of their glory with neither accolades nor fame.

Every day now he has to deal with being the sibling of pop music's biggest and most controversial stars. This book won't be without its controversies, but it will attempt to tell the truth about three sons whose lives were shaped by a doting mother and a violent father. Two of these sons have made themselves stars of some social significance, at times bogged down in a swamp of sycophancy. Oasis are hip, and to use that ambiguous word that lies on the fine line between praise and damnation, they are trendy. Everyone wants to be a part of them and new-found friends spring up everywhere, because when you become public property there's often little hope of keeping old friends. Fame is a strain and the wealth it brings ultimately pays for a large luxurious prison in which to sit and watch the world go by.

But was it dreams of wealth that spurred on Noel and Liam Gallagher? In over fourteen years of dealing with bands, I've seen musicians struggle, come up trumps, then turn into arseholes and drop out of sight, but I've never experienced such sheer will and ambition as that shown by the younger Gallagher brothers. There's a burning demon inside that's being exorcised through fame and more importantly through music. Workaholic isn't the word. The wearying, gruelling tours, one after another, endlessly pushing themselves to the limits – the determination they display is not normal. Even now, after two top-quality albums that will stand up for years to come, there's no slacking. What is this obsessive, compulsive and at times self-destructive extremism covering for? A lack of self-esteem, maybe caring too much, or a desire to prove to themselves that they have worth as human beings, that they are the best? Maybe this is why those young kids living on Britain's council estates love Oasis. In their music there's sadness, hope, determination, a wish to belong and be recognised and a daydream fulfilled almost to the point of futility. If you could bottle all those things, you'd make a million every time. This book attempts to explore where their determination came from, that void the music fills and the unique circumstances that made it all happen so that they will, like the song says, Live Forever.

Paul Gallagher is Oasis's number one fan. From the outset he has kept diaries and scrapbooks following their climb to the top of pop's tree. He shares the experience of growing up with them, and he shares some of the more negative aspects of fame. Now, though still the older brother by blood, he finds himself in awe of the very people he should be closest to, and the paradoxical change in his behaviour to them since their fame has put a strain on the relationship.

Paul, 30 years of age, is known to his long-time acquaintances as Bod. He shares the same famous Gallagher eyebrows as his brothers, the same bright pale blue eyes. Though thicker set, he looks like the brother of Liam and Noel, and that's the problem. At Manchester's Holy City Zoo club in September '95, I looked on as he was buried beneath an avalanche of autograph hunters and Oasis fans. 'Will you pass this on to Liam for me?', 'When is Noel back in town?', 'Can you get us tickets for Earls Court?' and 'What do you think of Blur?' The flipside was all the snide jeering. 'Oi, you City supporting twat. You're the one your brothers said had no talent, you're the one who's good at digging holes. Is Noel financing this band you're managing? Did Noel get you your job at Creation Records?' Fame by association is tougher than the real thing.

Paul was signing on and trying to finance the band he was managing at the time. He was a regular gig-goer and I kept bumping into him around town, sometimes at his band's gigs, sometimes at the Roadhouse club on Newton Street or at the university. He told me he wanted to write a book on Oasis called *Brothers*. He was getting fed up with the way the press were hounding him and his mother, and was stung by several statements his brothers had made about him publicly, but generally he just had a story to tell and saw an opportunity to get it off his chest. At that time I was working on a book about Manchester United and growing up in Old Trafford. I'd been speaking to a few publishers, so I offered to pass the numbers on to him. Then one night in the Roadhouse he said, 'Look, I'll give you the story and you write it for me.' Paul mentioned that he'd been keeping a diary and scrapbooks on Oasis ever since they started out and that he'd mentioned it to Noel who'd sullenly replied, 'You might as well write a book, everyone else has.'

So the Oasis book called *Brothers* was to go ahead, but we had to have somewhere to start. Paul is a naturally nervous and shy person; he smokes and bites his nails all the way down to the quick. He told me that throughout his childhood the only times he ever felt properly relaxed were during those four or five weeks during the summer when their mother's brother, Uncle Paddy, would drop them − Noel, Liam, their mother and himself − off in Charlestown, County Mayo, in Ireland. Suddenly the tension would ease and his fondest childhood memories are of those long sprawling summers in the Irish countryside.

So we started there.

Ireland is a magical place. Both my parents are from Dublin so, like Paul, I understand that strange things occur there. We headed for Mayo, both relaxed, enjoying the *craic* at various inns along the way, and I got to know Paul better. Paul and myself are complete townies and Manchester boys to boot, but the bright sunshine and the scenic wonder of Ireland was bringing the child out in us both. There were hills and fields and brown bog and as we crossed the silver Shannon between Clondra and Scramoge, it was all we could do to stay in the car. Travelling down the road marshalled on each side by tall hedges of ivy and mountain ash and ditches sprinkled with wild parsley, we journeyed on past river meadows brought to life by patches of bright yellow heather, and we couldn't help but feel in a holiday mood. Paul slipped a cassette of the Jam into the tape machine and we smiled as Paul Weller sang 'In The City', and marvelled at the endless magical colours around us. Welcome to Ireland, welcome home.

Paul's grandmother and various aunts and uncles still live in Charlestown, and are the Sweeney arm of the Gallagher family. I tried to imagine Paul, Noel and Liam as young boys, leaving the greyness of a Manchester council estate in Burnage for long, heady summers in this part of the world. If there was a glimpse of something different, something to stir the poet in them, surely this was it.

Paul told me how as kids they'd get a bit bored around here as there wasn't much to do. They'd wander the meadows, muck about in the haystacks, watch the men cutting peat from the bog. They even tried fishing, unsuccessfully, in the many streams known for their trout. He and Noel went off playing football with little brother Liam in tow, scratching at the bites left by the clouds of midges which swarmed all over in the summer months. He told me how once Noel had fallen into a badgers' pit as he went to retrieve an over-hit football from amid the bracken, and had to be pulled out. The area was full of badgers and they were renowned for their ferocity.

Landmarks were pointed out to me along the way. We stopped at his grandma's house and Paul related how his grandma had said: 'When I first met your father, Tommy Gallagher, he came in the door and he looked an ever so nice man. He could have had it all. Three fine sons, a fine wife and a fine home and he lost it all. You're better off without him.'

We passed his Uncle Paddy's farm. His Uncle Paddy, the eldest of his mother's brothers, had returned to Mayo from Mexborough in Yorkshire having taken early retirement, and now spoke with a bluff Yorkshire accent. Their uncle Paddy took them on trips to the beach at Enniscrone or to the holy shrine at Knock and tried to inject some culture and love of the great outdoors into their mischievous bones. Paul told me how their mother would push Noel, Liam and himself into the church and make them pray for a few minutes, how the place frightened them, and how either their mother or Uncle Paddy bought them each a set of Knock rosary beads. Knock was quite an eerie place – Ireland's answer to Lourdes – and the site of many documented miracle cures.

A turning on the road after his Uncle Paddy's farm took us up a narrow path to the tranquillity of Bushfields parish church where his mother made her first Holy Communion, and as the road widened out into dual carriageway we passed through Swinford and on to Foxford where the family of Paul Arthur's (Bonehead), Oasis's rhythm guitarist, are from.

We stopped at Casey's bar in Charlestown. Several well-dressed, middle-aged and older men wandered in and out. James Casey's pub is a cosy affair with a large pool table and chairs around the corner bar. Mr Casey himself is a bespectacled, lively and witty little man. He asked Paul how the family were doing.

'Ah, Jaysus, it's terrible how the press are on at your brothers all the time. I had two very smart, well-spoken gentlemen from the *Sun* in here just after their Dublin show, nosing around and wanting to go off bothering your grandma. Now she really hates all the interfering and just wants to be left alone.

'Noel was in here a while back drinking. I even had a bunch of young ones come in the pub from out of town asking, "Which stool did Noel Gallagher sit on, where was he sitting, when is he coming back in?" and a whole load of other questions. Things around here are a bit quiet at the moment. You can tell Noel to give my pub a few more mentions in the press; it's a great advert.'

We drove on into Sligo and as the broken fields stretched either side of us and the ever-beckoning Ox mountains loomed ahead, and we zipped past the painted villages with their tall church steeples, it was time for Paul to answer some questions. Why do a book on Oasis, why talk about your brothers, why have the accusing fingers of strangers pointing and jealously remonstrating with you for cashing in? It was difficult for Paul. The stress of being an older brother – bullied and cajoled, treated like a younger brother by his siblings – was plain to see. He smoked a cigarette, and I could see his bitten fingernails out of the corner of my eye. Then he began.

My head feels a bit worn out by all this Oasis stuff. I suppose it's time to be pessimistic and look back at my life and what I've done. Would I change anything, if I could live it all again? I'd like to have been stronger mentally, maybe played football better. I wouldn't have let people annoy me the way they have, although I wouldn't want to be a hooligan, either. I'm happy that I'm laid back and not quick-tempered. But as things stand, I do get stressed out and I do take things very seriously, some-times too seriously, and then I go off at the deep end.

I think I only get stressed out because of the desire to succeed which is burning inside me and always has been. If you look at Noel and Liam, we've all got the same need to prove ourselves. With all the pain and suffering we went through as kids and the beatings we got off our dad, we were made to feel small; we were belittled constantly. I need to prove to myself that I can do what I set out to do and not what somebody else wants me to. I spent my childhood desperately trying to please my dad, trying to be as Irish as he was, looking for approval, only to be ridiculed for it. That's why I want to do this book. The same with the job at Creation; it'll help me prove something to myself. The constant pressure I'm under doesn't make it easy. I'm quietly confident in my own ability and I'm a good organiser. People do listen to me; numerous people have always come to me for advice. If I can help someone in any way I will. That's probably in Noel's nature, too. Liam? I'm not quite sure where that boy's coming from at the moment. I think I'm being totally honest when I say that we've all got a burning desire to succeed after being constantly put down throughout our childhood, and that's what drives us on.

We were basically poor. My mother would scrimp and save, work her fingers to the bone to make sure we got everything that other kids had. I mean she made sure we were always smartly dressed. I never went on any school trips like my mates who went skiing or to Spain. The furthest I got was to Bollington in Cheshire where you went out to pray for three days on a retreat. It was one of those catholic boys school things – spend three days praying at a cost of £5. At the time I just thought, Well, at least it's three days away from my dad; yes, it was a retreat all right.

We grew up with a lunatic of a father. He never really had a gentle side to him. My mam called him a street angel and house devil. When he went out everyone would love him, when he came in we saw the real him. I used to work with him, go DJing with him when he needed a hand with the equipment, and I'd hear people say, 'Ah, Tommy Gallagher, he's a lovely man, so genuine,' and I used to think to myself, You don't know the half of it.

He's out of my life now and this story's got to come out. I need to get it out of my system. Noel gets rid of his anger through his songs. That's why they're so sad and poignant. It comes from within, from what he suffered and went through growing up. The same with our Liam – that's where the anger and bitterness in his voice comes from. My anger is only starting to show now, because it feels that as a result of their huge success and fame, my brothers are indirectly trying to put me through what I've been through before. I need to talk about the past to clear my mind, so my mind won't be clogged up any more. For 30 years I've carried it round; for 30 years I could never fall in love; for 30 years I've felt inadequate and insecure; but I'm not going to feel that way for the next 30 years, so help me God. I've got to get this out and off my chest. My mother feels the same – that we should close that chapter, get the skeleton out of our closet for good. We don't want to see him back.

Our father was a very, very violent man and not through drink, just total violence. I don't think he could handle kids. He couldn't handle the three of us. I don't think he even likes the three of us. I just think he got married too young. He wanted to live the life of a single man and he couldn't adapt to bringing up three boys. I don't hate my father or love him. I don't hate anybody. I just think he's a very sad man. I don't feel sorry for him; I don't feel anything for him except anger. Anger that he wasn't stopped, that he got away with it for so long; maybe he's still getting away with it. To release that anger I have to write this story, and I just hope that Noel and Liam acknowledge what they went through. To them I say 'Don't be ashamed. We didn't do anything wrong.' They should just read this book and say, 'Cheers our kid.'

I'm no psychologist, but as we sped along those country roads in Ireland's western counties, I began to understand the shame and humiliation Paul talked about. The more you feel it, the more used to it you become, so that it seems not as bad as it might have been. The same at school as at home; dozens of kids standing around to watch your shame, with nothing you can do but hide your tears, with all those violent emotions swelling up inside. It's hard to have sympathy for other victims, other ones who are bullied. After all, if they're getting hit, that means you won't be, so you just feel grateful it's their turn and not yours; it'll be your turn to cry tomorrow. Then there's the guilt you feel: guilt at being glad that it's your brothers being hit instead of you, relieved it's someone else on the receiving end. Like the punishment doled out to Paul by his father, it is something a person gets used to – becoming obedient to the regularity of the beatings, used to feeling small, until inside you become a living statue, afraid to feel anything, thinking that emotions are simply cramps that will creep up one day and unsure of what they will do.

We played a tape of 'Some Might Say', and as the lines 'Some might say we will find a brighter day' rang out from the speakers, that old Irish magic kicked in again. The clouds parted and the sun, which had been hiding for hours behind palls of drizzle, opened up on to the snaking road before us, turning it silver like some fairy enchantment falling to earth.

Terry Christian, 1996

Chapter 1

The mother's story

Sweeney: The Sweeneys, McSweeneys and the McSwyneys are the descendants of the Gallowglass Warriors who came from Scotland and arrived in Ireland in the fourteenth century as mercenaries, primarily for the O'Donnells. Initially they settled in the area around Fanad, in County Donegal, from where they fought as Gallowglasses for the ruling O'Donnells, as well as for other chieftains, for almost three centuries. In the fifteenth century, members of the family went south and fought for the McCarthys of County Cork and eventually established their own territory near Muskerry in that county. With prosperity and expansion, the Sweeneys further established themselves in County Kerry. The name today is found in its greatest numbers in Counties Cork, Kerry, Donegal and Mayo. The Sweeney motto is 'Tugha tualig abu' – the Tulaig territory for ever – and the meaning of Sweeney is 'pleasant'.

County Mayo in the Irish Republic, and a mere 60-minute flight seems a million miles away from Manchester. Miles of green bog and moorland stretch endlessly towards the mountainous Atlantic coast. Swinford lies on the border between Counties Mayo and Sligo, just south of the Ox Mountains and 25 miles south east of Mayo's biggest town, Ballina. It was here on 30 January 1943 that a daughter called Margaret (Peggy), was born to Margaret (née O'Brien) and William Sweeney. Peggy, the fourth of eleven brothers and sisters, tells the story in her own words, without bitterness and with objectivity and a good deal of humour.

I was christened in Charlestown, County Mayo. My father was a labourer who worked for the local council. He came from Sligo. As a family we were very poor, but I can't remember very much of my earliest childhood. I do remember we never had shoes or socks. In the winter time we wore Wellington boots, something of a luxury, and in the spring and summer we went everywhere in our bare feet. For breakfast in the morning we'd have a cup of strong tea and a piece of dry bread. For dinner we had potatoes boiled in their jackets and a cup of milk if we were lucky, and then for supper another cup of tea and a piece of dry bread. That's basically what we lived on when there were just the four kids. Altogether there ended up eleven of us. The eldest was my brother Patrick, followed by John, then Bridie. I was fourth, followed by my sisters, Kathleen, Helen, Anne, Una and Pauline. The two youngest were Willie and Daniel.

I walked to school at Corthoon, Charlestown, about half a mile from our house, using a short cut across the fields. We'd be in school all day from nine in the morning to three in the afternoon, fighting off hunger because we'd no lunches to take with us. At night the girls slept six to a bed, three at the bottom and three at the top. Probably the biggest day for me was when, aged seven, I made my Holy Communion at Bushfields church. I'll always remember my mother had to borrow a dress from the daughter of a neighbour for me to wear; I'll never forget that, it was a long white dress.

Things didn't improve when my father left home around that time. He just disappeared, never said goodbye or anything, and we didn't know where he went. Come to that, I never really knew where he came from, just somewhere in Sligo. I can hardly remember him except that he was tall and dark, and not a very nice man. He never really spoke to or even acknowledged any of us kids. My mother couldn't afford to look after us when he'd gone, and so we were taken into care. Kathleen, Helen, Una, Anne, Bridie and myself had to go to a convent in Ballaghaderreen, just up the road in County Roscommon. We lived there for the next six and a half years. The nuns looked after us well; we had regular food and our own beds and we quite enjoyed it there.

I left school aged thirteen and a half and went straight out to work. My first job was in a grocery store and pub called Tom Durkins, doing kitchen work for a pound a week, working from eight in the morning until nine or ten at night. You couldn't even sit at the table with the owners to eat, because you were just the kitchen help, so you had to sit in a different room from them – but that's how people were in those days.

My second job was at Eamon O'Hara's in Charlestown, a confectionery store. I looked after their four children. The O'Haras were a very nice couple and treated me like I was one of their own, even taking me on holiday with them when they went to Galway in the summer. After two years of working there I had to go back home because my mother was very ill with her heart and needed me to look after my brothers and sisters. I was sixteen at the time, and seemed to be the one that was expected to look after everyone else. It sometimes feels as if I went straight from being a kid to cooking for and looking after other people's kids. Even when I was working in town and earning a pound a week, my mother would come in on pay-day for money to buy groceries for all my brothers and sisters at home, which would leave me a halfcrown occasionally. My mother didn't believe in giving me any spends. She was too worried about making sure she could look after us and do her best for us, which is why to this day we all love her dearly. My mother's always been there to talk to us and give us advice when we were feeling down and I'll always appreciate what she must have gone through looking after all of us. My older brother Paddy was the same. He was very good to Paul, Noel and Liam when they were growing up, taking us to Ireland to visit my mam every year. Otherwise I would never have been able to afford to go over with the kids.

Anyway, I stayed at home for about a year and a half, but when I was eighteen I decided it was time to move on.

It was then that I first came over to Manchester, just to see what it was like really and get away from home. I went with a friend of mine, Angela McIntyre, who had sisters and brothers in Manchester, and they put me up for a night or two. It seemed a very big and strange place after coming from the country. I was a bit overawed because it was so totally different. Within a day or so of arriving, the daughter of Angela's sister took me into town to help find me a job, and I started working at the old Central railway station, which is now the G. MEX centre, wiating on tables. I lived at the station and worked shifts, either from 6 a.m. until 2 p.m. or from 2 p.m. until 10 p.m. I was homesick all the time for the first six months, but I didn't dare go home as there was nothing there for me. I earned £3 a week after my food money was taken out and from that I sent home a pound a week for my mother. There were a lot of Irish people in Manchester at that time and we stuck together, I suppose. We used to go dancing at the Astoria club on Plymouth Grove which was an Irish club [later to be called the Carousel and more recently the International 2].

After about a year, I had to go back to Ireland because my mother was ill again and the younger ones needed looking after. While I was in Ireland keeping an eye on my mother, I got a job looking after five priests at a college in Swinford. As housekeeper for the five of them, responsible for cooking, cleaning and washing, I was paid £16 a month, which was good money compared to what I'd been getting in Manchester. When she was better, my mother said I should go to America and make a better life for myself, but I didn't want to go. It was too far away, although to go for a visit is something I've always dreamt of. So after about eight months, I came back to Manchester. This time I shared a flat with my sisters, Kathleen and Bridie. Then Helen came over, followed by Anne and a little later, Una. My oldest brother Paddy was already in England, working in the mines in Mexborough, Yorkshire, and John was already here too, living in Birmingham. I'd been back in Manchester about two months when I met my future husband, Tommy Gallagher, at the Astoria club, in January 1964.

Looking back, I can't see what was good about Tommy Gallagher. He was always tight with money – wherever we were going he'd always meet me there so he didn't have to pay for me to get in. It was an odd courtship. He'd go away for a month at a time working, sometimes two months, and never phone me to say where he was. When he came back, we'd go out, then he'd go away again. I never knew where I was with him. He'd spin stories and weave a whole web of lies, but he had the charm and I'd believe his excuses. In retrospect I'm sure he must have had another woman, but he'd make me believe he was telling the truth. I think he always lived a double life.

Before I got married I started to see the other side of him, the quick temper, but by then I couldn't back out because everything had gone ahead and all the arrangements for the wedding were made. I remember a friend of mine saying, 'If you're not sure, Peggy, don't get married, because it's a long hard road; don't get married if you're not sure.'

By this time my father had got in touch with my mother again because he was dying. All those years we hadn't heard from him, he'd been living in Birmingham. My mother came over to see him, and even she told me that I was far too young to get married and that I shouldn't do it. In the end I just went ahead with it and got married on 27 March 1965 at the Holy Name church on Oxford Road in Manchester. It wasn't a particularly big wedding. There were about 40 people there including my mother and my sisters Bridie, Kathleen and Helen. The only member of Tommy's family at the wedding was his brother Sean, who was the best man, and Sean's girlfriend, Kathleen.

Afterwards, we lived in a one-bedroomed flat at 33 Mont-gomery Road in Longsight. Tommy still kept going away working. It was when I got pregnant that I really started to see his bad side and the violent temper he had, but I got married for better or worse and thought you had to make the best of it. My mother always said you make your bed, then you lie in it. There was no divorce among the Irish community in those days.

I was working all the time I was pregnant, and Tommy would still go away working on the building sites, only coming back at the weekends. In those days, it wasn't unusual for Irish people to travel to work in Grimsby, Bridlington, Wales, all over. I didn't like Tommy going away. He'd be gone maybe three weeks at a time and I hated being left on my own in a one-bedroomed flat. Just before I had the baby, we moved into a two-bedroomed house – 2 Sandycroft Street, Longsight. I gave birth there to a boy, which was the best day of my life, because I thought this one's mine and no one can take him from me.

When he was born, I wanted to call him Gerard, but his dad wanted him called Paul after Pope Paul. He must have had a win on the horses or something that week to be getting so holy, but I got to choose his middle name, Anthony. He was christened at St Robert's church, just up the road. When Paul was seven months old, I got pregnant again with Noel. There wasn't really much violence when I had Paul but before Noel was born, Tommy got really out of hand. One time there was a big row – I couldn't tell you what it was about – but he kicked and smashed and dragged and beat me. It was terrible.

Noel was born in the same house on 29 May 1967, so I had two babies, one newly born and the other 16 months old. Once I had the two boys, Tommy started to get jealous about the attention I gave them and they gave me. He used to say that the kids thought the world of me; yes, he was jealous, all right.

He was never the type to bother with small babies. He wouldn't feed them or change them, so I was looking after the two of them, getting up in the night with them, and I still went out to work. I had no choice. It was all I could do to feed the three of us. Paul and Noel grew up not really knowing their dad – they were just scared of him. If they cried he hit them, if they stammered he hit them – he'd hit them to try and get the stammer out of them instead of trying to coax it out. Because of that I had to take Paul and Noel to speech therapy for a good four years before I had Liam.

Paul went to school at St Robert's in Longsight when he was five and I took Noel to nursery underneath the local gospel school. I never took Paul along to the nursery because I didn't believe in it at the time. I thought it was better to keep the kids at home until it was time to go to school. Paul was very clingy and didn't want to go to school. Every morning when I took him, he'd cry to come back with me. I'd go back for him at dinner time and take him home for his lunch, and I'd have to stop in the sweet shop to buy him something to make him go back to school with me again in the afternoon. I knew it was because he was very quiet and shy, partly because of his stammer. He was very much a loner, always on his own. In the meantime, I'd take Noel up to the nursery a couple of mornings a week and he loved it, playing with the other kids. When it was time for Noel to go to school, he was very different from Paul. He loved it and mixed in well with the other kids. Once Noel started going, it helped Paul to settle down and get more used to it.

They were the best times in my life, when I had the two of them. But their father wanted the single life and wanted to be out all the time. I was quite content with what I had, but not their father. He was always picking on them. He'd stuff food down their mouths if they said they didn't want it. He wouldn't let them beat him, he'd say.

I was still having to go out to work and things didn't get any easier. We went to Ireland one year and brought back Tommy's seven-year-old nephew, William, to live with us. His father, Tommy's brother, had been killed in an accident. William stayed with us for six months but it didn't make any difference to Tommy. He still didn't stay in at night. He was

always out drinking and gambling with his friends, leaving me
to look after three kids aged seven, six and four.

Then I became pregnant again. Liam was born on 21
September 1972 and two weeks later we left our house on
Sandycroft Street as it was due to be demolished and went to
live in Burnage, in a three-bedroomed council house.

After one or two months in Burnage, everything started to
go drastically wrong. Tommy had no patience with Liam at all.
Liam wasn't well as a baby; he had eczema and he was born
with psoriasis. He was ill for over six months, crying morning,
noon and night. His father would sooner go out than look after
the child. Tommy was doing really well at the time. He had his
own business and he'd bought a car, but he was still going out
every night. With Liam being so ill, I had to take him to the
doctor, sometimes twice a week, for almost a year. I'd be
standing at the bus stop in the cold with a young baby and
Tommy would drive right past me in his car, and wouldn't give
his own wife and sick child a lift to the doctor's.

By the time Liam was eighteen months old, I'd decided to
leave their father. I'd just had enough of him. He was out with
different women every night; then they'd be on the phone
looking for him at all sorts of times, asking where he was. He'd
come back home, taking it out on me and the kids, and yet still
be the perfect gentleman to everyone outside. I left the house
one night with Liam and I was going to leave Tommy there and
then, but I went back. Noel and Paul were in bed and I just
didn't know how to go about getting a house or getting my own
money at the time. I had no idea of how to go about it at all.

Paul and Noel had transferred from St Robert's school in
Longsight to St Bernard's primary school on Burnage Lane,
and they loved it there. Paul was in the school choir. Noel was
a bit of a daydreamer and a right storyteller. By the time Liam
started at primary school, Paul had moved on to St Mark's
secondary school (now called Barlow High) in Didsbury and
Noel was in his final year at St Bernard's.

All this time their father carried on. The things I put up with.
Tommy never wanted to pay rent or gas; he never wanted me

to pay electric bills. When they came in, he'd throw them on the floor and tell me not to pay them because it was only a corporation house we were living in. It was unbearable. He knew I'd be out at work and he'd promise me he'd be in to look after the kids when they came in from school, but instead he'd be out with another woman taking care of her kids and picking them up from school. Noel and Paul were coming home from school with no one to look after them at all. I used to leave Liam on his own and tell him not to answer the door until Paul and Noel had come home; then all three had to stay in the house on their own. Sometimes their Auntie Una looked after them for a bit, but I'd the worry on my conscience of leaving the three of them at home alone while I had to go out to get some money to feed them. Meanwhile their father was off with his fancy woman, practically living with her, looking after her two kids, bringing them up and down to school, and he'd his own three in the house that he didn't give a damn about.

When Liam was four years old, I put in for a legal separation. The papers were served on him and he was told to vacate the premises. He told the court officials he'd leave but as soon as they were gone he'd come back again. He'd break the windows, break the door. I had to let him in the house; if I didn't he'd wreck it. I got an injunction out on him and he was told to get out of the house again. He said he would, but he still didn't go. I couldn't ring the police. One time when he came back in and I threatened to call the police, he cut the phone line with the hedge clippers and said he'd kill me. Then he pulled the phone out of the socket.

It carried on like that all the way through Liam's childhood. Liam saw it all going on. Paul and Noel would be out a lot of the time but they didn't escape their father's violence. Sometimes their father would go out at night and come back in the morning at quarter to eight. He'd drive up the avenue cool as you like, come in the house and all hell would break loose. He'd tip the house from top to bottom, ransack it, then demand the boys get up out of bed. He'd tip the bed over so Paul and Noel would end up with it on top of them. It was all because of the other women and his guilty conscience. I told him dozens of times to get out and he'd just laugh and say he wasn't going anywhere because it was his house so why should he go? He's still there to this day.

One night, when I'd reached the end of my tether, I took Liam over to my sister Helen's. I'd decided just to take Liam and go. The next thing, Tommy phoned Helen and said if I didn't get back to the house he was going to set fire to it and Paul and Noel would go up with it. I had to rush back home and I remember thinking, Jesus, he'll set the house on fire and burn them all because I said I'd leave him. When I got back home, Paul and Noel were in bed and Tommy had gone out.

Another time Tommy was with his fancy woman, and her husband caught them. He ran out and drove off in such a hurry he smashed the van into a lamp post. He phoned me at five o'clock in the morning and told me to tell the police that he wasn't living at our house any more and that he was gone. I told him and his fancy woman at the same time that I wished the both of them had got killed that night in the van because I had just about had enough of them.

When I'd go to Ireland in the summer with the three kids, he'd have different women up in the house and not a bit of shame in him. I'd come home and find things moved around and in the wrong places and then he'd try to pull the wool over my eyes, but I cottoned on to what he was doing. He'd tell me I was mad, that I should be in Prestwich having psychiatric treatment, that I needed locking up. To be honest, at the end of 20 years of living with the likes of him you begin to think it yourself. The only thing that kept me sane was the thought of my kids. I was determined he wouldn't get me down because if anything happened to me, what was going to become of the three of them? That's what kept me going. I thought, Once I get out of here, he'll never step inside my door again. He was a street angel and a house devil, that's the only way I could describe him.

In the Easter holidays, he'd have Paul, Noel and Liam up at the allotment. He'd make them go and the three of them would walk behind him, because they didn't want to walk with him. It was two miles to the allotment and then he'd get the bus round to his fancy woman's house with the stuff he'd have them growing there and leave the three of them to walk the two miles home. He didn't give a damn if they never got home.

He'd tell Noel to come in by eight, and Noel would purposely come in five or ten minutes late. Tommy would have arranged to go out drinking with his mates and his women at eight, so couldn't wait for Noel coming in. He'd come back in a fit of temper at all hours of the morning and pull Noel out of the bed and kick him just because he thought Noel had got the better of him by disobeying him and coming in late.

At night before he went to bed, he'd count all his loose change on the dresser – all the 2ps, 5ps and 10ps – and if any went missing he would go mad. When Liam was small, he'd sometimes take 10p and go down to the shops and Tommy would go mad. At this time he had his own concreting business and was earning anything up to £900 a week. He only gave me about £30 to run the house, pay the rent, gas, electric, and clothe and feed the family.

Even though we were legally separated, he still expected his meals cooked and his washing done. He didn't expect his life to change one bit. If there wasn't a dinner on the table when he came in, he created absolute murder. Sometimes he'd buy his own little bit of food and put it in the freezer. I used to cook it for the kids, and he'd come back in and ask where that chicken had gone, telling me how much it had cost. I'd tell him that I'd given it to the kids, and he'd go mad. 'It was my chicken. Get them something else?'

He was a selfish man – all he ever thought about was himself. As long as he had the best clothes, best shoes, his wallet full of money and he could go out every night in the week, he wasn't bothered about anyone else. He always said it was me and the kids that ruined his life. 'You're in my way,' he'd say. If he wanted to go and live with somebody else, I wasn't stopping him. I wanted rid of him. He just didn't have the guts to get up and get out. That kind of thing went on from when Liam was about two right through until we left when he was twelve, only it got worse and worse and worse until in the end we could take no more.

When they were old enough, Tommy wanted Paul and Noel to work with him in his concreting business on the building sites but they didn't want to, Noel especially. Tommy would tell me to make them go to work, and so I used to tell them to go just to keep the peace. He'd bring Noel and Paul out at five or six o'clock in the morning and some nights it was eleven o'clock when they got home, and he still wouldn't want to pay them. On Friday they'd ask him for their wages and he used to tell them to go to bed so they could be up early for work the next day. He'd tell them not to give any money to me for their upkeep if he did pay them. He didn't want them to be out and he'd say to them, 'Why should I give you money when you'll only spend it doing drugs and running riot? Go to bed.' That would be at eight or nine o'clock at night.

He hated giving them a wage. He hated them going out buying clothes, going to the pictures or buying records. The funny thing was, he wanted to be out all the time himself. He thought he should knock the hell out of Noel and Paul, work them really hard and not pay them at all, but that he should go out every night of the week, and come home and tell us all how it cost him £50 for a round. Basically Noel and Paul worked and he spent their wages, when he'd have been better off giving it to his family.

We had to get out because we couldn't stay in the same house as him. If the kids wanted to watch anything on the telly he always switched it over. Liam would come in from school and want to watch *Playschool*, and he'd tell Liam that *Playschool* was no good for him. Then Liam wanted to watch *Dr Who* and he'd tell him *Dr Who* was no good for him. He never let him watch cartoons or anything. He took over the television all the time, he was that spiteful. Then he'd play Irish music at full blast so everyone could hear him, and open the windows and the doors. That's what you had to put up with; music – morning, noon and night. If any of the kids' friends came to the door to call for them he'd tell them to f*** off and that they weren't there.

In the end Noel threatened to kill him. He was violent with all the kids; fighting with them, punching them and battering them. They were all saying to me. 'If we don't get out of here soon, mam, we'll kill him.' I asked the council for another house. I was on the waiting list for three years before I was offered one. I used to go down there in a terrible state, explaining what it was like putting up with him and his tempers and his coming and going with his fancy women when I was out at work and that I just couldn't put up with him any more. At first the council asked me why I didn't get him to leave. I told them he wouldn't go.

He'd got taken off building sites. People didn't want to work with him because of his shouting and bawling, roaring and fighting. Eventually he lost his concreting business because he wouldn't turn up for it. He wouldn't get out of bed unless I woke him and got up with him. He'd be in a mood, come in, smash the house, smash the glass in the door, and when he'd upset everyone he'd get dressed up to the nines and go out the door, head up in the air, not a bother on him, get in his car and you wouldn't see him again for two or three days. Then he'd come back again at the usual time on Monday morning, looking for his breakfast as if he wasn't doing a thing wrong. Then Paul and Noel got too big for him and started to retaliate. They just wouldn't put up with it any more.

It was almost like fate when their father had to be taken to hospital with a bad back in October 1983. When the ambulance men carried him out that night, I said a prayer that he wouldn't come back. None of the boys visited him. It was two months before he came home again because he went to a convalescent place, and I can tell you it was two months of great peace we had. Suddenly all the boys were able to bring their friends in the house. Noel could have all his mates around upstairs playing records, making cups of tea, and we could actually relax and sit in as a family because their father wasn't there. Eventually he came back from the hospital, but in the meantime the possibility of a council house had come up. I couldn't tell him we were going to leave because he would have killed us. Noel and Paul were threatening to leave, and if they'd both gone their own way I was worried how everything would turn out because it would have left just Liam and me.

Eventually, we moved out in 1984, to the house I live in now. There was nothing in it, only the four walls and the sink in the kitchen. The council offered me the house on the Monday and I told them we could move in on the Friday night when their father had gone out. Tommy went out that Friday night as usual, and I knew we'd be gone when he got back. I arranged for my brother-in-law, George, to come over to help us. We were still moving stuff out at two o'clock in the morning; it was a real midnight flyer. The new house was in a terrible state with no paper on the walls and just bare floorboards, but I wasn't bothered. I'd sooner live like that with just the floorboards because we had peace at last. I haven't seen Tommy from that day to this.

I always told him that one day he'd come in and we'd be gone, but he was always smug, saying 'You'll never leave me, you'll be here all the time.' I'd say I wouldn't be here at all except for the kids. Then Tommy would get really annoyed, saying, 'I never want anything off those three bastards.'

'You will,' I'd say to him. 'You'll want them long before they'll need you, because at the end of the day, if you haven't got your family you haven't got anything.'

As I said, we couldn't move out of the house while he was there because he always said he'd kill us. He'd wreck every bit of furniture and we'd take nothing with us when we went, he'd make sure of that. I think he had a feeling that night that we were going to go, because he asked Liam, 'Has mam got a house?'

Liam denied it because Liam wouldn't tell him anything. During the week he'd asked Liam, 'Where does your mam go in the day when she goes out and doesn't come in until four o'clock?'

Tommy had noticed that I went out in the morning when Liam was going to school. I was going up to the new house to see what I could do with it; then I went on to my job with the school dinners. I came home at four o'clock when Liam would be coming back from school, got the boys their tea, and then I'd be out again cleaning the place up ready for us to move in.

The saddest thing is how he treated the kids. Liam was twelve when we left and not once in all the years that followed did his father ever so much as send him a letter or put £1 in a card for him. Birthdays came, Christmas came, his 18th and 21st birthdays – nothing. It was the same with Noel and Paul – their own father never even dropped so much as a card round. After they stopped working for him, he never once tried to get in touch with them, never wrote to them and never supported Liam. He was told once he had to pay £50 a week for Liam, but he never paid a penny because he didn't see why he had to support his son. So that left us living on income support.

When we moved things got better, but Liam was very affected by it all. He was still in school and twelve is a funny age. He was very psychologically affected by his father; so was Noel but Noel is deeper than Liam and kept it all to himself. Noel and Paul were still working for their father for a while to bring money into the new house. They were probably more worried about me than about themselves. Anyway we got settled in the house and we got it all together and made a nice home of it, and our lives started to change. We started to recover, and all pulled together. I was still working as a dinner lady at school, keeping an eye on Liam. We managed. Then Noel went off with Inspiral Carpets. In the meantime, I got divorced from their father. I wanted him out of my life altogether. I never wanted any contact with him or to see him again, neither did Noel, Paul nor Liam. Paul and Noel couldn't carry on working for him. Liam and Paul might have seen him the odd time since then and just raised their hand but they've never spoken to him.

I remember at school, Liam was a very different kettle of

fish from Paul and Noel. Even when he was five he loved being noticed. He wanted to be the top of everything. He wanted to be the nicest dressed in the class, he wanted to have everything before the other kids, he didn't want them to have anything before him. If they'd have a school play, Liam would always want to be in it. The first time, I remember, he was one of the three wise men, and another time he played King Herod, but couldn't remember his lines so he ended up singing them like Elvis. He was always in every school play and always made sure he was picked for the best macho part; he used to tell the teachers he wasn't doing any sissy parts. In the nativity play at Christmas, Liam made sure he was Joseph.

When Liam was eleven, he began at St Mark's secondary school. From the very first day he knew exactly what he wanted to do – nothing. From day one, you knew he was going to be trouble because he had no intentions of doing anything. He was always a joker, always full of life, always on the go and loved to be the centre of everything. He was full of mischief from the outset. I worked at the school as a dinner lady for a couple of years. I'd see Liam come in the dinner hall and he'd be the picture of innocence, then you'd catch a glimpse of him as he was leaving and he'd be after giving someone a belt and a teacher would be grabbing him by the scruff of the neck. Afterwards the teacher would come to me about him. He wasn't trouble as such, just full of devilry. He had to be cock of the class, hang out with the best group, and generally be better than everyone else. It was like he was born to that. Liam loved attention and he loved people to notice him, but other than that he wasn't trouble, he just found school very boring. There was nothing to keep him occupied.

One time he turned up at school with his hair dyed. He'd asked one of his mates' sisters to put a blond streak in it and his hair turned orange. He went into school with it the next morning and was sent home. It cost me nearly £10 to buy a dye to get his hair back to its proper colour before they'd let him back into the school. Then he had his ears pierced, and he was sent home again. They'd tell Liam to take the earrings out of his ear and he'd go back to school the next day, brazen as you like, with the earrings still dangling, saying they were his ears and he'd do what he liked with them. Then he turned up without a uniform. The teachers would tell him he had to wear a uniform, and Liam would say he'd wear what he wanted to wear.

I paid more visits to that school over Liam than I can remember. Every time the teacher sent for me, I would have to go up there and grovel for them to take him back. He wasn't happy in school. I tried to explain to his teachers that a lot of it was to do with his father. I'd try to persuade the headmaster, hoping he wouldn't expel him. Meanwhile Liam would stand there like butter wouldn't melt in his mouth and promise me it would never happen again, 'Honestly, Mam.' But it always did and I'd find myself up at the school grovelling for him again.

They expelled him at the age of fifteen − I can't remember exactly what it was for. He was out of school for three months because the headmaster just refused to have him back. They wanted to send him somewhere where they could deal with his needs, but I think he was frightened of that. They wanted him to go to a school where there were more outside activities, where they could take him rowing and that type of thing, but Liam wasn't having any of it so, as usual, I had to go back up to the school and grovel again to the headmaster for them to take him back. I think the headmaster felt sorry for me and decided he'd give Liam one more chance but if he stepped out of line he'd be put off the premises immediately. So Liam went back to school after Christmas. He was due to leave the following May anyway, and he was on his best behaviour, like a little angel, from that day up until the day he left. When it came to the end of the final term, he didn't want to leave.

However he did. His teachers had got him a job at a fencing place on Parrswood Road. The money was good, about £60-odd pounds a week. He used to leave at eight o'clock in the morning and be home by four. Everything was fine for a couple of weeks until the day they asked him to clean the outside toilets. It was his turn. Everyone took turns, but Liam said he wasn't putting his hand down a toilet and cleaning it for anybody, so he left. He got a job with a friend of his, fixing illuminated signs, but was laid off. After that he went to work for a gas subcontractor with Paul. Noel had worked there earlier, and had a cushy job in the stores, handing out bolts and tools and spending all day playing his guitar. They were all living at home at the time and things were fine. Although Liam started out as a labourer with Paul, he managed to get Noel's old job in the stores, which suited him down to the ground because he loved daydreaming. Liam didn't really know what he wanted to do. He usd to say, 'I'll be famous one day, Mam, and you'll be proud of me. I wasn't put on this earth to dig holes, I was put on this earth for something special. I can feel it in my bones.' When he was on the dole he used to sign on and the people at the dole office would ask him what he wanted to do and he used to say he was going to be in a band. I used to tell him to come down from the clouds, that he was living in cloud cuckoo land.

Noel did well with the Inspiral Carpets. That's what he wanted to do at the time, but I knew his ambition was to be in his own band. When he came back after his first American tour with the Inspiral Carpets, he decided to move in with his girlfriend, Louise Jones, a very nice girl. He was 22 by then and he'd been going out with her for a while. I never saw the Inspiral Carpets live. I used to watch them on the television to see if I could catch a glimpse of Noel but I never did. By the time Noel came back from America, Liam was in a band and Noel immediately wanted to join it, and that was how he came to be in Oasis. They used to rehearse five nights a week at the Boardwalk club in town and then play up and down the country. They'd come back after every gig, and I'd ask if they had any luck. Noel would always answer 'No not yet, Mam', until one night after he'd been in Scotland. He came back and I asked him if he had any luck and he said, 'Yeah, I think we got a record deal.' He was so excited. I said that was great and Noel told me that they'd all got to go down to London next week. So I asked him where he'd get the money from, and he replied: 'Oh, our tickets will be at the station, we're getting our fare paid. We're meeting Alan McGee.'

By then Liam was really into the music. He kept on saying how he could feel it in his bones that they were going to be famous and one day he'd be this big rock and roll star and he'd make me very proud of him, but he'd still not a penny of money on him. I'd say, 'Yeah, yeah, Liam, I've heard it all before, now will you get off your backside and get yourself a proper job because I can't keep you any more.'

It's strange how things worked out. Noel was always very quiet, you never really knew what he was thinking. His father left a big scar on him; it affected all three of them. That's why Liam is so aggressive now, because he's got all this hatred built up. Liam never wanted to move out of the old house, especially the way we had to go in the middle of the night leaving all their friends behind. We couldn't tell anyone we were going. Those lads had to leave the place they grew up in. Paul had lived there since he was seven, Noel since he was five and Liam from when he was two weeks old. Paul and Liam used to ask me why their father couldn't go instead, but he would never have gone. Tommy would have carried on living his life the way he always had, bringing his women backward and forward, humiliating us with all his violence, abusing us all and taking his guilty conscience out on us. I had many a black eye with him. Liam would ask what happened to my eye and I was always making excuses saying I banged into the door or something.

For 20 years and more none of my family knew what I was going through because I kept it all to myself. If they did notice anything, I covered up. If they asked where Tommy was, I'd just say he'd gone to work. I'd never say he was out and he hadn't come in, that he had other women ... and other children. Because I was that ashamed, none of my family really knew I was leaving him until I actually moved. I never told them anything about a house, or what I was going to do or what I was up to. I just kept everything to myself. I'm sure that if I hadn't moved out then I would have cracked up. I would have ended up in hospital because it had all got too much for me.

But now it's all behind us. For the past twelve years, we've been happy. When I came into this house and sat down, I didn't care what I had in it so long as I could walk in my front door, close it and know he wasn't going to be there. I had over 20 years of violence, and none of us could take any more. The violence was terrible, even to his own sons. In the meantime, Tommy ended up having another son which he totally denied, but I know for a fact he exists. Why he wants to be a father now to Paul, Noel and Liam when he was never a father to them when they needed him, I'll never know.

Chapter 2

The young Liam John Gallagher

I remember going to Liam's school parents' evening. He was driving his teacher, Mrs Walsh, around the twist. She said to me, 'Well, I don't know how you put up with him. I feel sorry for you because you've got him all the time. I've only got him for so many hours and to be quite honest at the end of the day I have to go home and take a tablet.' That was when he was at primary school.

Peggy Gallagher, 1996

My youngest brother, Liam, hates being called the baby of the family. Now our Liam is a one-off on this planet, and we should be grateful for small mercies. He's always had that sullen expression on his face, like somebody's just pissed on all his fireworks, but take it from me, he's laughing inside half the time. The rest of the time he's whining. My earliest impression of Liam from the day he first started walking and talking was that he's the cheekiest lad ever born to woman. He never gave me a minute's peace from the moment he could talk – taking the mickey, winding me up, and then he'd start on Noel; I swear we should have put something in his tea to slow him down and shut him up. That boy is an expert at being noticed. Nothing was ever good enough for Liam. He never wanted to hang around with kids his own age, he always wanted to tag along with Noel and me and all our mates: 'Go and play with your own mates, Liam,' we'd say. 'No, I want to come with you. Mam, Paul and Noel won't let me play out with them.' Then Mam would shout: 'Paul and Noel, you take him with you or you won't be going anywhere.'

So, we'd take him to the park with us, like some little mascot. But you always had to watch him or he'd be wandering off, or start messing about. We'd be playing football and he'd be running off with the jackets we used for goal posts, or moaning that he was bored. In a pique, we'd end up blasting the football at him, or chasing him and putting him down on the floor, and he'd say: 'Wait till I tell Mam.'

If he was playing around with his own mates and he saw me and Noel with our friend Paul Hewitt or anyone else, he'd be over in a flash.

'Piss off and play with your mates.'

'No, I don't want to.'

'Then piss off home.'

'No, I just want to stay here with you.'

Paul Hewitt, who was the youngest brother in his own family, liked the idea of Liam as an adopted younger brother and would always say, 'Let him stay, he'll be all right.' He took our Liam under his wing, and Liam made him laugh, but he used to drive Noel and me round the bend when he was out with us.

Poor Liam was my mam's baby but he always wanted to act bigger and older than he was. We were always being pushed by our mam to take Liam with us and look after him. It was a full-time responsibility and a nightmare liability.

I recall one hot and glorious summer day, a gang of us decided we'd cycle over to Red Rock in Cheadle for the day and get a taste of country living. At Red Rock there was a stream that flowed into the River Mersey and we could swing across on a rope that hung over it. Just as we were setting off, our mam uttered the dreaded words, 'Take Liam with you.'

Despite the fact that we kicked up an almighty stink, she wouldn't take no for an answer. So with our mam's warnings about keeping an eye on Liam and looking after him ringing in our ears, we set off for Cheadle and Red Rock. It was a boiling hot day and we were sitting around chatting and sunbathing. Liam was bored hanging around, and because we were ignoring him he wandered off on his own. Unfortunately, he wandered off to the stream and tried to swing across on the rope. He slipped on a rock and fell into the stream which was fairly deep and had a very strong current. Now neither Noel nor myself could swim and we really panicked because we knew Liam couldn't either. We were frozen, helplessly watching as our little brother was being swept by the current towards the deep murky waters of the River Mersey, clueless about what to do. Liam's foot got tangled up in some rubbish or debris in the stream and he couldn't drag himself out; the water was flowing all around him. Luckily Paul Hewitt didn't hesitate. Paul went straight in and dislodged Liam from his untimely and near fatal brush with the bottom of that stream. We told Liam not to tell our mam when he got home, but as ever with our Liam, he couldn't keep it to himself. A few days later he grassed both of us to our mam, telling her all about his impromptu swimming lesson in the River Mersey. Typical of Liam, but one thing's for sure, if it hadn't been for Paul Hewitt, Liam wouldn't be here today.

Liam was funny when he was a kid, but he was always trying to get my back up and then hiding behind our mam. When he got on my nerves I'd shout at him or tell him off, and he'd always be giving me cheek and answering back. If I got up to teach him some manners, he'd run off. Everything was a game to him. He was hyperactive. If he was annoying our Noel, he'd just give Liam this look; a stern gaze, drooping his eyebrows. Liam knew then to shut up. I bet Noel wishes he could shut Liam up like that now.

Liam always had to let you know he was around. He'd be about four or five when I was starting secondary school. I'd pick up my exercise book and there'd be about five pages left in it. 'Mam, I'm bored. Paul, can I have some paper to draw on?' I'd see all this lined paper on the table with his little doodles on it. Another trick, which went on for several years, was he'd get my exercise book and write stuff on the front. I'd get to school, take my exercise book out and it would have 'Liam is cool' written on the cover, plus all kinds of graffiti as befits a six or seven year old. So I'd have to cover it with brown paper. Then it would be: 'Paul, can I play some of your records?' I'd reply, 'No you can't, don't go near them.'

Half an hour later, *screeeeech*. I'd run upstairs and there would be Liam purposely scratching all my records one by one. I don't know about rock and roll music, but if Liam had been into hip hop, he could truly boast that he'd been scratching records since he was four. 'Hey, man, when punk was big in 1977, I was really getting into scratching.'

My guitar had been gathering dust for a few years but Noel played all the time. Not to be left out, Liam decided he wanted to start playing music properly. He played the recorder and then wanted a guitar so I let him use mine. The trouble was, Liam didn't stand out enough during his music lessons with just a guitar, as too many other kids had them. So one day he came home and asked our mam to buy him a violin. That way he'd really stand out in the music group. My mam got herself into debt, buying him a violin for about £35. OK, it wasn't a Stradivarius, but then our Liam wasn't exactly Nigel Kennedy. The most comical thing my mam remembers is nine-year-old Liam insisting that he go to school with both his violin and guitar, one in each hand, just to show the other kids that whatever they had, he had more.

I can't remember any great tunes being scraped on that violin or any catchy melodies strummed on that guitar, but Liam kept up his music lessons on the violin until he left St Bernard's primary school and started at Barlow High (which had just changed its name from St Mark's and gone co-ed). Pretty soon after that, Liam decided he no longer wanted to play the violin as it was sissy. He dumped his guitar for the same reason (also probably because he realised that he'd have to practise to be as good as Noel) and decided to be a hooligan instead. Those famous musical instruments got passed around the family. The violin went to my Auntie Helen's daughters, Sharon and Tracey, and were in turn handed on to my Uncle Dan's kids. I'm not sure about the guitar. We might still have it at home somewhere, in which case, as the original owner, I'll reclaim it and auction it off to the highest bidder at some stage in the future, either for charity or just for a few quid spending money and posterity.

The lesson to be learnt from all this is that, although I originally had a guitar, Noel had more talent playing it, so I dumped it; I couldn't compete. Liam gets a guitar and a violin. He might not be as good on the guitar as our Noel, but he thought he'd outmanoeuvre him by becoming a violin virtuoso, too. When he went to secondary school, he learnt that at eleven and twelve you get more respect off other kids for bashing people in the head than for playing the guitar, and that in Burnage, anyone who plays the violin is a sissy, so that went out of the window too. If you can't be the best why bother at all; it's that sad. We must have been a right pain in the backside for our mam.

Our mam was always on at us not to be so mean with each other. Maybe if we'd had an older sister we'd have been more even-tempered and generous towards each other. But she really did protect Liam, not only from us but also from my dad. I think my dad threatening Liam would always be the final straw with her, and our dad knew that. She knew the effect our dad had had on Noel and me; all the problems with our stammers, my being bullied and constantly whingeing, always trying to ingratiate myself with everyone, how quiet and moody Noel was, staying up in his bedroom on his own for hours. Liam was spirited and a live wire and there's no way our mam wanted that beaten out of him. Although he was a right pain in the neck and I know he has his hang-ups and insecurities, he's always had a belief and confidence about his manner that he can thank our mother for giving him.

When I was about seventeen and Liam was ten, he wanted

to borrow some of my records for his school disco. Now Liam wasn't really into music at that age, but after his teacher had said to the kids, 'Bring some records from home,' there was no way Liam was going into school empty-handed, so he asked to borrow mine. I told him to get lost. 'Ask our Noel.' In the end our mam told me not to be so selfish. I foolishly relented and said he could borrow them as long as he looked after them and didn't scratch them. So Liam marched off proudly to St Bernard's school for his mini pops end-of-term disco, clutching about a dozen of my coolest and best seven-inch singles: the Jam, U2, Madness, the Specials. I think the other kids would have taken stuff like Adam and the Ants, but our Liam had to be better than them. Sure enough, when he returned with my precious vinyl, not only had he scrawled 'Liam G.' across the middle of the labels, but they were scratched to bits and jumping all over the turntable. I'm still waiting for an apology now. APOLOGY – there's a word our Liam's never learnt from that day to this. As ever, our mother defended him, telling me, 'He's only young, he didn't know.'

As he got bigger, he got worse. He was always grassing us up, he was a right little squeak; he'd have you banged up big time. I had to bribe him to shut him up. We'd be in the living room at home and Liam would pipe up with, 'Mam, guess what Paul did?' I'd be sitting next to him, hand over his mouth, whispering, 'Don't say anything and I'll give you 30p . . . 50p.' It got up to a pound later on as he got older and it's a good job I did a regular paper round to pay him off. Our mam would be in the kitchen just out of earshot. 'So what was that you were up to, Paul?'

I'd be sitting there with one hand clamped over Liam's mouth trying to do a deal with him saying, 'Oh, nothing, Mam, it's just our Liam messing about making up stories again.' He'd get you shot. That was the result of having to take Liam everywhere with us. I'm sure our mam had him keeping an eye on what we were up to, rather than the other way round. He was an eight-year-old spy; he shouldn't be in a band called Oasis, he should be in Supergrass!

Probably the worst trouble Liam ever caused anyone was when he was playing football outside in the street. One day he was kicking his ball against one of our neighbour's hedges, making a big hole in it. When the bloke whose house it was came back in his car, Liam didn't move so he parked in our dad's usual parking space by way of protest about Liam damaging his hedge. Well, our dad drove up, found another car in his space and Liam said that it was our neighbour who was the culprit. Our dad went round there and shouted at the man to come out. By then the neighbours were well aware of Tommy Gallagher and his temper, so this guy just popped his head out the door and told him to go away. My dad went and got his spade and hacked the guy's wooden gate in two. Our neighbour called the police who came round and had a quiet word with our dad about his violent and threatening behaviour. My dad would batter any of us for nothing, yet our Liam was out of order booting his football into this geezer's hedge. He refused to stop when asked, so the guy parks his car in front of our house, Liam tells our dad and my dad cuts the neighbour's gate in two. Bonkers!

The Weetabix kid, that's what we called Liam. He lived on breakfast cereals. At breakfast, lunch, tea and dinner, he was either tucking into Ready Brek or Weetabix. He wouldn't eat normal food like potatoes and meat, just Ready Brek. If he went to the cupboard and that box of Ready Brek was empty, he'd start a big inquiry.

'Who's been eating my Ready Brek? Don't you go near it.' He was such a fussy, whingeing type. 'I don't like my food messed with, this drink's too hot, too cold, who's been wearing my jumper, why is this shirt really creased?' But nothing like the fuss over his Ready Brek. Our Noel would chomp his way through Frosties or something, but if they ran out he'd have to be very stealthy about smuggling himself a bowl of Ready Brek or Weetabix; they were Liam's. When he was really young it was Farley's rusks. He'd have them on their own or with hot or cold milk and devour them morning, noon and night. He was a psychotic, pre-adolescent cereal killer.

When he was about nine or ten, I'd have to take him to the odd Manchester City match, usually on my mam's orders: 'Are you going to the match today, Paul? Ah well, take our Liam with you, he really wants to go.'

I'd have to walk up to Maine Road and make him hold my hand. You had to keep a tight grip on him too, otherwise he'd just wander off. He was a real live wire and couldn't sit still for a minute. At the match he wanted everything. It wasn't a football match, it was a walking shopping list.

'I'm starving, can I have some chips?'

'You've just had your dinner. Here you are, now shut up.'

'Can I have a Wagon Wheel?'

'Will you get me a programme?'

'Can I have some Bovril?'

'Can I have some crisps?'

'Can I have a hot dog, burger, scarf, souvenir poster?'

It was cheaper taking a girl out for the night than taking our Liam to the match. It was like Pacman versus English soccer. If City had scored as many goals as items of food that he ate, they'd have won the double. He must have had a stomach like Dr Who's Tardis – small outside, huge inside. When I'd protest to our mam and ask why Noel couldn't take him to the match, she'd say, 'Noel's too dopey. He'll start daydreaming and forget Liam's there and lose him.' So I was stuck with occasional match duty, watching our Liam chew a half-cooked hot dog with his mouth open.

Playing football with Liam was something else again. He was probably the best footballer out of the three of us – he'd have to be, wouldn't he? – and was the only one who played regularly for his school team. He was pretty fast and nimble, but used to just lose it if anyone kicked him accidentally or hurt him when they tackled him. A total hot head, he was skilful but prone to start fighting if anyone left him flat on his face.

He was always very fiery-tempered and constantly fighting with other kids, usually older than him. Liam was the one who'd provoke the fights by being cheeky. He hated being beaten. Once when he was ten he had a fight with a bigger lad of thirteen. This older boy had knocked Liam down on the ground about three times, but Liam kept getting up saying he was going to kill him. I intervened and literally had to drag our Liam off home while he was struggling like mad to get this thirteen year old. I told Liam that the older boy was too big for him, and would batter him, but Liam just replied: 'I don't care, I'm gonna kill him.'

When he went to secondary school he decided he wanted to start putting gel in his hair. He used to ask me to do it for him. He was that paranoid about his cow's lick showing, I'd have to put about two tons of gel on him to slick it down. I'd act as his personal beauty aide and he'd whine, 'Put some more on, it's still showing.' I'd end up putting half a tub on. You'd think he was going for a night on the town; I've never known a kid spend so much time getting ready for school. Then he'd go off to Barlow High like Mr Cool, with all his hair slicked back like some 1950s throw back.

The girls at school all thought Liam was Mr Cool, too. Every morning throughout his secondary school years, there'd be two, usually three, but sometimes as many as five girls calling for him to walk him to school. I used to answer the door when I was getting ready for work, and there'd be three young girls there saying, 'Is Liam in? He's dead fit [Mancunian slang for rather attractive] your brother.' I'd think, Jesus, you don't have to live with him. I'd call Liam and he'd pretend to be annoyed at these girls pestering him, but he loved it really. Stardom is nothing new to our Liam. He swaggered off to school every morning with his female escorts like God's gift. Fame? That boy's had it since he was six. Yes, even then the girls from the other end of our street would come to play down our end just to shout, 'Oohee, Liiiaaaam.'

Liam was well aware of the effect he had on the opposite sex and started to tart himself up at an early age. I caught him shaving, using all my gear, when he was thirteen. He used to do it all the time and try to put it back thinking I wouldn't know. He'd steal my aftershave, use my deodorant – he was always up to something. He actually grew a little moustache when he was fifteen.

While he was growing up, his best mate, before he met Dave Coates, was Mark Shenton. Mark had an older brother, Steve, who used to hang out with our Noel when they both reckoned they were punks. Liam once got Mark Shenton's sister to put a blond streak in his hair; it turned orange and he got into trouble at school. Basically he was saying, 'There you go, girlies, a new hairstyle. Gossip over that one in the yard.'

I'd come home knackered from work and ask our Liam to go to the corner shop for some cigarettes and a newspaper. He'd say, 'I'll go for a pound.' I'd answer, 'You what! It's only a couple of hundred yards away.' Then he'd say, 'A pound each way.'

I'd be that knackered after working all day, I'd end up paying it. By the time he was sixteen, the price had gone up – he'd want a fiver. It would have been cheaper to ring a taxi to go to the shop and deliver them. But Liam would never back down.

Our Noel never fell for it. He wasn't having any of that off Liam when he tried it on. Noel would just say, 'Forget it, I'll get them myself.'

I don't think my mam would disagree if I said she did spoil our Liam. Well, let's face it, she spoiled all of us. We all like to think we were a great help to her, but like a lot of lads in Irish families, we never even washed up so much as a plate after dinner, especially Liam – although he would go to the shops for her and wouldn't charge for it, though he'd end up charming or whingeing a fiver out of her later. I suppose it's always the youngest, and the one who causes parents the most bother and worry, that they fuss over the most. This meant that Liam was never particularly adept at taking criticism or losing gracefully. He was always the most aggressive of the three of us and always in scraps and scrapes in school – and out of school for that matter. To help hone his aggressiveness, Liam decided he wanted a punchbag for Christmas. Noel and I were too big for him by then. After beating it to a pulp for a few months, he joined Ardwick boxing club. He was about twelve or thirteen years old at the time. It turned into the usual debacle. Unfortunately for the young pugnacious Liam, at Ardwick boxing club the kids did more training than boxing, especially when they first joined. It was a good three weeks before Liam got his first bout in the ring with his own human punchbag and it was to be his last. Liam's temper always gets the better of him, even now. That lad is ready to row even before he's heard the reason for the argument or the other person's side of the story. On this occasion Liam got gloved up for his first bout of boxing with another twelve year old at the club. The other kid could box and our Liam couldn't, which meant that Liam got hit, and Liam hates being hit. Finally his famous Irish temper – a present from my dad's chromosomes no doubt – just snapped. Liam tore the gloves off his hands and just steamed into the kid he was sparring with, grabbing his hair, punching him, kicking him, literally battering him senseless. This poor kid fighting Marquis of Queensberry rules got a pasting and Liam was dragged off him, disqualified and thrown out of the club in disgrace for being too violent and not able to control his temper. As I've said, Liam always had to be the best, and he normally showed his displeasure with his fists. By the next day, everyone at his school had heard the story and knew what had happened at the boxing club. Liam became the kid not to mess around with, but it didn't stop him fighting, fairly or unfairly. Liam went on to become the cock of the school. Everyone knew him, and that is exactly what he wanted and expected.

I'm not going to comment on his immaturity. After all, it's a hard thing to accuse a twelve year old of. But as he got older, Liam stayed pretty much the same. He still can't control his temper. I don't think he wants to; it seems to get him his own way. At home we'd fight and argue as brothers do. We used to have two varnished wooden souvenir shillelaghs; these are, for want of a better way of describing them, knotted heavy sticks, Irish clubs if you like. As Liam got older, they started to be brought down from the wall and swung with abandon during our more heated disputes, until my mother finally removed them. We must have driven her mad, especially when we'd start arguing and fighting after getting away from my dad to some supposed peace. Anything could end up with an argument as far as Liam was concerned; in fact I'm sure there must have been a few kids at school who could beat him in a fight, but they were probably not as addicted to the buzz of violence as he was, or that obsessed with getting their own way. Liam would just steam in as soon as he got angry, and this no doubt unnerved and shocked many of his opponents. They were beaten mentally before they'd laid a finger on him. He's not the biggest bloke in the world, but he was big enough, especially when his eyeballs started rolling. If I was going to end up fighting with him, I'd get a few stiff jabs in early and retreat; it was the best way to handle it.

He ended up with a reputation for being a bit of a psycho. I don't know if he was a bully at school, but it's hard to imagine he wasn't. If you are the cock of the school, you have to bully to keep the psychological presence up and discourage any challengers. You've always got to be meaner, more vicious. You want the other tough guys in the yard on your side and you want to remind them as often as possible that you're number one; otherwise you'd be having fights every few weeks because people would say you'd gone soft. Maybe bullying is the wrong word for it, but Liam is bullish. He shouts and rants and raves and makes his presence felt. There's a saying that all bullies are cowards, but I disagree, unless you are talking about older kids bullying younger ones. I suppose it's all fuelled by fear, but more a fear of losing power and control. In fact, at school Liam would be pushed around a bit by one of his mates, a lad called Darryl who was the cock of the year above Liam, again for the same reason. Although Darryl liked our Liam, he still had to show the other kids that he wasn't scared of him.

The problem is, when you are the undisputed cock of the school, you are expected to get into fights with the hard guys of other schools. It all went rather seriously sour for our Liam when three lads from a rival school, St Thomas Aquinas, came down to sort him out. One of them pulled out a hammer and smashed it down on Liam's head. Liam just went wild, punching and kicking these three lads until one by one they went down. They must have been unnerved and frightened by Liam's fierce retaliation; after all, when you hit someone with a hammer, you don't expect them to just shake it off and give you a good hiding. He looked a right state with blood streaming all over his head, face and clothes, like an extra from some Stephen King splatter movie. All the girls in the school were crying, as Liam was the lad they all fancied, the school heart-throb. The teachers didn't think so, though, and he was suspended indefinitely from school, and not for the first time I might add. After three weeks of kicking his heels at home, my mam went and begged them to take him back, which they finally did after making it clear that this was it; if he ever stepped out of line again he would be out. I don't know if it was the suspension or the fear of being sent to another school or that blow on the head with a hammer, but he did behave perfectly after that.

Recently, I've noticed Liam becoming more paranoid. Maybe he's suffering from that rock star disease that Dave Stewart calls 'Paradise syndrome'. He called me up not long ago and asked whether I thought he should get himself checked out in case that hammer blow had caused him any serious long-term damage. I reassured him that he was a mad barmy bastard before he got hit with the hammer!

When it actually came to the time for Liam to leave school, he didn't want to, even though he was seventeen. That school yard was his kingdom. He had respect, all the girls loved him, and all the lads admired or feared him. He was worried about the outside world and what lay in store for him. I couldn't wait to leave school, but when the day came, despite all the front I put up about wanting to go, I was really scared. I knew inside I wasn't ready. Looking at Liam now, I think things were pretty bad for him when he left school. A lot of those insecurities he managed to hide behind his aggression, he had to deal with on his own because Noel and I were off doing our own thing. I think music has saved him. He's the cock of the pop world now, but I wish he'd realise that he doesn't have to prove anything by physically fighting or threatening any more. However, before you start believing the whole hard man image thing with Liam, bear this in mind. He might give you a slap or a nasty dig at the slightest provocation, but he's scared stiff of spiders, moths, bees, wasps – in fact anything that creeps or crawls. How he puts up with half those journalists and hangers-on, I'll never know!

As he got older, things would go missing from my bedroom – Adidas bags, shirts, the lot. He'd lend or give them to his mates. Everything of mine that Liam took out of the house had a strange habit of never coming back. It was my shirts that really bugged me, especially my Ben Shermans. I'd complain and our mother would say: 'Leave him alone, Paul, you've plenty of money for shirts.'

As recently as last year, when Oasis were on tour in the States, he borrowed CDs by the Sex Pistols and the Who to play on the tour bus. When he came back he returned the empty cases. I asked him: 'Where are the CDs? Empty boxes are no good to me,' and he replied, 'Don't worry, our kid. I'll buy you some new ones. I've got loads of money now.' I'm still waiting!

I had to laugh when I saw Noel and Liam on the Brat awards and Noel pointed out our Liam and said, 'He's got about seven different personalities.' He was dead right. With me, he's dead tight, but then he may well be exacting revenge for the fivers I refused to lend him when he was on the dole. He can be incredibly generous with his mates, buying them trainers and clothes and getting the beer in for them when they go out. Two of his mates tried to take advantage last Christmas time, when they travelled down to London for New Year's Eve. They went to Brown's club where Noel and Liam were regulars, blagged their way in saying they were bosom buddies of Oasis, ordered bottles of champagne and had them put on Noel's bill. Our Noel wasn't too chuffed and I think Liam thought they were well cheeky, especially when Noel wanted Liam to pay the bill as they were his mates.

Last year Liam rented a villa in Portugal to go on holiday with all his mates. He asked the management company to sort out a flight for him and they booked him on a first-class ticket to Faro airport for about £480 one way. Well, Liam went mad because his mates couldn't afford that amount of money and he wanted to go with them, not first-class. So he rang me in Manchester and I booked return charter flights for him and his mates, for about £140 each. It's good that Liam has stuck by his mates; I think he always will, because in the main they all seem to have stuck by him.

I should talk about Liam and his girlfriends here, but I don't think this book is long enough. When it comes to the side of his personality that deals with women, our Liam is what people call a babe magnet. Some women do want to mother him, sure, but Liam's all man and he's fun to be with. Girls have always fancied him and he can even be quite sweet when he wants to be. He can be temperamental and murder to live with – I think even our mam would agree with that – but even his ex-girlfriends, who he had storming rows and acrimonious splits with, still ask after him affectionately, and not just because he's now a pop star. After all, Liam's always been a star. Patsy Kensit seems to have done our Liam good. She's not on a big star trip, she seems plugged into the real world, and my mam's very taken with her. Patsy's life has been very different from our mam's and I think our mam does find all the film-star bit fascinating. But that would not be why our mother likes Patsy. No, she sees her as a good steadying influence on Liam and admires her for being able to . . . well . . . would 'put up with him' be too strong a phrase?

Liam's the one who gives Oasis their appeal to the kids, or as one writer put it, 'Noel is the heart, Liam is the soul and the spirit.' But I think in terms of talent he's more than just a pretty face. Although the song he wrote with Bonehead, 'Take Me', was very similar in style to the Stone Roses, it was a good song and I'm sure when he can sit still and muse one day, he'll get round to writing some more. If the day comes when Oasis split, Liam will still be a star and have a successful solo career – he just needs to settle in himself, but then that's probably not Liam. If he fancies doing an album of covers, I've got a few suggestions:

LIAM GALLAGHER – *MAD FOR YOU*

I Wanna Be Adored – Stone Roses; I'm Bored – Iggy Pop; I Want It All – Queen; Mr Vain – Culture Beat; Somebody's Gonna Get Their Head Kicked In Tonight – Rezillos; I Am The One And Only – Chesney Hawkes; Saturday Night's All Right For Fighting – Elton John.

As for Liam's relationship with Noel, here's a few of his observations on his older brother:

I'm not into slapping anyone around, but it's like there's days he's needed a slap and I've given him one, then there's days he's slapped me. But it's not right for other people in the band. Me and Noel will walk off stage during 'I Am The Walrus', they'll carry on playing and then come into the dressing-room and we're fighting. So we've had a word with the management and just tried to chill out.

He's not writing for me, he's writing for himself. I mean, he writes some bits for me but he's the man. He writes the gear and I think it's good 'cos then you've not got loads of people around saying 'I think we should do this or this'. I mean, it works for some bands and they get nice things out of it. But he's got it sewn up, he's got hundreds of songs that are just mega, totally different from what we've got now. He'll never run out.

I fuckin' hate that twat there. I fuckin' hate him. And one day I hope I can smash fuck out of him with a fuckin' Rickenbacher, right on his nose.

Chapter 3

The young Noel Thomas Gallagher

Noel would go out with his satchel to school in the morning and come home at the usual time. If I asked him what he'd had for dinner, he'd tell me in great detail. If I asked him where his homework was, he'd say he'd done it at school. Eventually the school rang up and said Noel's not been in school for three weeks.

Peggy Gallagher, 1996

Noel was a likeable if quietish kid, friendly to the last, but prone to bouts of moodiness, a trait he's carried on through to adulthood. He used to love his action man, taking it everywhere with him when he was younger, like some sort of security blanket. He was very military-minded between the ages of three and seven, with loads of toy soldiers and tanks, and the usual toy cars. His favourite, though, was a toy wigwam which he was never out of. He loved it so much that whenever we played cowboys and Indians, he'd always want to be one of the Indians. Whether we were playing cops and robbers or cowboys and Indians, Noel would never die gracefully – he'd never fall down dead. If he was shot, he'd say you missed. Even if you pressed a cap gun up against his back and went bang, he was prepared to argue the toss, and survived many an imaginary bloody encounter that way.

At football, Noel was quite skilful, a silky little player and fairly nippy on the ball. But he'd shy away from a bruising tackle so he never fulfilled his potential on the football field. I think he belonged to the Jean Pierre Papin school of thought with regards to soccer, believing it would be a better game if tackling was banned altogether (or at least tackling him).

If anything ever seriously bothered our Noel, he'd never talk about it; he always preferred to keep it to himself. Noel was a total daydreamer. He was always telling stories about what he'd got up to. We were pretty skint as a family at that time, but Noel would spin stories to the kids saying we had this and that, and we'd done this or that. I got a bit resentful about his stories, so when he'd been bullshitting some kid that he'd scored ten goals playing football in the park, I'd stand there and say that he didn't score any at all. Not a very endearing trait, but because he had a way of making his stories interesting and funny, it niggled me; perhaps that's where the first seeds of the Gallagher brothers' resentments were sown. On other occasions some kid would come up to me and say, 'Your Noel was telling me he did this, that and the other.' I'd confront our Noel on these occasions about his stories, and our Noel would say, 'Don't tell Mam.' To be fair, I didn't – usually. Mind you, our Noel grassed me up a few times.

Noel shared the same friends as me in our area. We spent most of our spare time playing football in the local parks. At home he'd try to steal off to his room and play with my guitar before he got one of his own. He also borrowed a new harmonica our dad had bought, but he couldn't master it so he never bothered after that. Noel wasn't aggressive in the way that Liam was, but he was a fighter, even when he was really young. I think all the younger kids around our neighbourhood were, mainly because of this big fat bloke who was about seven years older than me called Jimmy Doherty.

Jimmy Doherty was huge. Because of his weight, he got

bullied by all the kids his own age, so in turn tried to lord it over every younger kid on the street. Jimmy always said that he was fat because he'd been in hospital when he was younger and something went wrong. So it was nothing to do with the fact that he always had a meat pie or sandwich in his hand. I think the only thing that went wrong with Jimmy Doherty in hospital was that his mum didn't leave him there when he was born. Actually, he's a really nice bloke nowadays, but he was horrible then.

Jimmy's worst trait was stirring up fights between nice quiet kids who normally got along fine or who had nothing to do with each other. Two of the quietest eight year olds around our way were Noel and a lad called Paul Bardsley. Later on in life their paths would cross musically, but at that time they just knew each other. They weren't bosom buddies, but there was no animosity between them. Jimmy Doherty decided one day that he'd like to see these two lads have a fight. Paul Bardsley explains:

I knew Noel. We were just kids who'd hang around in the same gang, playing football and stuff. You know how kids are; there's loads of you and one day you're mates and the next day you've fallen out. Then this Jimmy Doherty, who I was a bit frightened of anyway after he'd nearly strangled me to hand over a strawberry sherbert, told me that Noel Gallagher had been saying all these things about my mate, Neil Daley, who was also a mate of Noel's. Jimmy was trying to stir a fight between Neil and Noel. I felt quite annoyed and as Neil didn't really want a fight, I said I'd give Noel a fight instead. Then Jimmy Doherty said Noel had been calling me names and saying he'd beat me up. I was really sensitive as a kid, and all the other lads round our way got excited about the fight and said that I'd better be ready, because Noel wanted to have a proper boxing match with me. I'd never thought of Noel as being dead tough, but once Jimmy Doherty started on me, I began to think Noel must be a bit of a hard case and I got really worried. It was stupid really because Noel was definitely getting all the same bullshit. I was that worried I decided to train for the fight with Noel, on the Incredible Hulk punchbag that I'd got for Christmas.

The fight was set three weeks before it actually happened. The whole idea is comical now, but at that age, it was really upsetting. In the end Noel and me stood off from one another. I remember Noel did this little Teddy boy dance first and leaned over and kissed his girlfriend, Janet Doyle, before we started. John Maloney said that the winner would be the one who drew blood first, and I should make sure I got in on Noel first. I jumped in and punched him, Noel thumped me back, and then my sister came out and called me in for my tea. That was all the excuse I needed, so I jumped over the fence and ran in. So much for all my training on the Incredible Hulk punchbag.

All the mums in that neighbourhood knew what Jimmy Doherty was like and tried to keep an eye on him. He was always trying to stir fights between the kids.

Jimmy Doherty fancied himself as the local puppetmaster but Noel wasn't a nutcase like our Liam. He was always quite shrewd and calculating. Mind you, there was no point in Noel or me being right nutcases when we had mates like Youngy and Paul Hewitt.

The fact that our mam and dad were really strict never kept us out of trouble. I think Noel thrived on doing the wrong thing and was never that bothered if he got caught. Looking back now, it was probably partly his way of getting back at my dad, and partly to win back the attention which he'd had off Mam before Liam came along.

Noel was a fast runner and really good at doing a fosbury flop over the adjoining garden hedges. We'd often do that for fun; run through all the adjoining gardens leaping over their hedges or diving through them, trying to get the adults to come out and chase us. In the summer, Youngy would have his tent set up permanently in his back garden, and Noel was always keen for us to join him under the canvas. At the age of seven, Youngy decided to take up smoking in the privacy of his tent, so Noel, Paul Hewitt and I would sit with him and his single cigarette and box of matches, while he attempted to smoke his ceremonial tobacco like some Indian chief.

Paul decided, for a laugh, to set fire to the canvas. One minute we were watching Youngy as he smoked his cigarette, the next we were scrambling out as flames engulfed his toy tent. By the time we'd got out of the blazing flames and tried to put the fire out with water from Youngy's kitchen, Paul Hewitt was in his own house as if he'd had nothing to do with it. Youngy's mum went mad at us and told our mam, who gave us a clout and made us stay in for two days. Paul Hewitt was at home laughing his head off.

Youngy was a bad influence. He used to steal money out of his mum's purse all the time. Once he took Noel and me on the bus to Belle Vue Zoo and fun fair with his ill-gotten gains. Whenever he was around, we always seemed to be on the verge of trouble.

Our old man, though, used to use me and Noel as a cover – he was almost comical if you didn't have to grow up with him. He was christened Thomas Augustine Gallagher. I mean, Augustine; he'd have more confessions to make than half the parishes named after the original saint. As well as beating our mam and hitting us, he always had loads of different women. Noel and I became a cover for him. At one time, he used to drive a Lancia Fulvia. He'd take Noel and me out with him as an excuse. I remember a few times when I would have been about eight and our Noel six. My dad would stop the car outside a particular house and say, 'Stay there, I'll be back in five minutes.' Noel and me would be stuck waiting in the hot and stuffy car, with the sun beating down on us, for up to three hours. At the time, we weren't really sure what he was up to, but we twigged later on. Other times he'd take us to the park where he would have arranged to meet some woman, who was usually married herself. He'd say he was nipping off for twenty minutes and we'd be left in the park kicking our heels for another three hours.

Once Noel wanted to go on a camping trip with the cubs. All his mates were going and he loved tents. Grandma Sweeney was over from Ireland staying with us at the time, and my dad was on his best behaviour in front of her; he had his street angel face on. He had promised Noel that he could go on this trip, but said he was going out and Noel would have to wait until he came back before he could give him the money to go. Noel was waiting ages for my dad to come back, and his head was in bits because he really wanted to go that badly. It was nearly time for him to go, if he was going to catch the bus, and my dad still hadn't returned. My mam didn't have any money, so my gran, realising how much it meant to Noel and thinking my dad had genuinely been held up, gave him the money to pay for the trip and a relieved Noel made a dash for the bus.

When my dad got back, he hit the roof.

'I told him he wasn't to go until I came back. What does he want to be off with the cubs for? Where did he get the money from?'

Well, my mam didn't dare say she'd got the money for Noel from my gran as my dad didn't want my gran thinking badly of him, so she said she'd borrowed it from one of my aunties and that my dad had better pay her back. My dad played absolute hell over it. I can't remember whether our Noel caught it off my dad when he came back – my mam always says that my dad was worse when it came to hitting our Noel than he was with me, but I had a few nasty ones off him, too.

Noel had a fair few accidents. Once in Ireland, when he was about five or six, he tried to ride this big dog like it was a horse. Well, the dog wasn't amused and savaged his arm. He's still got the scars today.

The sorriest I ever felt for Noel was when he was having a go on a makeshift swing at school. It was attached to a tree by ropes and swung out over a steep embankment. Noel was swinging out high and the rope snapped. Noel ended up breaking both his arms. No more guitar playing for a while, but that might have been when he started trying out the harmonica.

On another occasion, there were six or seven of us kicking a ball about in the local park, using two oak trees as the goal posts. Some local bullies, John Maloney and these brothers from a mad Irish family – who spent so much time between them in Strangeways prison that we used to joke that they had their own family cell – kept trying to nick our ball. Then they decided they'd have a game of darts against the trunk of one of the trees that we were using as goal posts.

I slid across for the ball, over the goal line, and felt a sudden sharp pain in the top of my head. I reached up with my hand and to my horror felt the plastic flight of a dart protruding from my skull. The local bullies scarpered in every direction, and none of my mates would pull the dart out. I started to panic, I felt that weak with shock. I couldn't go running home to my mam with a dart sticking out of my head; I'd have to tell her who'd thrown it, and they'd be back to get me for grassing them up. She'd go mad, anyway, because she'd told me not to go near any of them. I was standing there asking everyone to remove the dart and everyone was backing off as if I might explode at any minute. Then our Noel strolled up, cool as you like, and tugged the offending object out of my sore and bloodied head and I didn't feel a thing.

Three weeks later, I was the hero for our Noel when one of the mad Irish brothers shot a feather-tipped dart out of an air gun into the back of his knee. It was almost buried all the way in, and I had to tug it out. They were strange boys, always messing about with sharp, pointed projectiles, and using us Gallagher brothers as moving targets.

Noel was in many ways like an older brother. He probably wasn't as daft and impressionable as me. I think a lot of younger brothers have a certain amount of thinly disguised scorn for their slightly older siblings. Being the eldest, I always felt under pressure to act in a certain way. I took great delight when the other kids nicknamed Noel 'Brezhnev' after the Russian President famous for his huge bushy eyebrows. The fact that I had the same hirsute adornments over my peepers never crossed my mind.

Noel's nickname really took off during the 1982 World Cup. Our Noel was fifteen at the time. A big five-a-side tournament was organised on Cringle Fields near our house. All the lads entered teams named after the World Cup entrants. I was the goalkeeper for West Germany and we were the eventual victors of our little tournament, but Noel's team didn't fare so well. There was a lad called Tony Rafferty, a couple of years older than Noel, who was captain. Our Noel was a good player but lazy. Those summer afternoons, you'd hear Tony Rafferty screaming at Noel: 'Fuckin' hell, Brezhnev, chase the bleeding ball.' Or, 'Come on, Brezhnev, call that a pass?'

Everybody laughed, and of course Tony Rafferty, like any amiable half-wit who comes up with one funny line, started using it to death. Unfortunately for Noel, as just about every lad around Burnage was taking part in this five-a-side tournament, the nickname became popular. Noel hates having the piss taken out of him, not because he's precious but, believe it or not, he's hypersensitive; we all are.

It's funny how our Noel ended up playing the guitar. Our dad had a guitar and an old accordion hung up on the wall. He'd dabble around with them, and I suppose he could play them after a fashion, but he didn't exactly encourage us to become contenders for Young Musician of the Year. Like everything that belonged to dear Daddy, you weren't allowed to touch it. Noel had eyed up that guitar and he may have dabbled around with it, but my dad would have slaughtered him if he'd found out. If I'd known Noel had a death wish, I'd have suggested the bottle of orange-flavoured Junior Disprin as an easier bet. In fact, I was the first to get a guitar and Noel used to play with it; he'd have been about eight then, which is six years younger than Eric Clapton when he started playing. Our Noel was really into the guitar, and could play it better than me, despite the fact that I jealously tried to restrict his time on it and refused to show him any more than a few chords. In the end our mam bought Noel a guitar out of the catalogue for about £25 or £30 and paid it off weekly. He was seriously into playing the guitar like some junior junkie. He'd have taken it to the toilet with him if he could; he probably did. Once again my mother scrimped on behalf of one of us, and did without so Noel could have that guitar. Noel was quiet, but I think he appreciated what a sacrifice my mother had made and so was determined to play it; show our dad, too, that whatever he could do, Noel could do better in his own way.

Noel strumming on his guitar was an incessant, but almost comfortably familiar sound in our house at night. Then he got an electric guitar and an amp and it was, Hello, rock and roll will never die. He'd crank the volume up and have that guitar squealing out all kinds of tunes and riffs. It would drive us mad when we were downstairs watching TV. My mam would shout upstairs for him to turn it down, and he'd pretend he hadn't heard her. Then I'd go up and knock on his door, and shout for him to turn it down. He would – for five minutes, then it was back up to Woodstock level.

Noel always hated our dad, almost with a vengeance. He was always picking on him. He used to drive our dad mad by just sitting there saying nothing. Our dad would be ranting and raving at Noel to answer some question or telling him to do something, and Noel would just sit there as if our dad wasn't even in the room. I'd often say to him, 'Just do it and stop him going on', but Noel was fighting his own battle. I remember once my dad got so mad at him, he grabbed hold of him by the V-neck of his school sweater and ripped it straight down the front. It must have been a new move he'd perfected as he'd done exactly the same to me the previous week, ripping my jumper and kicking me like a dog. I felt bad for Noel when he was victim to all the roaring and shouting and different beatings from my dad, even if it was partly provoked by his own obstinacy, but there was always a part of me that was just glad it was him on the receiving end this time and not me.

Noel used to annoy my dad by rejecting his Irishness. He

didn't want to do all the things expected of Irish kids, and it wound my dad up. I wouldn't say my dad disliked Noel more than me or Liam; it was just that Noel knew how to get at him and genuinely wasn't interested in being like him, whereas I went along with being Irish. Our Noel was determined not to kowtow as often as I did, as far as our father was concerned, but it was a draining and dangerous game to play and only annoyed our dad more until it became a battle of wills. Our dad was always going to win in the end and Noel would normally end up doing something he hated. Still, in our Noel's mind, he could feel superior to me for standing up to him. They were crazy games in the Gallagher family.

Noel had always had a lot of friends, certainly more than me and probably more than Liam. Noel had different mates for different interests. He had certain mates who he was in the cubs and scouts with and others for school. He had mates to play his guitar with, like Paul Bardsley and Neil Daley, and then when he wanted to get up to no good he had mates like Paul Hewitt and Youngy to hang around with. I think one of the things Noel worries about is not keeping in touch with them. Certainly since Oasis have taken off, Noel hasn't had that much time to get in touch, and it's ironic that if you become a bit of a star, mates don't phone you; they think you're too busy. One famous sporting superstar and ex-millionaire even came up to me at a party recently and said, 'Listen, I'm on my arse at the moment. You couldn't lend me £40,000 to get by?' It's great, mixing with the stars.

Noel was always popular with the girls. He had girlfriends from the age of eight onwards. Later in life, he'd bring them home to get my mother's verdict. He was always the steady type, Noel, and liked to have a relationship on the go. He was engaged when he was eighteen, to a girl from Levenshulme called Diane. Despite romantically buying her an engagement ring from our mam's catalogue, it didn't work out. I think he was just experimenting with the idea. I saw her not that long ago pushing a pram around; I think she said she had three kids. Louise Jones was his first big love. He went out with her for six years and moved out of our home to live with her when he was 22 or 23. Louise is really into going out and clubbing and she's quite tough with a strong personality. Noel needed and liked that about her. She could be as moody as him, as well, so they were like soulmates for a while. Around Manchester, Louise is considered quite a catch. Soon after splitting up with her, Noel admitted, 'I don't think I'll ever get over it.'

About a year after they split up, he met his current girlfriend, Meg Matthews, through her friend Rebecca De Ruvo, the MTV presenter. Noel seems quite happy and settled now and our mam likes Meg a lot.

So how can I sum Noel up? He's very ambitious; he always was. He's not fantastically confident but quite brave, funny, intelligent, a bit paranoid at times and incredibly big-headed and very moody. I sometimes think that Noel does think he's better than everyone else, and I don't mean just musically. He loves music and likes to hang out with cool people, always wanting and needing to be the best; but then all the Gallagher boys do. If Noel were to decide he wanted to go solo and do an album of cover versions, I'd imagine these would be the suitable songs:

NOEL GALLAGHER – *MOOD SWINGS*

Heaven Knows I'm Miserable Now – Smiths; Moody Blue – Elvis Presley; All Or Nothing – Small Faces; This Charming Man – Smiths; With A Little Help From My Friends – Beatles; I Don't Want To Talk About It – Rod Stewart; Simply The Best – Tina Turner; Teenage Depression – Eddie and the Hot Rods.

Noel's got a strong love-hate relationship with Liam. Like I say, we've always been like that with each other. Liam goes mad at Noel when he slags him off, but that's because Noel's better at it than Liam. Noel explains:

Our kid doesn't have to slap his arse with a microphone. The Beatles never did any of that, did they? Me and our kid don't want to be rock stars but when you come and watch us, we are. We actually do not get on. We disagree on everything, except that we're members of the same band. At the moment it's quite funny, but if it's like this in two years we'll have to put a stop to it. Our kid's not got the faintest idea what's going on, not a clue. I think that's so cool. He's fresh. He'll be one of the greats because he doesn't know. He's not trying to be a rock star. He'll upset loads of people and just carry on and not give a damn. I just leave him to it. I give him the songs and say, 'Right, sing that and keep out of my way.'

Success has made Liam more stupid. He was pretty cool at school, but since being in the band he's gone completely off the wall. Now Liam's crazy. He is mental – madder than mad – he's out of control. He's beyond therapy.

If I lived in America I would have blown his head off by now and completely regretted it. Since I live in England, I just give him a black eye or something every now and then. I don't hate him but he pisses me off sometimes.

He doesn't write lyrics, doesn't play any instrument, doesn't write anything. All he's required to do is stand there and sing and look good. And I think he gets pissed off by the fact that he doesn't actually do anything because he can't. I don't know, I think he just winds me up on purpose. I think it's just boredom. I don't know what to do. We can't even agree to disagree.

Chapter 4

The young Paul Anthony Gallagher

G allagher. Today's Gallaghers are the descendants of the O'Gallchobhair sept, who were located in County Donegal. The name originates from Gall, meaning 'Foreign' and Cabhair, meaning 'Help'.

The O'Gallchobhairs were located in the Baronies of Raphoe and Tirhugh, where the sept had its stronghold centre at Ballynaglack, near present-day Stranorlar.

The Gallaghers excelled in two pursuits: from the fourteenth to the sixteenth century they were hereditary marshals of the cavalry of the O'Donnell armies, and a total of six Gallagher bishops were Bishops of Raphoe in the fifteenth and sixteenth centuries. Gallagher today ranks as the fourteenth most popular name in Ireland. It is the most popular name in County Donegal, the second most popular name in Mayo and the third in Sligo. The Gallagher motto is '*Semper paratus pugnare pro patria*' – 'always ready to fight for my country'.

My earliest memory is of sitting at a big table next to my baby brother, Noel, in front of a black and white TV watching the landing on the moon, back in 1969. I knew it was an event of some importance because the adults around me seemed to think so, and maybe it was because I can recall it. I thought it was dull at the time watching those small, fuzzy, white figures, but I suppose at three years of age you go along with these things. Moon landings happen every day, don't they? After all, one day I'd end up with two brothers living on a virtually different planet from me.

I can't recall the time when I was the only child. Our Noel was always around. Born sixteen months after me, we went through childhood being dressed identically by my mum, so that people thought we were twins, and being hit the same by my dad. We even had identical bruises. When you're very young you don't mind looking the same that much, but I kicked up about it when I was twelve; who knows the psychological damage that can be caused by wearing the same coloured jumpers, shirts and trousers as your younger brother every day?

Before I started school, I was pretty sheltered. We lived in a two-bedroomed end of terrace house with a cellar that was damp and fusty-smelling, where our coal would be delivered. We had a back yard with an outside toilet and a swing that my dad had built for Noel and myself. When I say swing, it was a bit of an eyesore. My father worked in the building trade, and was a handyman of the 'it's only temporary' variety. He'd obviously pillaged some site he'd been working on and brought home a variety of scaffolding tubes which he slotted together to make a swing with two pieces of thick, strong, dirty rope and a sawn-off piece of painted plank. I bet the other kids were really jealous even though it looked like a reject from Steptoe's yard. That swing was the centre of my world because I wasn't allowed to play out on the street. It was nothing to do with Longsight being a rough area, which it was and is, but more to do with living at the junction with a busy main road. I rarely ventured further than our back alleyway or entry.

The only friend I had locally was a young lad called Joey McGrath. We were enemies to start with; he used to run down the entry and kick our bins over so my dad would dash out and threaten to kill him. I wasn't too keen on leaving the safety of our back yard. The entry and surrounding area was populated by numerous stray dogs, with loud barks and nasty temperaments. I had a mortal fear of them, and to this day I'm still suspicious of those scavenging hairy brutes, whether they be dogs or heavy metal fans. On one of my few excursions outside, when I was about four years old, I snatched a young kid's glass baby bottle. He had Ribena in it. I'd asked my mam to get me some and she wouldn't, so I grabbed his. The bottle smashed and I cut my hand up. I was rushed to hospital and had to have stitches. I've still got the scar today, probably the only visible one of many I carry from my childhood.

Most of my mother's sisters were living in Manchester back then and because my dad was frequently away working or just out and about, my aunties were often round at our house, or we'd go visiting them. They did spoil Noel and me, always making a fuss of us, giving us sweets and buying us little presents. Noel especially was referred to as 'Mammy's little blue-eyed boy', until an even younger Gallagher came along to lay claim to that title. There's no doubt in my mind, though, that our mother was immensely proud of us and took great joy in trying to give us the best and going without so much herself.

Our favourite toys were cars. We had loads of them – Dinky cars, Matchbox cars, Corgi cars, double-decker buses, police cars, estate cars, Jags, even the James Bond Goldfinger Aston Martin with the ejector seat. Oh, and how could I forget those cement-mixer lorries, a few giant Tonka toy tipper trucks, and my Meccano crane, which I didn't know how to make. I basically had a toy building site, which was about as close as I wanted to be to my dad. I was scared of him, but I thought all kids were scared of their dads. He'd shout and roar and my insides would jump. He'd be on at our Noel and me all the time. He used to hit us hard, even at that age. I don't think we were that noisy or difficult. We probably got hit for crying, but he was the one who made us like that and made us so clingy to our mam. Normally when he stopped hitting Noel and me, he'd start hitting our mam. My dad was a really stock, muscular bloke. He must have weighed nearly thirteen stone, and I can still picture him punching my mam when I was about six years of age.

Because I was so sheltered and indulged at home by my mam and my aunties, I was frightened to death of starting at St Robert's Catholic primary school. It was in 1971, at the age of five, that I set off for my first day at school. I couldn't stand it; I even ran back out of the gates to go home again. Every day my mam would literally have to drag me there and I'd be screaming that I didn't want to go. God knows what our Noel who was three at the time must have thought school was like, seeing my daily hysteria. At playtime I was always on my own, the other kids used to make fun of my stammer. I had a really bad one, and so did our Noel. Our stammers were so pronounced that in the end our mam took us for speech therapy every week for four years to clear them up. It's a pity they couldn't have made my dad stop shouting at us and hitting us. The place where we went for our speech therapy was next to the old Victoria Baths in Longsight. We'd take a couple of hours off school and learn how to speak from the beginning again. It was highly embarrassing being five years old and being taught to speak like a one year old.

So the other kids at St Robert's school made fun of my stammer, mimicking it at every opportunity. They were a ready-made gang of kids who were nearly all from the Anson Estate over the other side from where we lived. They all walked to school together and played in the street together. Being taken to school by my mam must have been the equivalent of wearing a sign that said, 'Soft mummy's boy, please bully me.' I hated the place – the dingy outside toilets and a 60-year-old teacher called Mrs McCarthy who gave me long lectures on how to mix with the other pupils.

Sweets were my comfort at that age. It was around that time I was rushed to hospital to get my stomach pumped. I'd found a bottle of orange-flavoured Junior Disprin at home and eaten the lot. That would have been a real rock and roll suicide, overdosing on Junior Disprin at the age of five. I can see the Athena posters now: a moody infant, Paul Gallagher, who lived fast and died young, but had a headache-free time before he bit the bullet. What a nightmare for my mam: all because I was a greedy little git. Another bad habit was biting my nails, which I did all the way down to the quick. It was so bad that my mam used to coat them with that horrible bitter-tasting stuff to stop me, but I just got used to the taste, and I'm proud to say it's one childhood nervous trait I've kept into adulthood. My nails are still so bitten down I can't deal with the technology of the ring pull on drinks cans. In fact, when I'm drunk, my stammer returns and I start getting stuck on my words, which makes it two childhood hangovers I live with.

St Robert's school doesn't hold any pleasant memories for me. Even when the other kids were playing marbles, they wouldn't let me join in because I didn't have enough or I didn't have the sixer or bullseye or whatever the big marble was you needed to play. I felt sorry for myself in a way, and it's a good job too, because no one else at that place did. Perhaps I was just too nervous or maybe I just wanted constant attention.

Needless to say, given these circumstances I used to pick on my younger brother Noel, but not much. I was too busy trying to manoeuvre him between me and my dad. I got a bit of company when my cousin, Willie Gallagher, who was a year older than me, came over from Ireland to live with us. Willie was the son of my dad's brother William. My dad was very close to his brother and was heartbroken when he died in an accident at work. It meant that William's wife was left with four kids to look after in Ireland. Young Willie was a bit of a tearaway, a wild seven year old, and his mother couldn't cope, so he came to live with us. My dad wanted to adopt him; I don't know why when he never seemed to give a damn about Noel and me, and he was never around anyway. He never beat Willie, though, presumably because he was the son of his favourite brother. I suppose Willie was dumped on my mam for her to look after along with us, but I was glad to have him around. I don't know how he felt about being brought over to Manchester. It must have been horrible for him, but you don't think that way when you're a kid. Last year our Noel put Willie on the guest list for the Oasis gig at the Sheffield Arena and he came over from Ireland for it. He remembered the day my mam walloped him one across the legs. She'd told him to wait for her when he left school, but he ran across Stockport Road and nearly got hit by a car. My mam went mad. I think Willie lived with us for about six months and then my dad took him back to his mother's in Drogheda in Ireland.

Things got better for me at school when Noel started. He was a better mixer than me, and his stammer wasn't so pronounced by the time he started, so kids didn't make fun of him the way they had of me. Noel's always been popular; even at school. I suppose he's got a certain charm and a way of getting in with people.

It was around this time that we acquired a new little brother, a screaming, whingeing brat (he cried a lot when he was a baby, too). Liam was christened William John Gallagher, the William part being changed later to the Irish version of the name, Liam. My mother wanted a girl (who she now says she would have called Lisa), which is why she got pregnant again. All the way through the pregnancy she kept saying she was sure it would be a girl, but instead it was a bouncing handsome bundle of a boy who was destined one day to perform in front of thousands and started exercising his vocal chords from day one with all kinds of wailing, bless him.

A few weeks after Liam was born, we moved house from Sandycroft Street in Longsight to the plusher surrounds of a three-bedroomed council house in leafy Burnage. As far as council estates in Manchester go, Burnage would qualify as a des-res. Over all, it's a nice area and we immediately appreciated our move up the social scale.

Being the oldest in the family meant I could now have my own room. I'd shared bunk beds with our Noel before that. We had two plaster footballers on the wall; the blue one was for Chelsea and that was mine, the white one was for Leeds United and that was our Noel's. I don't know why we had them – we were both Manchester City fans. Leeds had drawn with Chelsea in the FA Cup final in 1970 and the replay had been at Old Trafford on the following Wednesday, the same night that Man City had won the European Cup Winners' Cup against Gornik Zabzre of Poland. The Leeds and Chelsea footballers were probably souvenirs of that FA Cup final and my dad had picked them up for nothing from a mate in the pub, an unsold token of a long ago final, but we kept them with us when we moved house. I'm fairly certain my dad didn't buy them for us; in fact, all my dad ever gave us was sweet FA. That's not really true. In a fit of generosity he did buy me a Celtic football mug at Manchester airport when I was six (like a good Irish Catholic boy), which is when my affiliation with Celtic started. There's a heady mixture; Celtic and Manchester City.

A change of house meant a new school and we started at St Bernard's Catholic primary school on Burnage Lane. I liked it a lot better there and it was nice that my old friend from Longsight, Joey McGrath, moved to Burnage at the same time as us. The council were pulling down a lot of the old streets in Longsight and rehousing all the families in council properties in that area. In fact, Joey and I went all the way through school together up to the age of sixteen.

We settled in well round Burnage and played outside a lot more than we could in Longsight. Not that everything was rosy for me – I got bullied by this kid at the top of the street. Paul Hewitt was the same age as me, but a lot bigger, and he made my life hell. I couldn't stand the sight of him, maybe because he seemed to get everything he wanted and all his own way most of the time. He'd grass you up and tell tales on you to save his own skin. He was clever and calculating but in a weird way very funny and sarcastic. Our Noel was very similar at the time. I admit I was jealous of that fact, but I suppose all siblings share a certain amount of jealousy about the craziest things. There being three of us, one always got singled out and picked on by the other two. At that time it was Liam, with him being the youngest and having replaced Noel as my mam's golden boy.

When I was eight years old, I had a three-wheeler bike. It

wasn't a trike. It was fast, state of the art, and had a box on the back to put things in. It wasn't quite as speedy as the other kids with their Choppers or Grifters, but almost, though it didn't corner very well. My dad sent me to the shop with a £5 note to get him some cigarettes. I put the money in the pocket of my shorts and rode to the shops. On the way I hit a bump in the pavement, but thought nothing of it. When I got to the shop, in a blind panic I realised that the £5 note had dropped out of my pocket. I was in tears as I went over every bit of ground I'd ridden along. I had to find it. Tears stung my eyes, blurring my vision, making it even more difficult for me to search the pavement in a thorough and logical fashion. How could I possibly go home and face my dad without his cigarettes and more urgently, his £5 note? My anticipated punishment made it worse. 'Please God, St Anthony (patron saint of lost causes and to a kid patron saint of finding things from a 10p piece to a football sticker), please let me find his money.' It was hopeless. My chest was heaving and I was crying fit to burst when I wheeled my bike into our front garden. My dad was waiting for me because I'd been gone for some time. He accused me of stealing and spending his £5. My punishment followed. It was severe.

Growing up as kids with Irish parents was difficult because the Irish have their own traditions. You end up thinking that the kids who don't go to mass, don't eat a Sunday roast and don't have very strict parents are the odd ones. No matter how messed up your life and your family are, I suppose you always think you're the normal ones. Within Manchester's Irish community, everything is for show. Show your face at mass every Sunday, show you're decent and upstanding, with no teenage pregnancies among the girls and no juvenile delinquents among the boys. Though we didn't have much money, our mother made sure we always looked smart, knitting us matching jumpers and scrimping and saving. It's that immigrant thing – they never want the indigenous population to think they are dirty, unkempt and uncivilised. I reckon the Irish like to wear nice clothes and look good when they can, anyway;

it's tied up with that Celtic vanity thing. Mind you, you see it in other immigrant communities, too. You rarely see a scruffy-looking West Indian kid, even though the family might have very little money and the same with the Asians. I don't know about those two communities, but the Irish do like to think of themselves as somewhat holier than thou with regards to the Protestant English, but then that's a different set of preju-dices. It always reminds me of the Irish comedian Dave Allen's joke, where a man dies and goes to heaven and meets Saint Peter who shows him a beautiful garden stretching forever in one direction with a huge wall down the middle. People are huddled together happily in different places. The man turns to Saint Peter.

'Who are those people over there?'

'Oh, they're the Muslims.'

'What about that lot by the river?'

'Oh, they're the Baptists.'

'Well, who are the guys having the big picnic?'

'That's the Jews.'

Finally the man's curiosity gets the better of him, and he asks, 'And what's over the wall?'

'Oh, that's the Catholics. They like to think they're the only ones who get here.'

That just about says everything.

Every stage in a youngster's life is marked out by the Catholic church and the sacraments. At six years old you make your first confession, at seven you receive your first communion – a fine tradition and anticipated enthusiastically by most kids as it means plenty of cash being handed over by relatives and being made a big fuss of for the day. My only objection to making first communion is that as a seven year old you're at that stage in life where you walk around with your front teeth missing. Finally there's confirmation, in which you are blessed by the Holy Ghost, adopt a saint's name and become a soldier of Christ.

We were all regular church-goers up until our teens, except for Liam. My mother got us washed and dressed up every

Sunday to take us. You could always spot the Catholic kids on a Sunday – they were the shiny clean ones wandering the streets literally in their Sunday best. We all made our Communions and were confirmed. I know it's a bit corny, but I still use my confirmation name as one of my middle names. The idea when you are confirmed into the Catholic church is that you are endowed with the Holy Spirit and take a saint's name to guide you along the way. I chose St Christopher, so I became Paul Anthony Christopher, Noel Thomas chose David and young William John chose Paul, no doubt in honour of me. Of course, nobody bothered to tell me at the time that St Christopher had been struck off the list of saints by the Catholic church as there was no evidence that he ever existed.

I'm not bragging when I say that I was the first of my mother's sons to show a talent for music by getting into the school choir when I was seven. I got some stick from the other lads at school because I was the only boy, but I loved it. Again, there appears that strange Gallagher trait we all share; wanting to be different, the best, to be noticed. The choir meant getting away from my dad and not having to be round at home when everything was going off there. Like Pavarotti, my voice was my instrument. It was my only claim to fame, the only thing I was recognised as having done well, probably to this date. We sang in mass every Sunday and on other special church occasions. Being in that choir meant everything to me so you can imagine how I felt when my dad put the brakes on it.

I was ten. I'd been in the choir for nearly three years and it was going to be a big event. In the Catholic church you'll see umpteen weddings, funerals, Holy Communions and confirmations, most of the run-of-the-mill sacraments, but you rarely get to witness a new priest being ordained. Well, on a Saturday morning, the St Bernard's church choir had been asked to sing at an ordination ceremony. We'd practised all the hymns and we were looking forward to it; it was a big deal and exciting to me. Then, my dad suddenly announces that he wants me to go off with him at seven o'clock that Saturday morning to a house in Bolton to help him lay a new concrete floor in some old lady's house. I was moaning about it like mad but my mam didn't dare go against him, and the more you said the more determined he was. God knows, I went to school all week and then on my days off I'd be made to go out concreting with my dad, all because he had this weird idea that I'd learn more about life going out working with him than going to school. I remember he said, 'Choirs are for sissies and girls. I'll take you out working with me and make a man out of you.'

So while the rest of the choir were off singing at this priest's ordination, I was standing mixing concrete for my dad in a house in Bolton; child labour, and unpaid at that.

When I returned to school on the Monday, I was told by our priests, Father Tainghey and Father Arkwright, that my vocal services were no longer required as it was deemed a cardinal sin for a member of the choir not to turn up to sing at the ordination of a young priest, a man who was following in the footsteps of many to sacrifice his life for the sake of the church. Meanwhile, I'd sacrificed my most precious thing in the world to help lay some old lady's concrete floor. Accompanying my dad on to building sites and working on people's houses on Saturdays became a regular thing for Noel and myself over the next few years, but why my dad chose that particular Saturday, I'll never know. It ended up with me being kicked out of the choir permanently and to this day it's one thing that really hurts; not any of the beatings my dad gave me, but getting kicked out of that choir.

We were wild young street urchins when we managed to get out and away from our dad's regime and the watchful eye of our mother. There was quite a gang of us. Besides Paul Hewitt, there were the Chung brothers, his next-door neighbours. I suppose they sound like some clearing house for straight-to-video Kung Fu films. In fact, the Chung brothers, who later changed their surname to Young, were half Chinese, but you would never have guessed. There was Mike who we called Youngy, and he was the same age as me. Vincent was a year younger than Noel, and Gerard was a year older than

Liam. We were all best mates. Then there was this kid called Paul Carruthers from Wales, who used to visit the area every school holiday. We imaginatively nicknamed him Taff. Taff was very quiet and shy until we corrupted him by getting him involved in all our mischief. I remember one day during the summer holidays, we played the Ouija board. I don't know why or whose idea it was. The glass kept flying off the table; it was totally eerie. For over a week I had nightmares that I'd broken some doomed witch's promise, that I was going to be killed by some strange occult group in Burnage, and then Paul Hewitt confessed it was him all along.

When I was eleven, I left St Bernard's primary school to go to St Mark's senior school, an all-boys Catholic comprehensive. I absolutely dreaded it. What if I couldn't make the transition? What if I still had problems mixing with new kids, and worse, what if I got bullied again?

I'd been toughened up a bit over the summer when we all went over as a family to Ireland for six weeks. It was one of the three occasions my dad took us over to stay with his relatives in Duleek in County Meath. Each time he tried to sneak us through on the ferry without paying. The Irish Sea is a choppy four-hour ride and we'd all end up being sick. My dad's Lancia suffered sea sickness once too, breaking down and being towed off the ferry while we waited around, embarrassed by his fits of temper. We'd stay in Duleek for the first week before we went on to County Mayo for the rest of the summer holidays. After dropping us off in Mayo, he'd return to Manchester to lead the single life.

It became a regular thing. Every summer we'd escape from our dad for five weeks or so by going to Ireland with my mam and her brother, our Uncle Paddy. Uncle Paddy lived in Yorkshire and he'd drive across to pick us up in his car and take us to Holyhead where we'd get the ferry across to Dun Laoghaire and then we'd all drive over to Charlestown, County Mayo, for a few stress-free weeks.

Around this time I desperately wanted some money for football cards, as I was mad on them for a while. This was the period when my dad was earning a big wage and yet he never gave us any pocket money. What was worse was the way he'd leave all his loose change lying out on the dresser in the bedroom, lots of it. I didn't know he counted every penny, so I stole 50p. When my dad found out he went absolutely apeshit, punching me and slapping me until I ended up on the floor. To stop him kicking me in the face I curled up in a ball hoping he'd stop, but he got frustrated and stamped on my head. One thing's certain, I never stole anything off him again – well, not for a while.

St Mark's was a bit of a mad house. We were nearly all of Irish descent and had more than our fair share of nutters. There was Ian Brewer the child bombmaker, always putting explosive concoctions together – a living warning for parents who think it's educational to buy their kids chemistry sets for Christmas.

We had some weird nicknames for our learned teachers, not the most imaginative but very descriptive. All these teachers, of course, later had the pleasure of teaching my younger siblings and it says a lot for them that between the three of us we didn't end up with so much as a grade five GCSE in basket weaving, although in Noel's case it might have helped if he'd turned up occasionally. But you could tell we were brothers; we were all streamed into the same group, and it wasn't the top one.

Chapter 5

In the name of the father

All happy families resemble one another; every unhappy family is unhappy in its own way.

Leo Tolstoy

Our father, Thomas Augustine Gallagher, came from a big Irish family although not as big as my mam's. He had five brothers, William (who died in an accident), Sean, Des, Pat and Dominic and one sister, Kathleen. I think their father was very hard on them and they had a tough time relating to him, but I'm not going to make excuses for my own father's behaviour. That whole strange uncharted land of relationships between Irishmen and their fathers is an emotional minefield. I remember the Irish-American comedian, Dennis Leary, saying that any loud bangs you heard in Ireland weren't necessarily bombs, but Irishmen exploding with tension about their fathers. I don't think he meant it as a joke either. Our dad was like a walking persecution to all four of us. Nowadays, I can't stand cartoons on the TV. Our dad would never let us watch them when we were kids. The only time we saw cartoons was if my dad was out, or if we sneaked downstairs at seven o'clock on a Saturday morning for all the different kids' shows. Our dad would sleep in if he wasn't working, because he'd been out drinking and clubbing it until three or four in the morning, or he'd be staying at some woman's house so the coast was clear for cartoon time at the Gallaghers. It was quite comical, like a stealthy commando raid on the television.

Normally, if we were watching anything and he was around he used to switch the TV off and start playing all his Irish records and tapes full blast just to annoy us; he knew we hated it. If that didn't work, he'd try his German oompah band records and all this unlistenable orchestral shite he had. The only things he'd let us watch would be nature programmes about otters and different animals, and that's another aversion of mine nowadays.

Football always played a big part in our lives. I remember being one of the first kids to get the new football boots that were being advertised by Kevin Keegan. As far as going to football is concerned, the first City match I ever went to was Manchester City versus Newcastle United at Maine Road back in 1971. My dad took Noel and me, and we used to mither him to take us again after that. My dad was so tight that the four or five times that he did take us, it would be three-quarters of the way through the game, with only fifteen or twenty minutes of the game left. He'd get us in free through the gates they opened at the ground to allow the early leavers to get out, then make us think he'd just given us the biggest treat in the world. We'd go in and my dad would ask, 'Excuse me, what score is it?'

'Nil nil.'

'See, what did I tell you? You've not missed anything.'

My dad was very strict with us. Every night we'd have to go to bed at seven-thirty or eight o'clock and in the summer time it was murder. It would be broad sunshine outside, and we'd be lying awake in bed while all our mates played in the street until nine o'clock, sometimes later. He was a spiteful person, and I suspect that he hated to think of us enjoying ourselves. Noel and I joined just about everything to get out of the house. The cubs, the scouts – we'd even volunteer to do bob-a-job to get away. Although we were Catholic lads, we both played football for the Boys Brigade team. Again, my mam scrimped so that we could have all the right woggles and uniform for the cubs. We never had to make do with second-hand things. Whatever we wanted, our mam would try her best to get for us. She could easily have said, 'I can't afford it,' but I think she had so little herself when she was growing up that she didn't want us to do without. She wanted us to have the best and be able to hold our heads up. I think everything she put up with from my dad, she put up with for us. To the outside world we were a model family, I suppose. My dad, although a bit temperamental, seemed respectable enough, and was generous in terms of buying drinks for his mates down the pub and club. We were all well-dressed kids who were in the cubs doing bob-a-job and went to church on Sunday. It was important to my mother, abandoned as she and all her siblings had been by their father; she wanted to give us what she had never had.

There was always tension at home between our mam and dad. Every nice trait our dad paraded to the outside world was merely show. In the privacy of his house with his so-called loved ones, the real demon came out, the Mr Hyde from the Doctor Jeckyll. Now I understand too well how our mam must have felt at the way our dad mistreated and humiliated her for all that time, and it makes me feel bad. I'm sorry for my mam now, at the way I misbehaved, and marvel at the way she coped with three boisterous lads like Liam, Noel and myself, who were always very demanding. She still managed to put up with my dad on top of it all. Everyone in the family trod around him on eggshells. It was impossible to ingratiate yourself, which is why later in life our Noel stopped bothering.

In case I haven't made it clear, my dad was an awkward type. He was always getting into arguments and fights with people; even the slightest thing would result in a ruck or a major falling out. He spent his time working with loads of Irishmen like himself. He DJed round the Irish pubs and clubs in Manchester and he played Gaelic football for a club called

Oisins. He wanted us to be Irish, so he could show us off to his mates and boast about how well-disciplined we were and how he'd keep us on the straight and narrow.

Oisins were a big organised club and they had junior teams, teenage teams, the lot. My dad had a falling out with them, or so he said. More than likely they threw him out because he was always fighting. To get his own back he decided to form his own junior Gaelic football club in competition with theirs, which he called St Bernard's after the local church and school, to play in the Wolfe Tone Under Twelves Gaelic Football League. Of course Noel and me were drafted in. I was eleven at the time and I'd just started at St Mark's; Noel was nine or ten and still at St Bernard's primary school. Gaelic football is like a cross between soccer and rugby and it's played with huge goal posts like you get in rugby. My dad took us to some old buildings and we had to help him remove six long wooden stair banisters, over eight feet in length, which he reckoned could easily be put into the ground for goal posts. We had to take all the clips off them and carry them down to Cringle Fields in Burnage, dig four holes and put the posts in, and then place the other two across the middle as makeshift cross bars. The things weighed a ton. We must have looked like the Clampetts off the *Beverley Hillbillies*.

There'd be about fifteen or so kids who'd turn up to these training sessions, most of them recruited by me from St Mark's first-year intake, and none of them had a clue how to play as the rules are quite complicated. Of course, Noel and I did it under duress. My dad would be really hard on us, calling us all the names under the sun, drilling us and ordering us about like Stalin or someone, putting us down and ridiculing us in front of all these kids we knew from school and church, kids that we had to face for at least 300 days of the year. We'd be wincing as he started shouting and roaring at these other kids, who'd take it out on me at school as retribution for the way my dad had picked on them in training. We'd do all the training, hump the goal posts back and forth and then my dad would delight in telling Noel and me that we hadn't made the team; we were substitutes. I knew we were just there to carry his goal posts and recruit his squad.

Inevitably my dad's dream team of St Bernard's folded after just one season. But I thought Gaelic football was a really interesting game. Together with Noel and some of the better players from St Bernard's, I joined Oisins, my dad's rivals. There were eight or nine Gaelic football teams around Manchester at that time, mainly associated with the bigger parish churches and Irish clubs. Nowadays there are over 30 different teams. I loved it – I even did all the circuit training. I used to pay £3 a week when I got older to go circuit training with Gus Wilson, the brother of the Tottenham Hotspur player Clive Wilson. He used to train us at Maine Road, and used to nearly kill us, pushing us all the way. It was like paying someone to torture you, but I thought it was cool, especially as his brother Clive was playing for Manchester City at the time. I was mainly the goalkeeper at Oisins. You had to be a bit of a mad bastard to be a goalie. I liked playing out field as well, but I was mainly a substitute, the standard at Oisins being a lot higher than at St Bernard's. I certainly wasn't the greatest player, but I was a tryer. After all, it was the only way I was going to be accepted after the way my dad had verbally abused all these kids who'd followed me from St Bernard's Gaelic football team to Oisins. Our Noel played all the way up to under-18 level and Liam played from the age of nine up until we left our dad.

We had a great time playing for Oisins. We played all over the place. Our big grudge games were always against St John Mitchell's in Liverpool – the Mancs versus the Scousers. The game got very tribal and we'd always end up fighting and rucking by the end.

Our dad wasn't a great bastion of morality. He gambled, drank, smoked, was violent, bossy, adulterous, and he was a top scally. He would never buy all the latest top 40 chart stuff. He'd just tape the chart rundown on the radio and stop the tape machine before the radio DJ started talking. Then when he was DJing, he'd dip the end of a song just before the radio disc jockey came in and start speaking on the microphone. He messed it up a couple of times, saying 'Happy anniversary Bridget and Joe,' with Alan Freeman crashing in underneath him. He used to have to buy the odd Irish record to play, but he mainly borrowed them off his mates or other people. He'd tape all the latest big-selling Irish records, make replica copies of that tape and use the original for his DJing work. He'd give me about 20 copies, a sort of 'Now That's What I Call Irish Music Volume 1' compilation, and send me on my bike to Longsight Market to sell them to this old Irish bloke who ran a stall there for £4 each. That old fellow was very pleased to see me. Visibly excited, he'd say, 'Ah, these are very popular. Can you get me another twenty for tomorrow?'

I'd cycle home, and hand over the proceeds of my market deal to our dear father, who'd count every pound.

My dad's bootleg tapes were bestsellers. He couldn't fill the demand. He'd spend all day taping these same records over and over again. I'd hang around listening to all those Irish songs played at full blast, usually with every door and window open so you could hear it way down the street. Then I'd be sent off on my bike with the latest batch to sell.

It's odd that I was scared of my dad, yet always tried to do what he wanted and like what he liked. Later on in life I went drinking at all the Irish clubs and pubs. I even DJed at them like he did. One night I was DJing upstairs at a function and he was DJing downstairs. I couldn't find any leads to connect my gear up, so when he wasn't paying attention I stole his – reward for the polite way he greeted me that night as I walked in. 'What the hell are you doing here?' I answered, 'And a very good evening to you, Father. My mother, my brothers and myself are fine, thank you.'

Our Noel was never into the Irish clubs and all that; he found them depressing, with too many bad associations. I reckon that's why my dad picked on him. Noel didn't want to be what he always called me – 'a plastic Paddy'. He didn't like the music, the accents, the bad jokes and the strange level of hypocrisy that existed in Manchester's Irish community.

Everybody knew everybody else. You were expected to go out
with a girl who was of Irish descent, get engaged, get married,
have kids and steer them through the same rituals of church
and school and that community which really belonged to
another time and idealised itself. The women looked after the
kids, washed, ironed, cooked, cleaned, kept house, paid the
bills, and were in effect slaves to the men folk, sustaining them
in their every need, just like Mother Ireland herself. It is a
matriarchal society which both idealises and oppresses
women. The Germans call their country the Fatherland, but for
us it's always Mother Ireland. I loved it; loved the clubs,
enjoyed the familiarity, the music, the comforting routine. I
think Noel felt shackled by it all and stifled. If there was
anything he was going to rebel against, it was all that hypocrisy
as he saw it; a life he didn't want being mapped out before him.
Those Irish tunes were the sounds of oppression. When Noel
wrote the lyrics to the song 'Whatever', was he singing about
escaping from our father and the Irish heritage he felt being
forced down his throat? He didn't want to be that typical Irish
lad at all. My dad used to give us Irish records sometimes, and
expect us to want to play them. It was aural brainwashing. It
worked on me, but with Noel, well, I can really hear that song:

> I'm free to be whatever I,
> Whatever I choose and I'll sing the blues if I want.
> I'm free to say whatever I,
> Whatever I like if it's wrong or right, it's all right.
> It always seems to me, you only see what
>   people want you to see.

I think Noel still sees those restraints and chains in everything
– in life, relationships, places and times. That's what we both
secretly admire Liam for; there's a wildness about him, a
sense of freedom. It's like he expresses how both Noel and I
felt inside, and if sometimes Liam can't quite keep a lid on his
dissatisfaction, he's probably healthier than the two of us
because of it.

Me and our Noel, 1971

'He's not heavy, he's our baby brother.' In the days when we could tell Liam what to do, 1973

On holiday in County Mayo in 1973 - Mam and her three little angels

Outside our gran's house in Ireland, 1974. Liam's still wearing the same style coat now

'If it's not a Vespa or a Lambretta, fuck it.' An unimpressed Liam, aged two

Stripped off in County Meath, 1974

My first communion, 1973

*Noel praying for a set of new teeth
at his first communion, 1974*

'The Weetabix kid' looking full of grace at his first communion, 1979

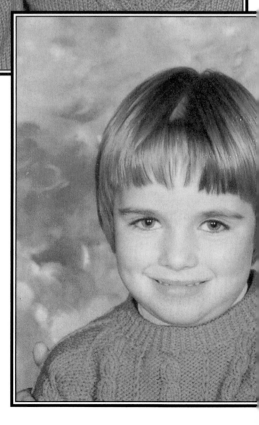

School photo of me and our Noel, 1973 – before Liam followed us there too

In cub uniform, 1974. I seem to be perfecting that famous Liam pose

School photo, 1977. Noel displaying those eyebrows at a young age and Liam looking decidedly chubby

In Grandma Sweeney's house.
Liam reads his latest book to us

With a stray dog we found in
County Meath. Our Noel had two
broken wrists – not much guitar
playing done on that holiday

Uncle Willie's wedding.
Nice suits

Rolling around in the hay. Young Osmonds, anybody?

Liam leaning against Uncle Paddy's car, 1981

Fishing in County Mayo. Without rods and tackle I might add

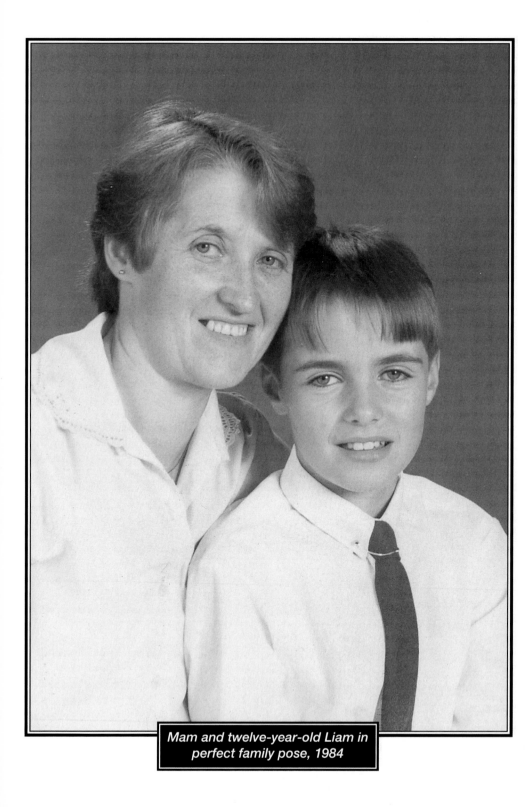

Mam and twelve-year-old Liam in
perfect family pose, 1984

Noel pointing the future out in 1984

Liam aged fifteen plus offensive
moustache

Liam didn't suffer that much violence from my dad, but he witnessed a lot of it, particularly against my mam. What lessons did my dad teach Liam by threatening anyone in the family who disagreed with him with violence and by shouting and roaring until everyone jumped to attention? He helped make us the people we are today.

Although Liam seemed to escape most of our dad's excesses, there were warning signs. Our dad sent Liam, who was six or seven at the time, to the paper shop to get him 20 Park Drive cigarettes. Liam came back with the Park Drive but he bought himself a 2p gobstopper with the change. When my dad asked him where all the change was, Liam confessed that he'd spent 2p on a gobstopper; the wrong answer. Our dad made Liam spit the gobstopper out and then stamped on it and said, 'There you go, that's what you get for not asking.'

Our dad certainly kept busy. For a time he and a partner had their own concreting business, called Holmcrete. In the evening, he'd be DJing in the Irish clubs, particularly the Ardri in Hulme and the 32 Club in Ardwick. He had his gambling and, for some strange reason, an allotment in Didsbury. The allotment was his idea of keeping us off the streets and out of trouble. We had our own patch of scorched earth to plough, rake and hoe. Every school holiday, our precious days were spent being marched two miles by our dad to the allotment and rain or shine we'd be out there, hearing orders being barked by Kommandant Thomas Gallagher: 'First you will dig up potatoes and plant more potatoes. Then you will look after the tomatoes. You, Noel, will exterminate the greenflies and will show no mercy. Paul, you will select the healthy strawberries from the unhealthy ones. Your orders after that are to water the onions and carrots. There will be no escaping.'

Once my dad had us organised, he left us to it, saying he'd be back to check. He wouldn't even give us the bus fare home. He used to tell us it was good for us to walk the couple of miles. Then he'd go off and get the bus round to his fancy woman's house with a bag full of potatoes and tomatoes and other stuff we'd be working our nuts off to grow for him.

Walking home that two miles, we agreed it was child labour. He was like some bloke out of *Oliver Twist*, like that fat bloke in the workhouse mixed with the temper of Bill Sykes and the meanness of Fagan. He might as well have asked us to climb up some chimney and sweep it. That was the Irish in him, really. In Ireland, it's not unusual for eight year olds to be out digging potatoes in the country areas. That's why they get really long summer holidays from school over there. Fair enough, but we lived in Burnage!

Our dad was a gambler. I don't mean just the horses, but like a lot of Irishmen he loved playing cards. He'd be DJing down one of the Irish clubs at night and he'd take Noel or me with him to help him carry all his boxes and equipment. He'd buy us one Coke with a straw for 5p, do his DJ stint, then he'd be playing cards for chickens, hams and turkeys and other stuff like that until two or three in the morning. I'd be really tired and bored. 'Dad, can we go home now? I want to go to bed. I've got to get up for school in the morning.' He'd just tell me to stop moaning.

Then he'd buy me another Coke and carry on playing cards. If he lost he'd be in a bad mood, and I didn't dare say anything to him. I'd try to pretend I wasn't there or I'd fallen asleep as we drove home later.

Of course, the next day in school I'd be tired out and falling asleep all day, not able to concentrate. I'd be in trouble with the teachers for not paying attention: 'We'll continue with the lesson when Mr Gallagher joins us from his slumber.' I used to dread those long nights working for my dad. It's horrible to say, but I was always glad if it was Noel's turn, although he would often take us both. Of course, when he got to be eleven (which in my dad's book was working age), our Liam had to do his stint as well.

As we got older, my dad would use his excursions to the Irish clubs to try and introduce us to what he considered a better class of people. I would be sitting there bored and my dad would say, 'Why don't you go and talk to that lad over there? He's a nice young fellow.'

Nine times out of ten I'd end up talking to the biggest and most boring dickhead on the planet, just because my dad was mates with the other lad's father. I'm not saying my dad tried to pick our friends, but he tried his best to get us away from the English lads we hung out with and put us with the sons of his cronies down the Irish club. I'd argue: 'But Dad, I'd rather be with my own friends.' My dad would say, 'Your friends are all thieves and junkies. Go away and talk to him.' When I was about fifteen, I'd be in the 32 Club or Ardri waiting for my dad, drinking Coke, and all these other kids I knew from school would be at the bar drinking pints of lager, having a laugh and chatting up girls. They'd see me with my Coke skulking in a corner or talking to some notorious dickhead. Noel detested those Irish clubs and our dad took a perverse pleasure in making him go. It was the usual battle of wills, and Noel didn't want to dance to that Gaelic tune.

Chapter 6

Young scallies

Make yourself an honest man, and then you may be sure
there is one rascal less in the world.

Thomas Carlyle

We all did a bit of thieving, like Fagan's young pick-
pockets. In my case any light-fingered pilfering was
just done to fit in on the streets. I'd always been
bullied by other kids when I was younger and the only way
around it for me was to be one of the lads. I went to school
with a lot of them, and I had to fit in at home as well. The only
way of avoiding contact with them would have been to stay in
and then you'd get bullied because of that, too. Besides, as
we got older, my dad didn't believe in letting us stay in the
house (on the few occasions he bothered to be there). He'd
drive us out with his Irish music and by not letting us watch
what we wanted on TV and picking on us. A lot of those lads
we hung out with were into crime. As long as they knew you
wouldn't grass on them they were OK with you, they'd be your
mates. The only way to assure them that you wouldn't turn
stool pigeon, was to go out and steal something for them. That
way they knew you could be trusted or they'd grass you, too.
It was mad, really.

We all did real scally things. We felt restricted at home so we went a bit wild when we got out. With the company we kept, it's a wonder we didn't end up in a detention centre. Noel and I used to hang out together and go nicking golf balls off the golf course or just muck about. When Noel was fifteen or sixteen, him and a mate robbed our local sweet shop. The woman there obviously knew him because he'd been in there loads of times. They just stuck their hands in the till and ran out with 12p or maybe it was 20p, hardly the crime of the century, but I think our Noel ended up getting a caution off the police and solitary confinement and a good hiding from our dad.

The first time I heard the Jam was when I bought the single 'In The City' in 1977. I thought Paul Weller was the coolest, hippest guy around. Our Noel now shares this sentiment, but when mod had a revival back in 1979, Noel was a punk rocker and a rockabilly with a big quiff and a confederate flag on his jacket. Liam wasn't old enough to be anything at the time except a nuisance. I wanted to be cool like Paul Weller, and accepted by the other kids. I had all the gear – an original American fishtail Parka, a brown two-tone suit, Ben Sherman-style button-down collar shirts, pencil-thin ties, white socks and black and white shoes with the pointy toes everyone called Jam shoes. The idea was to look as much like Paul Weller as you could and go around causing trouble. That's where I got my nickname. I was Bod the Mod, but I hate the name – which is why Noel and Liam still delight in using it. A guy called Leo Gallagher first coined the phrase. Youngy and I were odd bods because we were the only two mods in Burnage. As for my musical taste, I was into the Jam, the Who, the Small Faces, the Beat, the Specials, the Merton Parkas, the Lambrettas and Secret Affair. But it was the Jam's music that really struck a chord with me. It seemed to speak to me. 'This is the modern world, one day I will be on top,' I'd be singing in my head all day.

The first real aggro I got into as a result of my mod lifestyle wasn't from punks or rockabillies, but from our dad. I had a target and a Union Jack sewn on my Parka and my dad ripped them off, saying, 'Why don't you get an Irish flag there instead?' It reminded me of the old joke: 'Why aren't there any mods in Northern Ireland?' 'Well, would you walk around there with a target on your back?'

My dad banned me from wearing my Parka, or tried to. It didn't stop me. We thought we were real geezers, dead cool. Girls weren't a problem – we had a large choice – but the Teds and rockabillies had most of the best-looking women. Then there were the skinheads – National Front fascist tattoo-sporting dickheads who thought it was clever to start giving Nazi salutes in the street. They were all Joy Division freaks with their sluttish girlfriends and a hatred for stylish people, especially mods like Youngy and myself.

At that time, Noel was a bit mixed up. He didn't know what he was – punk, rockabilly, Smiths freak – he was all over the place. His favourite band were the Sex Pistols until he discovered the Smiths, and he looked a right balloon in his yellow tartan trousers with zips and rips everywhere. He got a lot of stick from our dad for it, but as ever, our mam would be in the background saying, 'Leave him alone.' Then he was a rockabilly, wearing a donkey jacket with a big Confederate flag on the back and a goon haircut. 'Don't Look Back In Anguish' would be a good title if our Noel was to relate one of his songs to those days, but I must confess that maybe the white socks that we mods wore weren't that great a fashion statement.

Meanwhile, in school I was joined by Sean Curly, the only other mod at St Mark's – that made a total of two mods in a school of 500 lads, most of whom were Teddy boys and Perry boys with their stretch jeans, funk belts, Fred Perry shirts and wedge haircuts with the sideways flick on the fringe. It was like a legalised blood sport, especially in the class of 1977–82. We were a throw-back experiment to the days of single-sex schools. All lads and no girls is tough to take. As soon as school finished, we'd go straight over the fence and across up to Parrswood School where there were hundreds of girls, but the fact that it was boys only in school added to the general atmosphere of malevolence. The great thing about being a mod, though, was that there was no compromise, and once a mod always a mod. It was quite eventful really. I had numerous fights and two Parkas slashed with Stanley knives on separate occasions. Later on, I nearly got knifed in Moss Side precinct when I went dressed up as a mod for a job interview at a dry cleaners there. We'd often wander down to Old Trafford and gaze at all the scooters in Horners, a famous bike shop in Manchester dating back to the sixties, dreaming about being a major face on the scene, a real-life player in *Quadrophenia*. It's strange how both my brothers have really got into scooters. Liam's still got an old one that he's never used at our house in Burnage, and even Noel's girlfriend Meg has got a scooter. It's good to know that what I got up to in my teens has come round back into fashion in London.

Although I wasn't keen on school, it was an escape from the tension and almost prison-like atmosphere at home when my father was around. We could never relax; we were on tenterhooks all the time. We were supposed to go straight home from school, have our tea, do our homework and then go into his homemade wood and plastic-sheeting greenhouse to pick his strawberries and tomatoes, in over 100 degrees of heat and humidity, covered in greenflies. Liam managed to get out of that, so Noel and I were on a rota, doing alternate nights. Yes, we rebelled, each of us in our own way. Our early lives were as stifling as that greenhouse and that's what that shabbily constructed torture chamber represented to me; my life as a child.

Music was an escape, and we were lucky to have Mr Sifter's record shop, owned by Peter Sifter. Sifters was our musical oasis in Burnage. The shop sold mainly second-hand records and rarities. Noel and I have bought records there for eighteen years. We used to love going through the racks of old vinyl albums, seven-inch singles and picture discs. It was like buried treasure to us. Sometimes I'd come across some rare seven-inch piece of vinyl and the hairs on the back of my neck would rise, I'd be that excited. Just the smell of that vinyl was enough; I was a total vinyl junkie. Which brings me to a very sad confession addressed at Mr Sifter himself. Dear Peter, when I was younger I spent nearly all my paper-round money in your holy acetate temple, but there were times when my finances were lacking and I did swap the price stickers around a bit so that I could afford that 10-inch, 12-inch or 7-inch single. There were rare occasions when the odd record disappeared up the front of my original American fishtail Parka, but I'll always repay you by advertising your shop as one of the biggest influences behind the greatest band in the world today. Any confessions our Noel or Liam might have as regards shopping at your store, I'll leave to them and their consciences.

While I'm on the subject of music, I'd like to fast forward a little to give you some idea of how people's musical tastes develop over the years. See it as a little trip through mine and my celebrated brothers' record boxes, if you like. As our Liam is almost six years younger than Noel and seven years younger than me, we'll start in 1986, when our Liam would have been fourteen. If back in 1986, you had sneaked into our Noel and Liam's bedroom, this is the vinyl that Liam would have been jealously guarding: Whistle – Just Buggin' Sounds Electro Volume One, Breakbeats USA and Breakdance Party.

Nowadays if you sneak into his bedroom, you'll see everything by the Beatles, John Lennon, various sixties and seventies bands, the Bee Gees, the Doors, the Sex Pistols, Neil Young and the Who.

In 1986 our Noel possessed everything by the Smiths, U2, the Sex Pistols, Easterhouse, the Damned, the Exploited and the Dickies.

Nowadays, you'll find the Beatles, the Rolling Stones, the Doors, John Lennon, Smaller, Ocean Colour Scene, Dr Robert, the Jam, the Who, Paul Weller and Cast.

Compare that motley selection with my refined record box in 1986. I had the Jam, the Specials, Madness, the Merton Parkas, the Style Council, the Who, Secret Affair and U2.

Nowadays I've added the Small Faces, Paul Weller, the

Stone Roses, Super Furry Animals, Teenage Fan Club, Northern Uproar, Alex Chilton, early Bee Gees, the Osmonds and Cast.

When I was fourteen and fifteen, I was open to corruption and vice of every kind. I didn't hanker to get involved in shady things; it was peer pressure and fitting in. Maybe it was all the bullying at school and at home that made me a follower rather than a leader. I didn't have our Noel's social skills – maybe I wasn't as bright – and I certainly didn't have our Liam's self-belief coupled with his hair-trigger temper. Strange thing, a bad temper – when you're an adult, it's seen as childish and immature, but when you're a kid, it gets you respect, and that's not a lesson you forget easily.

Because of the company I kept I got roped into all things parents warn you about. Glue-sniffing, petty crime, burglary, you name it – I was to some extent an accessory. I was finally accepted as part of the gang on the inside looking out and not the other way round; I belonged. We'd go to Errwood Road Park, Youngy, and a couple of others. We'd find a spot and get out some empty crisp packets. We'd empty a pot of glue into the bags and inhale and we'd be off floating, like a constant buzz, a bell ringing in your brain. Sniffing glue meant we could spend our dinner money on glue and cigarettes as the glue suppressed our appetites. We'd occasionally have cannabis, but that was a rarity and a bit expensive for us. Besides, we thought only old hippies did that sort of thing. Glue was our main vice and easily available. Shop-keepers didn't bother about selling us glue, especially me. I looked a nice sensible lad. I was quite shocked when Liam said that his favourite drug was glue. It was probably a wind up, but I don't know every single thing he got up to in his teenage years!

Glue bags fights were mad. Three of us wagged off school one bright sunny day and we were sitting under the arch of a disused railway line at 9.15 a.m. with our nose bags. We were so high we had no control over our faculties. There was a celebratory atmosphere as it was a few weeks before we were due to leave school. Well, we got a bit out of hand, and the next thing you know, we were throwing Evo Stick at each other. It clumped in my hair and I was absolutely panicking. What could I do? Youngy was in the same sticky situation. Anyway, we pooled our money and went to a barber's shop. We came out virtually bald, just looking like we had a couple of day's growth. When I got home that night, my dad went mad about it, reckoning I looked like a right skinheaded lunatic. I thought it was rather fetching, and so did the girls, so I kept it short like that right up until a few years ago, although the amount of time me and my number two haircut spent unemployed is testament to how prospective employers felt about such short, neat hairstyles.

Drugs aren't clever, nor do they make you big, and they're certainly not good for you. It's a bit corny, but the attraction was just to help me get somewhere different for a short space of time; leave behind the mundane nature of everyday life for a few hours. It was a form of escapism. It wasn't just glue that we did. Glue was merely our starter pack. Come October and November time, it was magic mushrooms, *Psilocybin* I think they're called, small thin mushrooms with a little nipple on the head. We'd pick them and eat 20 or 30 each while they were still fresh. I suffered a bad case of paranoia on mushrooms, akin to the Ouija board incident. I was in the local park and tripping that much I thought I'd been abducted in a space ship. I tried to jump down a flight of steps and nearly broke my leg. Then I started running home and in the sky I thought I could see what looked like a huge dog chasing a boy. Sure enough, when I turned around there was this huge Labrador chasing me. Well, as I've mentioned before, I was always frightened of dogs. I ran all the way home like Ben Johnson (well, there was no way I'd have passed a drugs test). As soon as I got home, I went straight to bed and buried my paranoia in a restless sleep, dreaming that I was surrounded by dozens of Red Devils trying to stab me with pitchforks.

I'd just daydreamed my way through five years of school at St Mark's so I left without taking any O-levels or CSEs. I didn't want to take any exams and I didn't have a clue what I wanted to do. I went for a few interviews, trying to catch my stammer as it stuck in my throat. I was nervous, and that was just talking to the careers' officer. There was a YTS place going at Bert Sibbets, a butcher's shop just around the corner on Greenend roundabout, Burnage. I only wanted the job because it was about five minutes from our house. I'd go in at nine in the morning and go home at five o'clock. In between I'd make beefburgers and sausages and muck about talking to all the young ladies who came in. I ended up working in the covered market in Manchester's Arndale Centre for another firm. We were really busy so they didn't have the time or inclination to teach me how to bone meat and be a proper butcher. I was just a dogsbody doing the beefburgers and sausages and scrubbing surfaces down all day, and for a crappy £50 a week.

For some reason we always ended up hanging around in Levenshulme, where the action isn't. When you're on the dole (I didn't last at the butcher's) and all your mates are working, it's the worst feeling in the world, but in Levenshulme neither Noel nor my good self felt any stigma, as everybody else was out of work and potless (broke, skint). We tried playing football all day, but it didn't fill the void and that emptiness we all embrace in adolescence. There was no future (I'm starting to sound like those punk records our Noel listens to now) and let's face it, we were basically a bunch of low lives with nothing better to do.

There weren't that many nice girls in Levenshulme, so we moved to pastures new. Reddish Vale in Stockport was a bit on the rough side, but the girls were more numerous and easily impressed, especially if you had a Manc accent. Noel's quiet exterior actually worked in his favour; plenty of girls would think of him as shy but strong and silent and deep. Self-obsessed and moody would have been more like it.

My eighteenth birthday was spent on a freezing night in the middle of January on Greenbank playing fields with two girls and a few bottles of cider. One of the girls, Paula, I took a particular fancy to and the night was a roaring success. That was my eighteenth birthday party, budget style.

At Reddish Vale, the local lads would all run off home when they saw a large group of Levenshulme lads, which is not surprising when you think what a state we all looked. Including Noel and me, there would have been about 20 of us. Noel only hung out with us occasionally as he was particularly fond of the ladies and spent a lot of time bearing his sensitive soul to them. I was glad he was there on one particular night, though, when we decided to go to the rougher end of Reddish Vale and really show those locals who was boss.

We started chasing these biker guys, calling them names and threatening to give them a kicking. Suddenly one of them stopped his bike, pulled out an air rifle and opened fire. He was joined by a very mean-looking bunch of 15 to 20 older lads – we didn't hang around to count. We ran for what looked like some school playing fields and outbuildings nearby, but first had to get over a fence. It was covered in that anti-climbing paint and I just couldn't climb over. Our Noel, who'd already got to the top of the fence, was pulling me up by my jacket which ripped. I was yards away from getting a group kicking when I finally scrambled over. We were running through what I thought was a school, when it dawned on me that it was full of headstones.

I didn't see the open grave. The shock of dropping six feet when I was expecting my trainers to hit solid ground knocked the wind right out of me. I could hear Noel shouting for me to hurry up. He came back and pulled me out of the freshly dug grave and we finally made the safety of Levenshulme, with me looking like a zombie covered in mud and dirt. My mam wasn't too pleased with the state I was in when I got home, but I could hardly say a bunch of nutters from Reddish Vale were out to kill us, and I'd fallen in a grave. She'd never have believed me. I can't wait to read our Noel's version of that story somewhere.

Noel started to think we were all losers and it was beginning to look that way to me, too. I had a mate with his own flat.

We crashed there at night sometimes, dropping acid with Youngy. Youngy was a bit of a chancer back then. He'd do anything.

One time, I came across Youngy and another couple of lads in a beat-up old brown Triumph Dolomite at about one o'clock in the morning. They told me to get in, so I went with them to Whalley Range, an area of huge old houses, big gardens, student flats and bedsits. I was told to wait, so I waited while they went off to do a few houses. I could hear an alarm sounding and by the time they got back with the gear the police had arrived. They tried to stop us, hanging on to the car, but we drove off, went too fast around a corner and, 200 yards from where we'd left the coppers, we crashed.

Youngy and me ran off in a different direction from the other two, through a back garden. Youngy ran straight into a washing line scoring a nasty welt across his neck. He was spluttering and choking, while I tried to get him to hush in the darkness. I ducked under it and left him, leaping over a wall into a larger back garden, full of trees and bushes. The police were searching for us. I could hear them shouting, calling to each other, knocking on doors. I crawled into some bushes and lay there, hardly breathing. Gradually the night became still and quiet. I spent five hours crouched in the dark, getting startled by hedgehogs. It was like one of those nature programmes my dad tried to make us watch. Paul Gallagher presents *Hedgehog Watch*.

Stiff with cold and tension, I tentatively rose from the bushes as light was breaking and then literally ran all the way to Levenshulme and our mate's flat. I finally got back to Burnage the next day and breathed a sigh of relief.

Two weeks later, while I was kicking around at home, there was a knock on the door – not just *a* knock, but *the* knock. Two coppers stood there.

'Bod.'

'You what?'

'You're Bod?'

'Some people call me that. Why?'

It all came out – the stolen car, injury to an officer, burglary, resisting arrest.

Liam, twelve years old, joined in with, 'It wasn't him, leave him alone,' and then Noel started: 'You dickheads. He hasn't done anything wrong.' Liam latched on to the comment. 'Yeah, dickheads.'

I got a large fine and a record. The other three got sent down. It was my first offence.

Horrible stuff. It amuses me when the press get so hot under the collar about our Noel burgling houses. I never saw any of the supposed gear all the time I was living there. He knew Youngy, who was notorious at one time, but I can't see it myself. Noel could have been a look-out as he was quick and crafty, but I'm not swallowing that burglary bullshit. The press will write any old shite. If you joke with them they make a headline out of it.

We carried on dabbling in drugs like amphetamines, or whizz as we called it, and LSD of course, which I didn't enjoy in the slightest. One of the last times I took drugs was in 1984 when I was eighteen. It was just before we left our dad. After that I didn't feel the need.

We thought we were being daring back then. Now it's just sordid. Take a drive down Claremount Road in Moss Side and see the crack dealers hanging out all day dealing right in front of the police and tell me something's not messed up. That's why I don't bother nowadays. I've had many an argument with record company types who've tried to get me to snort coke in bars and at different parties. They seem to get very defensive and paranoid when I refuse and say I don't touch the stuff. Cocaine to me seems a very expensive way to become seriously wired and anxious, and I've got enough neuroses in my life without enhancing them. One thing that strikes me particularly about regular cocaine users is how they can sit around and talk absolute bullshit for hours and seem to feel their opinions are really important. It just makes people cocky, big-headed and full of themselves and when they come down they are irritable, bad-tempered and paranoid.

Noel wasn't that big into drugs at that time. He'd have a bit of cannabis, but didn't every kid back then? I don't think anything stronger appealed to him. Noel got high on his Smiths records; he was that ultimate box-room rebel, waiting to break free. People nowadays make fun of the Smiths, but there was a definite power in their message, and Noel was never into any band with quite the same passion. They inspired him the way the Stone Roses later inspired and influenced Liam, and I don't think you could get a better example of what was unique about Manchester bands than the Smiths and the Roses. Noel has left most of his Smiths vinyl at our mother's house, and I sometimes listen to the track, 'It's Over'. Morrissey sings, 'I've seen this happen in other people's lives, and now it's happening in mine.' I wonder what dreams and thoughts our Noel had, listening to the Smiths, fantasising about the unlikely day when he'd be in a group as important and, in terms of sales, probably even bigger than them.

I was in Manchester all through the first summer of love in 1988 and right through the ecstasy binges of Madchester in 1989 and 1990, never touching anything stronger than a cigarette and a glass of Jack Daniels. The whole vibe made me high. That was a time to be in Manchester, a time to feel really alive. Drugs were part of that scene, but they weren't the scene itself. I never bothered doing ecstasy, but Noel was not averse to it, going to places like the Hacienda.

Chapter 7

Labouring on

Noel could handle being out of work better than me, because it gave him more time for his music, and he had Louise to keep him sane and confident. Our Liam just never took too kindly to getting his hands dirty or being told what to do and so could accept being unemployed, although I know the lack of money got him down.

Apart from the boredom, the worst thing about being out of work is the small amount of money you're expected to live on. The government try to force youngsters into dead-end, low-paid, menial work and call it training. All it means to me is stuffing sausages and wiping down surfaces in a butcher's shop with the added bonus of emptying out the rubbish.

My dad took the mickey when I was working at the butcher's, saying I should go and work for him and make double the money. I wasn't keen, but my mam wasn't working at the time and I needed to be out earning. Working for my dad was no treat. We'd all worked for him on the building sites at one time or another, at weekends and during school holidays. When we were younger, he'd have us on this windswept site in Liverpool or somewhere at seven in the morning, freezing to death.

He'd never want to pay us. I'd ask him for my money on

Friday and he'd just refuse to pay me, saying, 'What's the point of giving you money when you only spend it?' Trying to get your wages off him was an ordeal. I remember one time my Uncle George was working for him and my dad never paid him either. He was desperate for his money. He hadn't had any that week. He came round to our house to see my dad for his wages and my dad just punched him in the face and slammed the front door on him.

When he did pay me, I never got as much as he promised. I'd get my pay packet and he'd have made deductions like 25 per cent tax and National Insurance. I wouldn't mind, but I was on the dole at the time signing on for welfare. It was supposed to be a cash arrangement. He'd also subtract money for every bit of food I'd had from the chippy at lunchtime. When it was a hot day, and we'd be doing hard physical labouring, he'd tell me to go and get a big bottle of Coca-Cola from the paper shop. He'd drink most of it, then deduct it from my wages the following week. He was really tight.

Still, it was better in a way than what I'd been doing. I'd normally come out with about £100 a week plus my social security money. When Noel left school, he was in a similar situation. My dad paid better money than he could earn elsewhere, and as our Noel had also been dragged off to many a building job by my dad, he was familiar with the work. Now Noel is the hardest working man in pop music. He likes playing the guitar, writing songs and being in a band, so he will work hard. Get him on a building site, however, or doing something else, and that staunch work ethic is non-existent.

Noel once said that I had a God-given talent for digging holes. Compared to Noel, a one-armed dwarf with a bad case of arthritis had a talent for digging holes. Noel was never that strong physically and he was a right lazy git. He didn't take to any physical labouring jobs. But he was smart and had it all sussed. He could hide and doss about for hours without getting caught. His favourite scam was to volunteer to go to the chip shop at lunchtime. Three hours later, he'd turn up, our chips would be stone cold and when you asked Noel where he'd been, he'd say, 'There was a big queue.' His God-given talent then was for shirking and daydreaming.

We would end up arguing like mad over the menial tasks, like whose turn it was to brew up (in a tin can over a makeshift campfire with no mod cons like kettles or gas rings), and I'd always end up doing it. I could tell our Noel wasn't afraid of hard work by watching the way he fought so bravely against it.

Mind you, our dad was a hard worker and good at his job back then, even if he did take stupid risks like riding on concrete staircases as they were lifted up into position by the crane, and wandering about a site without a hard hat. He acted as foreman at work and spent all his time at home cracking the whip. I started giving him some verbal back and he'd freak out at me, raise his fist and start chasing me round the house. I was about eighteen by then. I'd answer him back, but I never actually hit him. Neither did Noel, but he really wanted to at times. I swear we couldn't warm to that man if we got cremated with him.

Our mam had been legally separated from our dad for years and we were desperate for her to find us another house away from him. Things started to go right the day my dad slipped a disc quite badly at work. He was taken into hospital for an operation on his spine and it was nearly two months before he came home. They sent him off somewhere to convalesce. For a couple of months we had a sneak preview of what life would be like without him around. I think the happiest people were Noel and our mam because they'd had the most to put up with from him. Just that shadow being lifted from us made a big difference.

The back injury meant both Noel and myself were unemployed for a while, so I went back to being a butcher. My mam carried on pestering the council to get us a house so we could escape from him because he'd refused to leave. Things came to a head when he returned from the hospital a semi-invalid, or so he cracked on. He'd spend all day lying on his back in the living room, making us step over him, giving out orders and expecting our mam to wait on him. The only times he got up was to hobble to the toilet or the bathroom, and of course to go out drinking and gambling at night round the Irish clubs. After two months of peace he was back, a bigger pain in the neck than ever.

Finally my mam got us a council house on the other side of Burnage, about a mile away. We did a midnight flyer when my dad was out one Friday night, and by the time he returned the next morning we were gone. The press never seem to get this right. To quote the *Daily Star*, among others:

> ... Tommy Gallagher's family walked out on him eleven years ago after songwriter Noel, then a teenager, beat him up in a bloody brawl following years of violence. Noel has said, 'The last time I saw him was when two paramedics were carrying him out of the house to hospital.'

I know it makes much more interesting reading than the fact that we did a moonlight flit when my dad was out drinking, and the press love those kind of stories. The paramedics story is a nice touch, too. In fact, both Noel and I worked on and off for my dad for a good while after we'd done a runner from the house, and witnessed many incidents of his violence and temper directed at his workmates, foreman, crane drivers, and anyone really who annoyed him or got in his way. Maybe he missed being able to abuse us physically and verbally at home. Who knows. As far as being a kind boss went, my dad wasn't exactly sympathetic. If you kicked him in the heart, you'd break your toe.

The house we moved to was in a bit of a state. We didn't have any carpets for the first three months or so, but it was good to get away. The only one who was down about it was Liam. He was only twelve and all his mates, including his best mate Mark Shenton, lived about a mile away. He used to look a forlorn sight walking off to play up that end of Burnage, and I know my mam was worried about him. She felt really sorry for him and that was what made it so difficult for her about moving out. She didn't want to take him away from his friends but she did want to protect him from our dad. Both Noel and myself were getting a bit too old to hit, but Liam was the age where he'd start coming up against him more and more. She used to tell Liam to be careful and not to go near our dad.

Those first few weeks of life without our father were sheer bliss. We could come and go without the threat of violence hanging over us, not that we took our mam for granted. We realised it was a big step for her and tried to help her all we could, mainly by trying not to worry her. It's hard to explain that sense of freedom; you'll hear it in Noel's song lyrics – those lines about breaking out and being free and his appreciation of what our mother did for us. He was now able to concentrate on his music without being dragged downstairs to pick tomatoes. Liam did resent it for a while, but only because his mates were all round our old house. As for my father, he never dared come round. I suspect he was glad to see the end of his responsibilities. He was supposed to pay a certain amount of money to our mam for Liam, but he never did. Our mother was a stronger person than he'd given her credit for. She'd have called the police if he'd have come within 200 yards and I'm sure Noel fantasised about taking some form of violent retribution should he show his face at our new house.

Relief for our Liam arrived a year or so after moving in the shape of David Coates, or Coatesy as we came to know him. David was the same age as Liam and had moved to Burnage from Yorkshire when his mum and dad took over the local Sam Smiths pub, The Sun. Coatesy was pretty quiet, but a really nice lad, and became Liam's best friend. This meant Liam soon stopped walking all the way down to where we used to live to play out, which pleased my mam. Coatesy is the best friend Liam has ever had, and I don't think fame can ever change that. It was a funny mixture, really; Coatesy was born and raised up to the age of twelve in Doncaster, supported Liverpool Football Club, and was a quiet, unassuming lad. Then there was Liam, a rabid City fan and the exact opposite in temperament; although he can be quite shy at times.

Money was tight at the new house, so in order for Noel and

me to make some decent wages we still had to go out to work on the building sites with dearest Daddy. He used to pick us up at the corner of the street in his van. We felt uncomfortable and so did he. He knew that Noel hated him, and we kept the conversation down to a minimum. He'd ask, 'How's ya mother?' We'd say fine (now that you've gone, you big lump) and that would be all the personal stuff out of the way. He wasn't bothered that we'd left. It may have been what he wanted all along, but it wouldn't have gone down well in that Irish community he was so fond of. There was a lot of shame attached to your wife and kids leaving you, and they must have been aware of his gambling and womanising. He never told his family in Meath. Our gran and uncles on that side didn't know for ages. Later he even told them that all three of us were working for him and doing really well. By that time he'd lost his business as well as his family, so whatever he said then was all for show.

Anyway, we kept our tempers with him and just got on with it. Most people dislike their work and their boss and the alternative for us was hanging around at home getting on our mam's nerves or getting involved with crime. It was hard work. Our dad's speciality was concreting. We'd use these heavy concrete beams, put blocks made of coal dust in between and then we'd have to fit ceiling hangers and grout them with wet cement. Grouting meant pouring a wet mixture of sand and cement over the beams, slabs and coal dust blocks and spreading it over with a brush. It was quite a delicate oper- ation and you'd often have to keep hosing down the slabs and beams with water to make sure the cement would stick and cover the gaps. Then you'd let the sun dry it off. My dad would always end up having an argument. He'd have us hosing the slabs and beams on a floor and there'd be brickies working underneath who'd be getting water leaking down on them and their bricks. As these guys started complaining, he'd be threatening to kill them if they didn't shut up.

They were mad days. Take a look at Mere Golf Club near Macclesfield. Gaze lovingly on part of Blackburn Rovers football ground and admire the Fisherman's Friend lozenges factory in Grimsby, because me and my famous songwriting brother Noel Gallagher laid concrete floors in all those places.

Noel has said about those days: 'All my dad would do is moan. I'd graft with me dad, me brothers, me uncles and cousins, and working on a building site on a cold January morning you end up hating them all.'

I can't really imagine the words 'graft' and 'Noel' in the same sentence, although one thing Noel did say, I would agree with: 'I worked with my dad when I left school, which was the worst thing in the world to do.' I'd do any job back then to get away from my dad. Unfortunately few of them paid as well, but in comparison they were hassle free.

I wouldn't want anyone to get the idea that during my many and varied dull jobs I was a shirker. I was rarely, if ever, late for work and grafted while I was there, but it's hard to build a great image of yourself when you are basically making a living skivvying for what was often less than the minimum wage. I loved nice clothes and they didn't come cheap and I was a young lad. It doesn't matter how fat, bald or ginger haired and ugly you are, if you've got money, women are queuing up to go out with you. The only way to be glamorous if you're working class is to be a gangster, a crook, a footballer or a rock star – and that's reality.

The best thing Noel and I ever did was to stop hanging around Levenshulme. I stopped because I started working for Norwest Holts laying gas mains. It was hard work I can tell you. Most of the people we left behind ended up in prison or getting heavily into drugs, and that's what happens when people get stuck in a rut without a job or ambition. It could easily have been Noel or me if we hadn't had a strong mother behind us to kick our backsides every now and then.

I moved on to Kennedy's Civil Engineering and got Noel a job there. When he first started he was working outside with me, 'digging holes' as he and Liam always put it. Noel couldn't handle the outside graft; in fact he hated it. I wasn't actually working in the yard when a JCB dropped a section of gas mains pipe on his foot. I know it was an accident but I always used to kid him on that he'd done it on purpose, like a soldier who shoots himself in the foot to avoid going over the top. By all accounts Noel was writhing around in great pain for some time before anyone helped him. This was typical of those big tough Irishmen we worked with. Noel was on the ground groaning in agony and the workers were all casually strolling past saying, 'Ah, Jaysus, dat's nuttin'. Sure just walk it off, ye'll be right soon enough.' I would have to check, but I've a fleeting memory that he was on the ground for over an hour before anyone helped him!

Every cloud has a silver lining and his foot injury meant he got moved into the stores so he could spend all day handing out nuts and bolts and sit around playing his guitar, daydreaming. That would be on his curriculum vitae: Name – Noel Gallagher. Hobbies – playing the guitar, listening to music, football (playing and watching) and daydreaming.

Later, when Liam came to work at Kennedy's, it was the same scenario. He didn't like the outside graft and he wouldn't let me or any of these other Irish blokes teach him how to handle a spade properly. It used to annoy me in a way. Noel said he hated it and Liam would say he hated doing that kind of physical labour, too. Did they think I loved it or something?

Liam worked on and off, but more often than not he was on the dole scrounging money from me and my mam. He ended up staying on at school until he was seventeen, which meant he kicked around doing odd jobs and signing on for eighteen months or so before he joined Oasis. Liam is really vain and he admits it openly. He was always posing about during his teens. I think if he ever had to go to hospital again he'd insist that his X-rays be retouched. Obviously he did it all for a reason: women. They all loved him. When he was of an age to start going out to pubs and clubs he'd head out to Altrincham and Alderley Edge where Coatesy's parents had taken over a new pub, The Vine. He'd come home bragging about all these posh girls he'd met and gone out with. He was a real live wire, Liam.

In Manchester town centre, he'd go to the Ten Cafe Bar

and when he was seventeen he became a member of the Solstice Club at the Academy in Manchester, a popular nightclub run by Anthony Boggiano, who was also managing the Inspiral Carpets. Noel was working for them by then, hence Liam's free membership. Solstice played a mixture of house music and indie stuff. There were some strange club records in Manchester back in '88, '89 and '90 – 'Tomorrow Never Knows' by the Beatles, 'Alone Again Or' by Love, as well as the Doors and Hendrix. The Beatles became quite hip again, thanks to the Stone Roses mentioning them in interviews and the fact that LSD was seen more in Manchester's clubs than ecstasy; well, it was cheaper. That club, like a lot of clubs at that time in Manchester, was forced to close down after trouble one week, when about 35 members of the Gooch gang in Moss Side turned up and were refused entry. No wonder we called it Dodge City. The clothing company Gio Gio had a famous T-shirt out at the time with a picture of the city centre on the front and the words 'Manchester: dedicated to dodging the rain and the bullets' written across it.

Noel was getting more and more into playing his guitar and started jamming with Paul Bardsley at another friend's house. Later Paul was in the Manchester band Molly Halfhead and now has a new band called Wireless. Paul and Noel ended up forming a band called Fantasy Chicken and the Amateurs. Mercifully they never played a gig. I remember Paul Bardsley would try and sing like Kevin Rowlands of Dexy's Midnight Runners fame. Later, Paul's band Molly Halfhead would have Oasis playing support to them at the Boardwalk, but that's a later story.

Chapter 8

Away-day blues

It's scary to think that although Noel, Liam and myself are different in many ways, we've all inherited loads of bad traits from our dad. One thing we gladly inherited from him, though, is our support for Manchester City Football Club. League Champions in 1968, FA Cup winners in 1969, League Cup winners in 1970, winners of the European Cup Winners' Cup in 1970 and League Cup winners in 1976. Since then absolutely nothing, and as Liam wasn't born until 1972 and did once say, aged five, 'I'm a United fan, me,' until Noel and I put him straight, I'm pointing the finger at him as the jinx. I'm sure Noel will agree when he considers the evidence.

The last time City won a m ajor trophy was in 1976, when Dennis Tueart (my all-time favourite City player) scored the winner with a devastating overhead kick in a 2–1 victory over Newcastle United in the League Cup final at Wembley. Noel and I had a chance to touch the Cup the following day. We were at Neil Daley's house (who was later to be in a short-lived band with our Noel) and Neil's dad used to play professional football for Preston North End with Man City's chief scout Ken Barnes. It was Ken Barnes's son Peter who scored the other goal in City's Wembley victory and you can imagine our delight when Ken Barnes brought the Cup round to the

Daley household to show it off. Neil took a photo of our Noel holding the Cup – a happy memory.

When you're Irish Catholic in Manchester everyone expects you to support Manchester United who have always been seen as the Catholic team, and by far the more successful. But as I've tried to make clear, my dad was always awkward. When he first moved to Manchester most of the other Irish blokes on the building sites were Manchester United fans, so to wind them up my dad supported City. Also City's ground was nearer to where we lived in Longsight.

Noel and I were always football mad ever since our dad first took us to see Man City versus Newcastle United back in 1971, a game Manchester City won 2–1 thanks to goals by the club's now chairman, Francis Lee, and possibly the best City player of all time, Colin Bell. All through my teens I tried to go to as many home games as I could, which was most of them. If I did miss a game or Manchester City were playing away, I'd sit all Saturday afternoon in my bedroom with my radio, a pools coupon and a big pad of writing paper. I used to flick across the dial between the football commentary on Piccadilly Radio and BBC Radio 2, writing down every score and every goalscorer as they came in, noting down all the details they gave on the radio, such as whether a goal was scored from a free kick, corner, header or long-range shot. I was there with the final results before the teleprinter, and that would be every game in the English first, second, third and fourth divisions and the Scottish Premier League. Noel and Liam would be out larking around and come in and say, 'What's the score, our kid?' I'd say, 'Two-nil to City, Tueart with a free kick and Channon with a penalty.' 'What's Liverpool's score?' 'They're winning one-nil, Kenny Dalglish with an overhead kick.' They'd even ask me daft ones like Bury, Bolton Wanderers and, of course, Celtic. Saturday for me always meant football and still does. For other kids it might mean reading comics or sticking plastic models together, but if I couldn't go to see City play, the only place I wanted to be on Saturday afternoon between

3 p.m. and 5 p.m. was in my room with my radio, pools coupon with all the fixtures, and a notepad and pen.

If that seems a bit sad, I don't care. I enjoyed it. It made me feel important, and I still do it occasionally, only there's no younger brothers around to update on the scores.

In 1981 Manchester City made it all the way to Wembley for the FA Cup final against Tottenham Hotspur. The team line-ups that day were:

Manchester City – Joe Corrigan, Ray Ranson, Bobby McDonald, Nicky Reid, Paul Power, Tommy Caton, Dave Bennett, Gerry Gow, Steve MacKenzie, Tommy Hutchison, Kevin Reeves.
Tottenham Hotspur – Milija Aleksic, Chris Houghton, Paul Miller, Graham Roberts, Steve Perryman, Ricky Villa, Osvaldo Ardiles, Steve Archibald, Garth Crookes, Tony Galvin, Glenn Hoddle.

I remember all three of us settling down in front of the TV for that one – even our Liam managed to sit still for five minutes. Tottenham had the better side on paper with England internationals Glenn Hoddle and Garth Crookes, Argentinian internationals Osvaldo Ardiles and Ricky Villa, and Scottish international Steve Archibald. City had a collection of over-priced youngsters and two old mercenaries in Gerry Gow and former Scottish international Tommy Hutchison, plus England's third-choice goalkeeper, Joe Corrigan. The final ended in a 1–1 draw after extra time, Tommy Hutchison scoring for Man City with a header and then scoring an own goal with a header past the hapless Joe Corrigan who was made man-of-the-match. Overall City were unlucky not to have won that first match. Tottenham were the favourites but City were more up for it, battling through, and deserved to edge it. In the replay at Wembley the following Wednesday, City were again the best side for much of the game and should have won. It was 2–2 after 90 minutes but in extra time Tottenham's class started to show through. City had run themselves into the ground trying to contain Glenn Hoddle and Ossie Ardiles, who had been one of the stars of Argentina's 1978 World Cup winning side. Ricky Villa, another member of that World Cup winning Argentina side, came on to score the winner for Spurs. City had been beaten by what people called a 'wonder goal', after Ricky Villa had taken the ball on a mazy run through the heart of City's defence before slotting it in the back of the net. My view on it at the time was that it was all the fault of Manchester City's sleepy defence, something they've carried on as a club tradition, much to my and everyone else's annoyance, for the past fifteen years. But in the final analysis, the reason City lost was because . . . our Liam's a jinx.

Yes, it's tough being a blue, as our Noel said in one of his little ditties. In fact, Oasis were going to do the official Manchester City song for the 1995 season, the title of which was 'It's Tough Being A Blue When You Come From Where I Do'. Due to problems about which label it was to go on, it never saw the light of day. Noel kept the tune and used it for the song 'Acquiesce', one of the great Oasis B-sides appearing on the flip of their first number one single in Britain, 'Some Might Say'.

Anyway, back to Manchester City; the most frustrating side in English football, unpredictable, either very good or very poor, seldom in between. They've got some of the most loyal fans in football, attracting gates of 30,000 plus even when they're not winning, which is often.

I remember Noel and even Liam being upset when City were relegated to the old Second Division back in 1983. They won promotion to the First Division in 1985, only to be relegated again in 1987. It was that first drop, though, that could have destroyed us as fans. We were young, we were heartbroken, but we decided to make the most of it. So to show our loyalty to the Blues, Noel and I went to nearly all the away games that season as well as the home games – Southampton, Oxford, Blackburn, Oldham, Nottingham, Burnley, Derby, Watford, Crystal Palace, Wolverhampton, small depressing towns, big depressing towns – a catalogue of back-end-of-nowhere-places for us Manchester boys escorting our team back to the First Division where they belonged.

Every Saturday we would go and meet up with the rest of the lads at the Mauldeth pub in Burnage, have a few pints of lager, then get on the coach to the match if it wasn't too far. Otherwise we might set off early in the morning or the night before. I remember once we went to Sheffield, a town famous for its steel. It was home to the finest knives in Europe and, boy, did those Sheffield United fans know how to use them. No wonder they're nicknamed the Blades. Those Sheffield United fans scared the shit out of us young 'uns from Manchester.

We'd gone down early on the train to get some serious drinking in before the match kicked off. What we didn't realise, though, was that we'd stick out like sore thumbs even though Sheffield's only 40 miles away. You see, being from Manchester and fashion conscious you are easily spotted among Yorkshire folk, not particularly renowned for that trait. We were ambushed by a mob of Sheffield United fans outside Rackhams store in the town centre. Noel was the first to get it, with his head pushed into the glass pane of a bus window. I ran over to help him and bumped into a girl pushing her kid in a pram, and then I saw nothing. Next thing I knew I was waking up in hospital with a numb head and a nurse telling me I was being wheeled in to have my head X-rayed for a suspected fractured skull. I was thinking, I didn't come 40 miles to spend all day in hospital. Noel was being treated too, but we discharged ourselves and went to get a taxi to take us to the game. As we were walking towards it, we saw all these bloodied and bruised Sheffield United fans heading for casualty, and we overheard them saying they'd been attacked by the Cool Cats, a well-known firm of Man City hooligans in the late 1970s. What they didn't seem to know was that the Cool Cats were long gone and City's big hooligan firms then were the Mayne Line and the Young Governors, who were probably the ones who had attacked them.

Anyway, Noel and I, much the worse for wear, finally made it to Bramhall Lane for kick-off and watched Man City play out a lame and tame scoreless draw. We eventually got home after the usual hitches of avoiding the home team's more psychotic fans, praying all the way that even though we were getting more accident prone (as far as our mam was concerned), we would live to see City another day.

The next away match that particular season was Oldham Athletic. Well, it wasn't so much an away match as a derby, as Oldham's ground is only about ten miles away from Maine Road. The rivalry was fierce and the Yonners (as we call people from Oldham and north Lancashire) were spoiling for a fight. We ended up with loads of other City fans behind the goals, and the Oldham lads were very aggrieved when City slotted their second goal of the game into the Oldham net. Fighting was breaking out sporadically throughout the game, and at the final whistle it all went off. We headed for the gates and were joined by more City fans. The gates were kicked in and destroyed, and it turned into a riot with City fans turning the burger stands over, even trying to set fire to one, and totally wrecking the place. I got separated from Noel, and when I met up with him much later, his trainers were all blackened where he'd ended up with all the rioting City fans who'd been kicking the hot-dog stands over.

We were loyal travelling City fans, but don't get the impression that Noel and I were football hooligans; that wasn't the case at all. Manchester's a city where you get to know people quite easily – you see each other around town. We are very friendly and, in the main, affable people. When you travel all over the country like Noel and me and our mates, following a football team, you obviously get to know the other supporters well, and the more games you go to the bigger the gang you travel with gets, because you have to stick together. Some of this gang would be out and out hooligans looking for some tribal violence, others would be fringe types and others would be petty shoplifters out for the buzz and the trip to a new town or city where the security in shops may be lax and the pickings rich. I'm not suggesting that either Noel or I fell into one of these categories, but I had a certain amount of sympathy for the stores in these small towns who wouldn't be expecting a half dozen or more Mancunians to descend on them with a few hours to kill before the match kicked off, and rifle through their shops. New jackets, shirts and jeans were the usual fare, but if you couldn't get them, then a few useless items – toiletries, ladies underwear, books anything really – would do. We weren't bad lads, just kids with a passion for Man City and an eye for an opportunity. Looking back it was sheer bravado a lot of the time, keeping a look out while some weasel-faced kid from Gorton robbed some useless item from a shop in Oxford or something. The real hooligans and hard cases were OK. I suppose they was my own kind of university days really, and all those chaps were Honour students – no doubt spending a good part of their lives saying, 'Yes, your Honour; no, your Honour.'

City's season hadn't been the best, but with two games left all they had to do was win away against Notts County and they'd be assured of promotion to the First Division where they belonged. Otherwise it would go to the last game of the season against Charlton at Maine Road and depend on other results. We were full of hope and anticipation. This was going to be a big occasion and not one to be missed. Noel and I boarded the coach along with 50 other faithful City fans in Burnage to make our way to Nottingham. About 67 miles down the road the coach broke down in some country village just outside Derby, 30 miles from our final destination. Well, we'd all had a few drinks on board and several of the boys were a little intoxicated, so a few people got off our bus and started running around the village like lunatics. As ever, misunderstandings abound. Someone, apparently from our coach party, had robbed a village shop and the police were called. We all ended up being taken to the station, even the driver. Well, we weren't happy at being banged up in the cells, so we started making as much noise and causing as much chaos as we could. After about two hours we were finally all released without being charged and we carried on to Nottingham, the coach having been repaired in the meantime.

We finally arrived at Meadow Lane, Notts County's stadium, at half-time, only to be informed that City were losing 3–0. A bad day had just got worse and there was more to come. It was obvious in the stands how disgruntled City's travelling fans were. All the team had to do was beat Notts County and we were in the First Division the following season. It was City's biggest game for years and here they were trailing 3–0 at half-time. It was a disaster – the City fans were going mad, like stir-crazy convicts about to riot behind the ground's perimeter fencing. Suddenly the City fans stormed the fences, ripping the metal apart like an empty Coke can. Thousands of City fans invaded the pitch and started fighting with police, stewards, security men and the opposing fans. Eventually the fans were moved back into the stands, thanks in part to Billy McNeil, Manchester City's Scottish manager, who went on to the pitch to appeal for calm and restraint. The City fans eventually settled down to witness their team storm back into the match, scoring two goals to make it 3–2 to Notts County. Alas, the City players had found their form too late in the game to score a third and fourth goal.

As the final whistle went Noel and I made our way out of the grounds to find our coach. When we arrived at the parking lot where our transport was supposed to be waiting, we were informed by a policeman, rather unsympathetically, that our coach was already on its way back to Manchester. We were left wondering how on earth we were supposed to get home. We didn't have enough money between us for one train fare let alone two. As we were debating what to do we saw five more lads from the same coach as us arriving at the car park. At least we had company with our problem and the seven of us pooled our money and decided that one lad would ring his mother and get her to pay for our train tickets in Manchester. It was a long, dull and slow journey which involved changing trains at Sheffield. We eventually arrived in Manchester rather downcast but more than ready to follow the up-and-down fortunes of Manchester City for another season of away-day blues. Luckily, the boys won their final match of the season at Maine Road 5–1 against Charlton Athletic and managed to scrape back into the First Division by coming third.

As far as I'm concerned, Manchester City were the team for the boys; the young scallies. Noel and I, together with our mates, agreed that we'd all have plenty of stories to tell our grandchildren about our jaunts across the country to see our heroes in sky blue. Manchester United fans are different from City fans. You always went to City with your mates, on the spur of the moment if you suddenly felt like it. For United you had to buy or book tickets weeks ahead. Around Burnage, all the United fans seemed to go to games with their dads or granddads, but City fans went with their mates or, in my case, my younger brother Noel, and occasionally Liam.

Noel and I had many memorable times following the blues home and away. The first celebrity we spotted at a City game was *Coronation Street* star Kevin Kennedy who plays Curly Watts. It was at a pre-season friendly in 1985. City were playing an Australian soccer league select eleven and actually lost (shouldn't be surprised, really) 3–1. What made us laugh was that as City boys we were quite fashionable, but Kevin Kennedy was standing in the Kippax wearing the scruffiest jeans and an old donkey jacket. Obviously his *Coronation Street* outfit – well, he was playing the role of a bin man at the time.

Another memorable day was 22 March 1986. Another derby and a rare trip for Noel and me to Old Trafford. We were with all the other City fans in the scoreboard paddock when all these Man United hooligans, or 'rags' as we used to call them, started showering us with coins. We were lucky we didn't lose an eye as the hail of 10p pieces (remember the old big ones?) and 50p pieces were raining down on us throughout the game. On the field it was quite a thrill: an own goal by United's Arthur Albiston and then one from Clive Wilson making the final result a 2–2 draw. A good result against the satanic enemy.

The next day was a trip to Wembley for Noel and me to see

Manchester City in the short-lived Full Members Cup final against Chelsea. We were really looking forward to it, although a bit confused as to why City had to play a final the day after what had been an exhausting but brilliant derby match. Although we were excited, we were also apprehensive, especially travelling down to London when you knew the Chelsea fans would definitely be up for some major hooliganism. The Chelsea fans had a deservedly bad reputation for football violence, and whenever teams from the north go down to play a London team, it's not unusual for the hooligans from other London clubs to band together against the northern invaders for the day.

We were scared witless making our way to Wembley. There were muggings and stabbings, group kickings and major GBH happening all around us. We somehow made it to Wembley but ended up in the Chelsea part of the ground. I would have ended up with my throat cut if Noel hadn't dragged me out of the way of one Chelsea lunatic who slashed at me with a knife. We were chased, with kicks and punches flying all around us, to the barrier which we had to scramble over into the City end. The Chelsea fans were still sticking knives through the barrier trying to get any City fan who wasn't paying attention.

The game itself was turning into a disaster for City. The players looked tired and lethargic after their exertions against United the previous day. With ten minutes of the game to go, City were getting slaughtered 5–1. We were in total and abject despair. Typically, City started to get it together. In the last nine minutes they scored three goals (I mean, three goals in nine minutes), building up our expectations, only to make us feel even more deflated at the final whistle by losing 5–4 . . . I suppose it's why we love them.

So our first trip to Wembley ended in defeat, and as City don't seem to be heading that way in the near future, I have to admit I've only unpleasant memories of the place. The worst thing is United fans are always travelling down to Wembley for a big day out, and by the time City reach the FA

Cup final again, Wembley will probably have been shut down, recognised for the shit hole it is, and a new national stadium will have been built in east Manchester to replace it. So us City fans will have a big day out a whole four miles away from where I live.

Our Liam went to City, but until he was in Oasis he rarely went with me and never, as far as I recall, with Noel. He wasn't interested in the same way Noel and I were. He was more of an armchair supporter. David Coates, Liam's best friend, supported Liverpool. That may be why Liam never went to see City that much; Coatesy was a Liverpool fan and I think most of Liam's other friends were United fans, so he didn't have many people to go with or that much money, and lost interest. The last time I went to see City with our Liam was the season before last against Blackburn Rovers. City lost 3–1. One of the City games Liam saw last season was against Liverpool and they lost 6–0. So I'll finish this chapter where I started – as far as Manchester City are concerned, our Liam is a jinx.

Chapter 9

D'yer wanna be a spaceman?

What inspired us about the Mondays and the Stone Roses was their success. I remember the Stone Roses selling out clubs and thousands being turned away. Then it dawned on me; I'd written that song five years ago and better than that.

Noel Gallagher

I t's hard for me to talk about my brother Noel. Although I can't recollect a time when he wasn't around, he doesn't encourage closeness. You certainly wouldn't say he was loud; in fact, he's probably shyer than either myself or Liam until he gets to know somebody. He's very suspicious and doesn't trust that many people. He's got his insecurities – who hasn't? He's very image conscious and likes to hang out with people who other people will think are cool. London is the sort of place where wanting to hang out with a certain in-crowd becomes an obsession, but nowadays Noel and Liam *are* the in-crowd. Let's face it, everyone wants to know them. Sometimes it's hard to imagine that Noel's a huge pop star who strangers stop me and pester me about; he's my brother. Sometimes I miss him, other times he gets on my nerves and I'm glad he's down in London or wherever he happens to be.

One thing's for certain; he can really play his guitar. I think it was Noel's lack of confidence or lack of pushiness that stopped him playing in a successful band before he eventually joined Oasis, although I also think it might have been fate. He had to believe he was the best and feel needed; that he was indispensable even. He certainly feels on top of the world nowadays. I hope he's happy.

Noel used to go to a lot of gigs even when he was quite young. I remember him going to see Adam and the Ants with his girlfriend when he was about thirteen or fourteen at the Apollo in Manchester, and going with her to see the Sex Pistols film, *The Great 'n' Roll Swindle*. As he got older he was always keen to meet other musicians and wished to be recognised by them for his talent. I think that's why Noel likes to hang out with Paul Weller and people like that now. As far as I'm concerned, Noel was talented enough as a guitarist and songwriter to talk with Paul Weller as an equal years ago, but I suspect Noel didn't think so. Maybe we should have helped him foster more self-belief and confidence, but that seems to be in short supply among people who share our background, until we go out and prove it.

Besides Noel, Liam and I were constantly competing with each other in every way you could think of − Noel and Liam still are. Recently Liam turned up at my mam's house in Burnage with Patsy Kensit and showed me his £20,000 Bristol car. They only make eight a year and although it was a 1981, it was very impressive. 'What do you reckon, Bod − better than Noel's Rolls Royce?' I should have slapped myself. Was this my brother, brought up on a council estate, now a rich rock star, getting to be like other rich people, where all they've got to talk about is what they've got? I just thought, Good on you, Liam. Pity neither you nor Noel can drive.

Noel was a keen follower of the local band scene in Manchester. I suppose he was subconsciously checking out what types of groups made it, looking for the ingredients that meant some would be successful and others would fall by the wayside. Noel had been a huge Smiths fan. He bought each single on the day it came out and went to see them play at the

G. MEX with New Order, the Fall, and some other Manchester bands from the old punk days in that one-off 'From Manchester With Love' concert in 1986. He even got Morrissey's auto-graph through our Auntie Anne who worked at the same BUPA hospital where Morrissey's dad was a porter. That boy was Smiths mad. He'd buy the seven-inch and twelve-inch singles, all the versions on cassette, all the imports, everything. He loved Morrissey and certainly bought his first solo album, and he thought Johnny Marr was the coolest guitarist in the world. He'd spend hours in his bedroom playing his Smiths records, playing along with them, learning Johnny Marr's riffs. His favourite was the instrumental track on the B-side of the single 'Panic'. It was called 'The Draize Train'. He drove us mad with that one. The Smiths and Johnny Marr really were crucial in helping Noel make up his mind that he was going to play music for a living. After the Smiths it was hard to imagine another Manchester band ever being as original, but Noel was always out, waiting to see the next big thing.

He'd done some taping and jamming around in Burnage. For a time Noel used to hang out with Paul Bardsley. Before Paul played guitar and sang with Manchester band Molly Halfhead and more recently Wireless, he and Noel had a little five-piece outfit called Fantasy Chicken and the Amateurs. Noel and Paul Bardsley took it in turns to write songs and sing, although I remember Paul Bardsley saying he once criticised one of Noel's guitar riffs as 'sounding like a cat crawling up an alley'. Noel pretended to be annoyed, but it was more than likely his rockabilly influences coming out. The band got their name from the Kentucky Fried Chicken take-away on Barlow Moor Road in Chorlton-Cum-Hardy, close to where they rehearsed. The other members of the group were Neil Daley on bass, who also went on to play with Molly Halfhead, Gary McCrowan on drums and John Thompson. They never got to play any gigs, and just fizzled out. Paul Bardsley told me he never saw Noel from that day, back in '85 or '86, until Oasis were on the same bill as Molly Halfhead at the Boardwalk in November 1992.

I remember Noel making his first demo tape of four songs back in '86 or '87. He recorded them on a four-track porta-studio with Mark Coyle, who later engineered and produced Oasis's debut album *Definitely Maybe*, sitting in with him twiddling the knobs. I thought those four songs were good enough then to have warranted a recording deal, but to be a success in pop music you need more than just talent and good songs.

Noel first met Graham Lambert of the Inspiral Carpets at the International 2 club in Manchester. It must have been fate because that was where, 25 years earlier, my mam had first met our dad, only then it was called the Astoria. It was 29 May 1988 and Noel was out celebrating his 21st birthday. The gig was James and the Stone Roses; not a bad bill. Noel just got chatting to Graham about gigs and playing the guitar. Noel asked Graham if he'd ever heard of the Inspiral Carpets. Graham laughed and invited him on to the guest list for the next Inspiral Carpets gig a week or so later.

In July 1988, the Inspiral Carpets released the twelve-inch EP, 'Keep The Circle Around', on Playtime Records. It was a big success thanks to John Peel at Radio One who gave the band a session and played the song a lot. Things went a bit wrong with the Inspirals just after the release of 'Keep The Circle Around' when their lead singer, Stephen Holt, left the band. I've heard various stories about the reason why, all highly amusing and some of them downright scandalous. Whatever it was that led Stephen Holt to leave the Inspiral Carpets just as they were starting out, it didn't stop him forming another band a year or so later called the Rainkings, also signed by Paula Greenwood's Playtime record label.

When he left the Inspirals, it was big news in Manchester. Everyone thought he was mad. The hottest ticket for would-be vocalists in Manchester was to get that job as singer with the Inspiral Carpets. Noel was a fan and got on well with Graham Lambert, who's got a great sense of humour, and he really looked up to the Inspirals' Clint Boon. Clint was a good musician and a veteran of several half-decent Manchester bands throughout the eighties. Noel was constantly praising him and hanging out with him. I think Noel saw him as some sort of mentor. Certainly Clint was no slouch when it came to understanding that a band had to work and rehearse and put themselves about in terms of publicity to build an audience.

Noel wanted to be their new singer. In retrospect I don't know whether this would have worked. Perhaps it could have worked out initially with Noel, Graham Lambert and Clint Boon writing the songs, but sooner or later Noel would have wanted to play the guitar as well and eventually take the music in a direction which wouldn't have been what the Inspiral Carpets wanted. Also, no matter who wrote the songs, the Inspiral Carpets were a democratic band. Everyone had a say, and all the money was split five ways. That kind of pinko-commie thinking would never have appealed to Noel. He's not into that caring sharing thing at all. Besides, too many people having a say in how the music sounds ends up taking its edges off, and rather than something weird and wonderful you get a watered-down common denominator – just look at what happened to Squeeze in the early eighties.

As fate would have it, they auditioned Noel but turned him down for the vocalist's job. The person who landed it was Tom Hingley who'd been singing with a student-type band called Too Much Texas. Noel was disappointed because they said his voice wasn't strong enough, but the Inspirals offered him a job with the band as a roadie and instrument technician. This gave Noel ample opportunity to expand his musical dexterity and get paid for looking after, setting up and playing about with guitar, bass, keyboards and drums. The fact that he could fiddle about with Clint's Farfisa organ, Graham's guitar and Noddy's drums during soundchecks and rehearsals and all those hours on end in various studios over four and a bit years, meant that by the time Noel left, he'd more or less mastered every instrument. Though he had to accept that he was never going to be the frontman, Noel's spirits soon revived. He was in good company. The Inspirals auditioned a fair number of people. One man who didn't even make the audition was the Charlatans lead singer, Tim Burgess. Mind you, he'd have been a bit *too* handsome for the Inspiral Carpets.

Noel's time with the band was like his Youth Training Scheme in pop music, but unlike my YTS as a butcher, he actually learnt something useful. Both Liam and I were proud of him. As the Inspiral Carpets became more successful, we'd brag to our mates about how our kid was sort of in this group and we always got places on the guest list at their concerts. Although Liam was never a fan of the Inspirals and would always have something detrimental to say about them, it never stopped him going. (Don't believe all that bullshit about the Stone Roses at Spike Island being Liam's first gig, either.)

Noel started flying off around the world with them. He got his hair cut in that famous bowl cut like Clint's and started wearing the loud big-patterned shirts, but drew the line at the British Knight trainers. In fact, by the time they had their first number one album with *Life*, Noel actually looked more like a member of the band than the band members themselves. I suspect that's the impression he wanted to give. Again Noel was subconsciously trying to be better than the rest of them – he had the image off to perfection, a mini Clint. Noel ended up almost being part of the band anyway. He roadied for them, sorted out the T-shirts and merchandising, worked in their management office, and took care of the group's sound-checks. That's how Noel became close mates with Mark Coyle, who was the Inspirals sound man, and Dave Bachelor, who was responsible for the front-of-house sound at the Inspirals concerts. The only dubious thing from my point of view was that bowl haircut. He used to spend ages in front of the mirror with a hairbrush and hairdryer getting the bowl effect just right. All that time taken, only to look a right goon. It's a good job he didn't live at home at the time, because with our Liam in the same house he'd never have had a chance to get in front of the mirror.

Towards the end of his time with them, Noel would play his own songs during soundchecks for himself or whoever was around at the time. He may have kept himself very much to himself, but it was like when he strummed his guitar in his bedroom at night – you could see it was a letting go of something inside him. I know it sounds corny, but that's the only way I can describe it. That was always something I envied about our Noel; he had that six-stringed companion to ease his ache.

For the most part Noel loved his time with the Inspirals: going to Europe, Japan and America, and being involved with a band who went on *Top of the Pops* and played to 8000 people at Manchester's G. MEX on three separate occasions, the place where our mam had first worked when it was the old Central Station and she'd just arrived in Manchester from Ireland. It was a buzz for him, as it would be for any 20 or 21 year old.

He never actually got to play as a stand-in, although it did look likely back in June 1990. The Inspiral Carpets were due to play in Austria and their drummer, Craig Gill (Noddy), was sick. Noel was all ready to make his debut on the drums, but Craig was worried and made a miraculous recovery before Noel got to play. I think Noel was disappointed, but I couldn't really picture him as a drummer. He's not loud, obnoxious or daft enough. Funnily enough, I was with Graham Lambert recently and somebody asked him whether Noel had actually got to play the drums at a gig for them, and then asked if Noddy was paranoid. Graham said that Noel was so good on the bass guitar and on Clint Boon's Farfisa organ that they were *all* paranoid. Graham remembered Noel's scheduled debut on drums and said that the band were really excited about how good he'd sounded in rehearsals, and couldn't resist letting Noddy know, so when it came to the time to fly off to Austria, Noddy made this lightning recovery. Noel would have loved to have had a go on every instrument. Not long after Oasis were signed, Noel did a little impromptu drumming on stage with Primal Scream one night, which annoyed our Liam; not that the poor lad would have been jealous or anything.

The Inspirals eventually sacked Noel around October 1991

just before their last American tour. He had his own ambitions and they felt his heart wasn't in the job any more. After that tour they took their own long sabbatical away from the business. People are dismissive of the Inspiral Carpets nowadays, and I was never their biggest fan, but four of their albums got into the top ten, and that deserves respect. Noel listened and learned a lot. He saw the business mistakes they made and the things they did well; how they at first benefitted from their Manchester scally connections only to be scorned for the same thing later.

It hurt Noel's pride to get the bullet from them and he bristled about it for a good while. I think he realises now that he'd have done the same thing. Anyway, life's too short to bear grudges about things that aren't meant personally.

Noel is very shrewd, and I think some of the people who moan saying he doesn't want to know them any more or has deserted Manchester are wrong; he's still playing a game with the media and winning. If there are friends of his he doesn't get in touch with, that's nothing to do with stardom, that's just Noel. He was never into keeping close mates – friends come and go. He's always been ambitious, and he wants Oasis to be a worldwide success. It doesn't matter if someone living in Australia knows that the band are from Manchester or not, it's being the biggest and best that matters to him. There's no room for parochialism and little England attitudes which, in the wider picture, can be harmful. Noel's very careful how he thinks things out and basically knows what he's doing. For all his arguments with Noel, Liam can see this too, and instead of shouting and going off at the deep end he should listen and learn just like Noel did. Noel's attitude is: 'We don't go to the US as representatives of England; we go as Oasis. We don't go round waving Union Jacks or anything. I don't really feel I have anything in common with any British bands except maybe Primal Scream and Verve and Paul Weller. There's a lot of competition, but it's as it should be. You really shouldn't be in a band if you don't think you're the best band in the world. If you're going to make outrageous claims like I do, you've got to back them up. You've got to go on the road and play. Not just in New York, LA and Chicago, but 30 or 40 dates in a row. You've got to play to people in their home towns. It's only fair to the people who bought the records.'

It sometimes seems as if Noel downgrades his time with the Inspiral Carpets, although he admits he learnt his dedication from them. It's true they had their disagreements towards the end, but I've honestly never heard any one of them out and about Manchester say a bad word about him. Whatever Noel may say about his time with them, when he'd sometimes moan to me and other people about various aspects of his job, it certainly beat working in the stores at Kennedy's Civil Engineering where he'd been before, and he learnt more than just the basics of rock and roll . . .

Chapter 10

A new creation

*L*iam never liked guitar music or guitar bands. He thought they were all twats. Then, when he was seventeen, he really got into the Stone Roses, albeit about two or three years after everyone else in Manchester. When the Stone Roses started out in 1985 playing around Manchester, Liam just wasn't into music at all; nor was Liam into the Stone Roses in 1986 and '87. He was into electro and hip hop. He was a bit of a break dancer and used to go off no doubt annoying the shoppers by spinning on his head in the car park behind Kwiksave in Burnage. That could be another book: 'My little brother, the Burnage B boy, the home boy without a posse.'

After Inspiral Carpets, the first gig our Liam went to was the Stone Roses at Spike Island in the summer of 1990. People talk about punk rock and the swinging sixties, but those were selective scenes. That whole Madchester scene reached everyone in Manchester; anyone under the age of 30 buzzed with it, and our Liam just couldn't wait to be a part of it. He loved everything about the Stone Roses and they in turn got him into the Beatles. Most of all at that time, Liam loved Ian Brown. He wanted to be Ian Brown. That's always the ticket for a good frontman – have young lads wishing they were you.

It was there at the Stone Roses gig, I think, that he decided for definite that he wanted to be in a band – in particular to be the singer in a band, to be Ian Brown. That whole Madchester music explosion was the reason for Oasis. According to Noel:

What people have got to realise is that there are four-teen-year-old kids who are into this band, who when the Stone Roses played Spike Island were nine or ten, so they've never known anything like that. All they've known is 2 Unlimited and the Prodigy. Then there are 20 year olds who were fifteen when Spike Island was happening and were into it, and now they've grown up they can see something in us that they got from the Stone Roses and Spike Island. But the important thing is that for the younger kids who weren't into music then, we'll be the first band they really get into. If we can turn them on to the Beatles, the Stones and the Stone Roses . . . then music goes on.

If they go out and buy a few Beatles albums and decide to pick up a guitar and start a band and influence the next lot of nine year olds . . . then rock and roll will never die.

Liam, still starry-eyed about his first experience watching the Roses, added:

I went to see the Roses and I just thought, This is top, I'm really glad to be part of it.

Liam's opportunity came when a local band called the Rain (not to be confused with Liverpool band, Rain, who had an indie hit with a song called 'Lemonstone Desired') sacked their lead singer. I knew several of the guys out of the Rain. Paul Arthur (Bonehead) always seemed to be in bands, and I'd seen him around for years, carrying his keyboards under his arm, going to rehearse with whichever band he was in at the time. He came from West Point, in between Levenshulme and Burnage. I didn't know Paul McGuigan (Guigsy) the bass player, but I knew Tony McCarrol the drummer, who was from Levenshulme. He used to go drinking in a lot of the same Irish bars and clubs as me around Manchester. There's not a lot I can say about the Rain, who mainly played in various pubs around Didsbury and Levenshulme. The line-up was Chris Hutton on vocals, Paul Arthur guitar, Tony McCarrol drums and Paul McGuigan bass. I only heard them once and they were pretty feeble – they had one song in their set about the Strangeways prison riot in Manchester in 1990 called 'We're Having A Rave On The Roof'. They used to rehearse in the cellar of a pub called Raffles Hotel. They'd played a few inconspicuous gigs, including upstairs at Squire's wine bar in Didsbury, but they were going nowhere. Then Chris Hutton left.

Liam saw this as his big opportunity. He'd already modelled himself to look like a young Ian Brown, and he even sang like him in those early days. Liam got in touch with Bonehead, Guigsy and Tony and arranged an audition. They were quite keen to have Liam in the band, but he put his foot down and said he wasn't joining a band with a name like the Rain. He said they should call the band Oasis and so that's what they did. Now there are a variety of different stories about where the name Oasis originated. There was the poncey explanation that it means an oasis in a musical desert. Noel says it came from the name of a clothes shop in the Underground Market in Manchester. In fact, the truth is that the name came from an Inspiral Carpets poster that was in Liam and Noel's bedroom, advertising a gig at the Swindon Oasis. I think our Liam just liked the sound and look of the name so thought, I'm having that, I'm mad for it . . .

When Liam first joined, the band was still rehearsing at the Raffles Hotel. As a rehearsal site, it was a bit limited. I had a word with Liam Dennehy who managed the nearby Grove cabaret club on Plymouth Grove in Longsight. The Grove was a big Irish club with a pub out front. The club part was only used at weekends, and I sorted it so they could just slip Liam

Dennehy a tenner every week so the band could use the club part, with its PA and stage, to rehearse in. Mr Dennehy's only stipulation, apart from me keeping quiet about our unofficial arrangement, was that Oasis were welcome on the premises so long as there was no drug-taking going on. After two weeks of rehearsing at the Grove, a young Irish pot collector caught a whiff of a different kind of pot. Unfortunately for Liam, Bonehead and company, he went straight to Michael Costello, the owner of the club, and told him that the band who rehearsed nearly every day in the Grove were smoking dope. Michael Costello didn't even know there was a band re-hearsing on his premises, never mind enjoying a sly joint in between songs. The band were kicked out and barred for life and Mr Dennehy was given a good dressing down by his boss.

Liam was well into being in a band, and to be fair to him, he doesn't always get the credit that he should for really going for it. Liam isn't the easiest-going person you are likely to meet, but he wanted to be in a band that much, he put everything into it. Nobody was as skint as Liam at the time. Oh, he'd do a bit of scallying to get a few bob, but the early Oasis had nothing. He was determined. Liam was on the dole at the time, but he really believed in the band even if nobody else did.

After they got kicked out of the Grove, Bonehead sorted the group out with a rehearsal room at the Redhouse in Ancoats.

The first gig they played was supporting Sweet Jesus at the Boardwalk on Little Peter Street in Manchester, 18 August 1991, with a line-up of Liam on vocals, Bonehead on guitar, Paul McGuigan on bass and Tony McCarrol on drums. There were only about 40 or 50 people in the club but among the audience were all the members of the Inspiral Carpets, Noel, his girlfriend Louise and me. Noel had just finished touring with the Inspiral Carpets, for the last time as it turned out. It was quite a grim gig and I remember our Liam being really nervous about singing in front of all his mates. He still gets nervous about it now, but that night you could tell! On stage he did sound very Ian Brownish, struggling with some of the notes, but although it was far from brilliant, as debut gigs go, I've seen plenty worse. Liam's attempts at doing a few Ian Brown-style steps on stage looked a bit goonish, so if you ever wonder why he stands still with his hands behind his back when he's singing on stage, you know now. The songs they played that night were all written by Liam and Bonehead. 'Take Me' was the only one which survived after our Noel joined the band and started sorting the songs out. Others included 'Alice' and 'Reminisce'. (Thankfully they left out 'We're Having A Rave On The Roof'.)

I don't think our Noel was particularly impressed that night, but he did admire the way that Liam had achieved what he wanted to achieve, which was to be the frontman in a band. Noel had always wanted to be in his own band, a band that performed his songs, but he was still with the Inspiral Carpets and he probably thought it was too early. Whatever the case was, our Noel kept all his cards close to his chest. I suspect that if that line-up of Oasis had been really good, Noel would never have joined because he wanted to shape a band himself. He admitted as much when he said: 'If I couldn't write the lyrics and the songs, I wouldn't be in the band.'

Also I reckon Liam would have told him: 'Get lost, we don't need you.'

The band had been rehearsing all this time at the Red-house in Ancoats. Then came the crunch move which I personally think brought our Noel into the band. They decided to start rehearsing at the Boardwalk. Noel had finished with the Inspiral Carpets by then and he'd been given a fairly generous pay-off of £2000. Towards the end he had been earning £500–£600 per week which meant he had a few bob in his pocket. That certainly made having Noel in the band doubly appealing to Liam. Noel was living with Louise in a flat on Whitworth Street in Manchester town centre, a mere five-minute walk from the Boardwalk. Now I know enough about Noel to be able to say that he can be a right lazy git at times, so the fact that Liam was now rehearsing with Oasis a mere five minutes away meant that Noel could join the band without too much inconvenience, but you'll never see that in any interviews: 'Noel, what was it about Oasis that made you want to join the group?' 'I thought our kid was a charismatic frontman and the band had potential, but most importantly they were rehearsing about 300 yards up the road from where I lived.'

So Noel left the Inspiral Carpets and joined Oasis on what must be one of the best free transfers of all time. History was about to be made, but not quite yet.

Noel knew that first and foremost what Oasis needed was songs, money and a lead guitarist. He fitted all those categories perfectly and he had the experience of touring all over the world with the Inspiral Carpets and seeing how they managed to become successful. Our Liam's reasons for wanting Noel in were the same, but not necessarily in that order – money, a lead guitarist, experience and probably lastly, songs.

It was no secret that Noel wanted to be in a band, but not just any old band. It had to be right and that for Noel basically meant his band. I think he saw in Liam what he wanted to be years earlier; a cocky, arrogant kid with a voice and a need and desire to be heard and noticed. Things started a little shakily and there were some major teething problems, the main one being that Noel walked straight in and started giving out orders. Liam resented this. After all, he'd been the one who'd got up off his backside, found a band, auditioned for them, got them to change their name – and then Noel comes back after being away for ages, swans in and takes over. That's where the whole battling Gallagher brothers myth started. Before they were in a group together, I can't remember Noel and Liam arguing that much. Nowadays, they are in the press constantly competing with each other in a show of sibling rivalry with the gloves off.

Noel made a big difference and quickly stamped his mark on the band. He had loads of songs and bits of songs that he'd written over the years, and he was trying to work a lot of these into the band, which was probably as time-consuming as writing new songs from scratch. It was five months after

Oasis's first gig that Noel played his debut gig with the band, and it was a vast improvement on that first one back in August.

But before then, Oasis played a one-off show on an outside stage during the Granada Festival, in late September or October. They only played one song, 'Take Me', and the bloke introduced them on stage saying, 'Welcome to Oasis who've just flown back from their tour.' Liam was mumbling to himself, saying, 'What tour? We've just come from Burnage, dickhead.' That little one-off was most noteworthy for a punch-up that nearly happened in the Granada car park. As Liam, Bonehead and I were making our way to where Bonehead had parked his car, a large flash-looking jeep was pulling in. Liam was daydreaming and only jumped out of the way at the last minute. The jeep's driver was Simon Gregson who plays Steve McDonald in *Coronation Street*. Liam was going mad, raising his fist and shouting threats at Mr Gregson, who had the temerity to give him the V sign. Liam answered back with: 'Come out here you twat and I'll fucking knock you out.' You could see then that Liam had all the right social graces to mix with his fellow stars once the band had made it.

Oasis's first proper gig with Noel in the line-up was at the Boardwalk, unsurprisingly, and was again not a particularly busy night. I can't remember which band they were support-ing, but with their new lead guitarist they certainly looked and sounded more like a rock and roll band with a mission, on that night of 15 January 1992. They opened with an instrumental of 'Columbia', because Noel hadn't written any words for it at that time. Still a bit of a favourite in the set, though, was the Liam and Bonehead composition 'Take Me'. Soon after the gig, Liam and I had an argument at home. He was on a star trip after playing to about 40 people.

Gigs weren't that forthcoming, so after much arguing the band went into the Out Of The Blue studios in Manchester to record a demo. As they didn't have any of Noel's compositions ready to go, they recorded 'Alice', 'Reminisce' and 'Take Me'. The tape sounded very Stone Roses, but Noel's extra little guitar riffs added another dimension, and although our Liam was still doing his version of Ian Brown, his vocals sounded stronger and more confident than I'd heard before. Our Noel now tries to deny that he had anything to do with that demo. When he was being interviewed by Pete Mitchell on Piccadilly Key 103 FM in Manchester just before the group's two sell-out shows at Maine Road, Pete played some of that first demo to Noel, and Noel once said he didn't play on it. I thought it was quite good and I can tell you now Noel played lead guitar on all those tracks.

It's a coincidence that Oasis's first gig outside Manchester was to be in the same area that Keith Richards and Mick Jagger came from, and the Stones started out gigging in – Dartford. Later, Oasis built their first keen following in Liverpool, where another famous British band of the sixties came from. At Dartford Polytechnic, Oasis shared the bill with Oldham band the Ya Yas, who'd supported the Inspiral Carpets on their last UK tour, and a band called The World Jones Made.

The order in which the bands went on stage was to be decided on the night. The Ya Yas were quite laid back blokes and nobody was that bothered at first. Because the Ya Yas had had a local single out around Manchester it made sense for them to headline but then The World Jones Made jumped up and started insisting that they should headline. Well, that was like a red rag to a bull with our Liam, who can be very forceful when roused. Liam shouted that there was no way Oasis were supporting some 'nondescript student band'. I've no doubt a few oaths and threats were uttered and in the end Oasis headlined with the Ya Yas second on the bill and The World Jones Made acting as a kind of warm-up for them both. Pretty persuasive at times, our Liam, but then he's spent his life getting his own way.

The gig went down OK, the venue being one of those glass and concrete, teacher-training college places which was built overnight in the sixties. The night itself was a typical student bash. The band seemed quite pleased with how it went and weren't even put out when one of Liam's scally mates went running out of the door with the blind charity box full of 50p pieces, which had apparently fallen off the bar into his hands as he was passing – you know the sort of thing. Still, it paid for the fish and chips on the way home.

The following night, 20 April, the band played at the Hippodrome in Middleton, some godforsaken place in north Manchester. They were supporting Revenge, the new Peter Hook band, once of New Order fame. Revenge was a dour band but because of Peter Hook's connection with New Order was thought by some people to be cool. I wasn't one of them and I was in full support of Oasis and my brothers that night. Among the usual array of girlfriends, Liam's scally mates and Noel's semi-music business contacts was Phil Saxe, head of A & R at the soon-to-be-defunct Factory Records. Phil was there that night to video Revenge's gig, using money that the label could ill afford.

The gig was the best I'd seen Oasis play to date, although they were still far from the finished product. They next played at Club 57 in Oldham, supporting the Ya Yas again, and followed this with two gigs at the Boardwalk in the summer – the first, in July, was their first proper headliner to about 40 people, and the second was a support slot in August. In the meantime they started to get a few write-ups. Steve Cowell, who wrote for a free Manchester paper-cum-magazine called *Uptown*, interviewed Paul McGuigan and Noel in a Manchester pub. Paul was on his lunch break while working for British Telecom. Liam wasn't there because he'd gone to sign on that day. Steve Cowell was really nice about the band, even swallowing Noel's bullshit line about the band having played to full houses at the Boardwalk – I didn't realise that the Boardwalk's capacity was limited to 40 people.

Penny Anderson gave them a good write-up, almost 1000 words, in *The Word* column in the *Manchester Evening News*. She said that the band's demo tape was the best she'd heard all year, despite the fact that their lyrics needed some work and the songs were a bit long. Like Steve Cowell, Penny had spotted a glimmer of originality. Noel was realistic enough in the interview to be philosophical about how far the band still had to go: 'Oasis music isn't pop or rock but somewhere in between – maybe pock. I've always been into guitars. We want to put keyboards on, but keyboard players don't look cool on stage, they just keep their heads down. There's never been a cool keyboard player since Elton John.'

Noel was well aware of the amount of work and time it would take to get the band to the level where people would be really sitting up and taking notice – the Inspiral Carpets being probably the hardest-working band to come out of Manchester unfazed by the idea of long and arduous world tours. Noel was aware of the pitfalls of being signed up too quickly and then being unable to deliver the whole package. He explained to Penny Anderson in the same interview: 'Someone said to us the other day that if it was 1987 we wouldn't have to try; two or three years ago at local band nights everyone would go. Anyone with a half decent tune was signed up. Now nobody wants to know, so you've got to go down to London. We haven't got a manager or anything like that, so we've got to do it ourselves. If we'd been around back in 1989 we would have been signed, but we would have been under serious pressure to deliver an album, but in eighteen months we're going to be five times as good. We're going to bide our time until we feel confident enough to come up and then really go for it.'

Noel was trying to do a manager's job for the band, hustling gigs and spending what money he had, or didn't have, on new equipment. Our Liam, meantime, was trying to dodge working for a living by scrounging fivers and tenners off me to go clubbing, while giving the people at the social security the runaround. The only job he wanted was to be a pop star.

Oasis were still just a local band, not even considered in the top ten up-and-coming ones. Looking back, they didn't deserve to be; it was still far too early. You hear all those goons boasting, 'I first saw Oasis back in 1992 and I knew then they'd be massive.' Bullshit. The people who say that know nothing about music. Oasis were noisy and raucous. It took a while for the songs to settle in and for them to discover how to put them across. At that period in Manchester, the bands who were doing it live were Puressence, the Sugar Merchants, Molly Halfhead, That Uncertain Feeling, Mr Robinson, Ultracynic and a hell of a lot of dance stuff like Rhythm Quest and Family Foundation.

In September 1992, Manchester hosted its first In The City international music seminar, and every band in Manchester wanted a gig, but very few managed to land one. Noel was desperate for Oasis to get involved and after some major hassling, got lucky, wangling a date on the bill at a concert going under the banner 'The In The City International Unsigned Talent Night'. This also featured Machine Gun Feedback (now known as the Space Monkeys and signed to the Factory Too label), Skywalker and Jealous at the Venue on Whitworth Street. Noel had already been turned down for a gig by Rick Michael at the Boardwalk and was just glad that he could get Oasis squeezed on to the bill for that particular night.

Oasis were due on stage at ten o'clock and there were a fair number of people in. I was amused to spot Gary Davies, the Radio One DJ, in the crowd. The guy stuck out like a sore thumb wearing these really bright clothes among the scallies and unwashed student crusty types. It's funny, looking back, how all these music writers and so-called trendy DJs go on about Oasis, how they played them first etc., and yet I can honestly say that the first national radio DJ to see Oasis live was none other than Gary Davies. Radio One should bring him back; he's the man with real cred, even if he does dress like a goon. Besides Gary Davies, there were a fair few A & R types there, including John Brice from Warner Chappel publishing, someone from Silvertone, someone from Rondor and London, and a few others, so I was told. I thought the gig was OK but it wasn't one of their best. Liam was still doing his loon-type dance and trying to sing like Ian Brown − very northern on the vowel sounds and slightly off key. Liam obviously did a great impression because all the London geezers seemed to reckon Oasis sounded like the Stone Roses.

I heard later that John Brice was interested in the band, but his bosses in London wouldn't even give him a budget to demo them, saying they didn't think that Oasis were good enough. I don't think Noel was that bothered at the time; he knew it was still early days, but he was beginning to come out in the open a bit more.

All this time, Oasis continued rehearsing at the Boardwalk next door to Puressence (now signed to Island Records), Medalark Eleven (who were about to sign to Creation Records and were managed by the Inspirals' former manager, Anthony Boggiano) and the Sister Lovers, one of whose members, Lorraine, went out with our Liam for a while. Noel was living with Louise in India House at the time. An old mate of his, Liam Walsh, and Alison Martin from Red Alert, the record-plugging company, also lived there. Noel knew Alison from his Inspiral Carpets days, and Red Alert was to prove very helpful to Oasis in the early days. Through them Oasis also got together with Terry Christian.

Oasis still didn't have a sniff of a deal at this time, and I can't honestly say whether I expected them to get signed or not. I'd seen worse bands with deals, but I was aware that they hadn't really played that many gigs and a lot of the time the sound in the clubs was a bit ropy.

The gig at the Boardwalk on 22 November 1992 was the first time Oasis encountered anything which resembled a crowd, with just over 100 or so people turning out on a cold Wednesday night. Oasis were bottom of the bill. Headlining were Dead Dead Good Records' dreadlocked thrash signings from Cheshire, the Cherries, together with Molly Halfhead, featuring Noel's ex-colleagues Paul Bardsley and Neil Daley. Molly Halfhead were signed to Playtime Records in the UK and Sony for the rest of the world, and had just had a few singles out. They were the band most people had come to see. Still, there were a few influential Mancunians in the audience – a couple of DJs from the local stations like Craig Cash and Pete Mitchell, Terry Christian and all the people from Red Alert. In fact, they were all mates of Noel and Louise. Then there was Steve Harrison from Dead Dead Good Records, another Man City fan, and all the guys out of the Inspiral Carpets.

Oasis were first on and blasted out six numbers: a version of 'Columbia', 'Take Me', 'Must Be The Music' (an acoustic one), an untitled number, a rocky, psychedelic cover of a house number called 'Better Let You Know', and, attempted for the first time live, 'Whatever', with Liam comically holding the lyrics in front of him. 'Whatever' is a song that Noel claims to have written later, but I know it was one of his earlier bedroom strummings and there must be a tape of the make-do version from that night somewhere. They'd been on stage for about 30 minutes, maybe more, and were just about to debut 'I Am The Walrus', when the Cherries, worried that everyone would leave after they'd seen Molly Halfhead (who were supposed to have been the headline band that night), pulled the plug on them. Well, there were a few words bandied about on stage with our Liam, Noel and Bonehead storming off, leading to a ruck backstage with the Cherries, in which Oasis were the victors. It wasn't a great gig, but at least our Liam had stopped gooning around on stage. He'd realised by now that he wasn't Ian Brown and he certainly would never be James Brown when it came to making some serious moves.

They were still sounding rough and amateur, like a local band, but they had improved a lot just over the past six months. As Noel said at the time: 'At first we did sound rough. A lot of people did say we were like some mad punk band. I think we were writing so many songs so quickly, that we just didn't realise we should be spending more time working on them, putting that bit there and this bit here on the chorus. Then one day we just got up and wrote our first pop song, 'Whatever', and I knew we'd have to wait before we could do it justice.'

* * *

Meantime, Red Alert were sending copies of the demo tape out for Oasis, prompted by Noel. They worked for a whole list of record companies including London, EMI, One Little Indian, Mute, Virgin, Sony and Neil Ferris's label Brilliant, who had just had a chart success with Bitty Maclean. Noel would go into Red Alert's office and use the fax machine and photocopier, setting up gigs and trying to hustle a deal. Needless to say, all these labels rejected the band. Oasis had something to aim for now and at least people around Manchester knew who they were, despite the fact that the band had not played many gigs and only one which was outside the Greater Manchester area. It is worth noting, though, that literally dozens of demo tapes were sent out to record companies, despite Noel's later kidology that he just passed out a few to acquaintances.

The band really started to find its feet in March 1993. The time spent rehearsing showed and they began to sound like they were getting somewhere when they ventured out of town to play in Liverpool at Le Bateau.

I have to admit that I've always liked Liverpool and Scousers; I think that secretly most Mancunians do, and Scousers probably like Mancunians too – but I wouldn't put money on it. Liverpool is a vibrant working-class city with a selection of good small venues for live music and that's exactly what Le Bateau club was. Oasis were supposed to be supporting a band called Small (now called Smaller). The band's singer and songwriter, Digsy, later became good mates with Noel. He used to be in a band who were signed to Virgin in the eighties called Cook Da Books. After Oasis had soundchecked, Digsy said Oasis should headline because they were better than his band. Well, Noel loved that, and it says a lot for Digsy. I can't imagine many Manchester bands as good as Smaller offering to let a support band move up the bill and headline instead of them, especially a band from out of town. In the end, despite the usual jibes from the audience of 'You Manc bastards' and the returned compliments, the gig was one of the best yet. I think Digsy did a lot for Noel's confidence and because it was a lively atmosphere which you never seemed to get at the Boardwalk, it rubbed off on the band, and they enjoyed themselves.

Oasis certainly seemed to go down well in Liverpool better than they ever had in Manchester. Manchester and Liverpool do have this big rivalry, being the two biggest cities in the northwest of England and a mere 30 miles apart. In recent years, Manchester has grabbed all the headlines in terms of both music and football. Personally, I think most of the so-called hatred is reserved purely for football, especially the rivalry between Manchester United and Liverpool. Sometimes you'd think the two cities were at war. But as I don't support either of those two teams, I don't care. Football may be a beautiful game but music is the truly universal one. Liverpool gave us the Beatles in the sixties; Manchester has given us the nearest thing to them in the nineties. It shouldn't really be a surprise that Manchester bands go down well in Liverpool and Liverpool bands go down well in Manchester. Both cities are very working class, and there's a traditional love of music in both of them, maybe because of the huge Irish connections. In the sixties Liverpool had the whole Merseybeat thing with the Beatles, the Searchers, Billy J. Kramer and the Dakotas, Gerry and the Pacemakers, and Cilla Black. Up the other end of the Mersey, Manchester had the Hollies, Herman's Hermits, Freddie and the Dreamers, the Bee Gees, Wayne Fontana and the Mindbenders, John Mayall's Bluesbreakers and the Mocking Birds, whose songwriter, Graham Gouldman (later of 10cc fame) wrote the Yardbirds' smash hit, 'For Your Love'. In fact the whole music explosion in Britain in the early to mid sixties was driven along by bands from these two northwest cities – so much so that *Top of the Pops* was first broadcast from a studio on Dickenson Road near where I was brought up. I know Manchester bands like the Buzzcocks, Joy Division, the Fall, the Smiths, the Happy Mondays, the Stone Roses and Inspiral Carpets always went down well in Liverpool, and that Liverpool bands like Echo and the Bunnymen, Teardrop Explodes, the Christians, and the Las always did well in Manchester. I suppose it's near enough the first out-of-town gig any band from either city gets to do. Audiences in both cities are curious about what's going on in the other. As Manchester and Liverpool encroach on each other, next century they'll probably both be part of the same conurbation, and then it will be the leading exponent of pop music in the world.

In April, Oasis were back in Liverpool, again sharing a gig with Smaller but this time at the Krazyhouse. The Krazyhouse is a dark-painted building near the Liverpool Lomax, and inside it's not that different from the Boardwalk. This was the night I first really believed my two brothers would make it. Just like a top footballer who's had a shaky start to his career and come through the bad times, our Noel suddenly hit a rich vein of form. I think it was the feel-good factor of having the guys from Smaller around. Noel had been writing a lot and had a whole batch of good new songs to bring into the set. It was here that the band first performed 'Live Forever', 'Strange Thing' and 'Bring It On Down'. The set was tight and sounded brilliant and the crowd were really appreciative. The night was buzzing.

At the end of the Oasis gig, the guys from the Real People, who were in the audience, decided to jump up on stage and do an impromptu 20-minute encore to round off the night. Now I know musicians like to get up and sing a song, but the Real People weren't really in a fit state. They staggered around on stage, blitzed out of their heads, singing out of tune, but the audience loved it, joining in. That's when you really start to see the Irishness in Scousers.

It was a great laugh being around Digsy and all his mates. It was when Digsy invited Noel round to his house for tea that Noel was inspired to write the lyrics to 'Digsy's Dinner' – Noel hates anything fancy and foreign and lasagne counts as that to him. Noel's eating habits aren't the healthiest and consist of a strange diet of pot noodles and burgers.

It was around this time that Oasis recorded their famous live demonstration tape with the aid of the Real People's equipment and studio facilities. It was the first time Oasis had something on tape that would really turn heads. The tape sleeve even had a message from Oasis to Chris and Tony Griffiths of the Real People, saying 'Special thanks to Roger Moore and all the Claggies'. Roger Moore referred to Oasis sound engineer, Mark Coyle, and claggy is a nice Mancunian term for people who've got a very poor dress sense – I'm afraid it's well known that the majority of Scousers aren't as fashion conscious as the Manchester scallies and haven't been since about 1980. The tracks on the tape were so good that several ended up being B-sides for later singles. The track listing was:

Side one – 'Cloudburst', 'Columbia', 'D'Yer Wanna Be A Spaceman', 'Strange Thing'
Side two – 'Bring It On Down', 'Married With Children', 'Fade Away', 'Rock 'n' Roll Star'

Oasis returned to Manchester's Boardwalk in May for the gig that at last started to establish them with their home crowd. It was a Wednesday night and there was a good turn out, maybe 150 people or so. It was still mainly the Mancunian music set, with Johnny and Ian Marr, Tim Burgess and Mark Collins of the Charlatans, the Inspiral Carpets and various journalists like Chris Sharrat from *City Life* magazine and assorted DJs from the local stations. Both Noel and I knew Ian Marr but we didn't realise his brother was Johnny Marr. It was through this connection that Johnny Marr first got on to Oasis and the band ended up with Marcus Russell managing them. Noel explained at the time:

I used to see this lad, Ian, down the Hacienda all the time in the late eighties and we'd chat and have a laugh. When I bumped into him one day in town he asked, 'What are you doing nowadays?' I told him I'd got a band.
'Oh, what are they called?'
'Oasis.'
'Oh, right, you'll have to get us a tape and I'll play it to our kid.'

I just thought, Big deal.

'Who's your kid?'

'Our Johnny.'

'Who's Johnny?'

'Johnny Marr.' Well, I dragged him round to the flat and gave him a cassette. Two hours later the phone rang and it was Johnny Marr himself. He'd heard our tape.

'This is amazing, can I produce your records?' I mean, we didn't even have a record deal at the time. Johnny helped us quite a lot, getting us a top professional manager. After he came to see us he actually phoned Marcus, who was managing Electronic, and said, 'I've just seen the greatest band of the last five years.'

It was at the end of the same month that Oasis landed their famous deal when they went up to Glasgow with the Sister Lovers to play at King Tut's Wah Wah Hut. There was nothing earth-shatteringly different about that day. No portents or omens of good fortune in the heavens, no rainbow hanging in the sky and no yellow brick road. In fact, from my point of view the day was a disappointment.

Noel and Liam decided that as they were travelling so far they wanted to do it in style and comfort, so they hired this flash Mercedes Splitter van with a CD player in it. I was meant to go with them, but they left earlier than they were supposed to. I was a bit miffed when I found out that they'd gone without me.

There are various stories about what did and didn't happen that night. Only a few people really know the truth and journalists are rarely concerned with that anyway. (Something our Noel learned from his time with the Inspiral Carpets was that if you feed them any old bullshit, and it makes a headline, they're only too happy to believe it. Our Noel should have a degree in feeding people stories.)

That day, Sunday 31 May 1993, Oasis rehearsed with the Sister Lovers at the Boardwalk. The Sister Lovers were mates of Creation signings, Boyfriend, who were also due to play at

King Tut's that night with another Creation band, 18 Wheeler. The Sister Lovers thought they'd sorted out with the promoter that Oasis could play too. Basically, the promoter was worried by the small turn out and refused to let Oasis play. Noel pointed out that they had brought seventeen people up from Manchester with them and, if they didn't play, things might get out of hand as they'd all travelled a long way and expected to see them play. The Sister Lovers and Boyfriend agreed that, if Oasis couldn't play, they wouldn't play either and eventually the promoter agreed to let Oasis play a short fifteen or twenty minute set. Anyway, the Manchester contingent would more than double the turn out in the club.

Supposedly, the presence of Alan McGee, head of Creation Records, at the gig was a coincidence. There is a good chance that he had been tipped off by Anthony Boggiano. Anthony had dealings with Creation Records and also knew Noel well from his Inspiral days. He was interested in managing Oasis, but then Anthony Boggiano would have saved any favours he might do Noel until the ink was dry on a contract. Alan McGee may have gone to check up on 18 Wheeler and Boyfriend, but according to Alan the story goes like this:

I'd had a big argument with my girlfriend, so decided to go up to Glasgow for the weekend. It was a Sunday night and I was out with my sister when we saw a poster advertising 18 Wheeler and the Sister Lovers. I mistook the Sister Lovers for my friend's band which has the same name. I needed cheering up so we went to the club. Someone pointed out all these guys from Manchester and said that it might kick off that night if they weren't allowed to play. When I saw them, I knew I'd just seen the greatest rock and roll band in the world and I know they thought I was mad when I offered them a deal there and then. It was a pure coincidence.

According to Noel, it was like this:

When we'd finished playing, this tall geezer with a ginger skinhead and glasses, wearing a denim shirt and white jeans, came up to me.

'Do ye want a record deal?' He was very smooth and handed me a card that said Alan McGee, President of Pop. I looked at it and said, 'So it's all your fault is it, then?'

He just said, 'Look, don't take the piss. You don't know me.'

'Yeah, but I've heard all the shit on your label.'

Actually, after we signed, they took us down to the Creation warehouse and I think the band came out with two cassettes between five of us. Well, we already had all the decent stuff like the Boo Radleys, Teenage Fan Club and Primal Scream.

Suffice to say Alan McGee was well impressed that night in Glasgow, and bought the band train tickets to go down to London to see him a few days later. Noel remembers.

Bonehead, Liam and I went down to see Alan at Creation in London. We were expecting it to be this big flash office. We got in a cab at Euston station and ended up in Hackney. Even the dogs wore shoes, there was that much broken glass about. It was a totally dead and derelict-looking part of town. We went up to this big green door hanging off its hinges and knocked on it. A bloke opened it and there was a sweatshop full of Asians. I said, 'We're here to see Alan McGee', and he pointed at another door. When we rang the intercom bell there were sparks flying out of it. It was like the three stooges with Liam, Bonehead and me instead of Larry, Curly and Mo. When we went into Creation, it was like a rubbish tip with empty bottles everywhere and people asleep. Then we had to go down to Alan McGee's office which was called the bunker, with a big door and a sign that read: Alan McGee, President of Pop. We just went in. He sent his

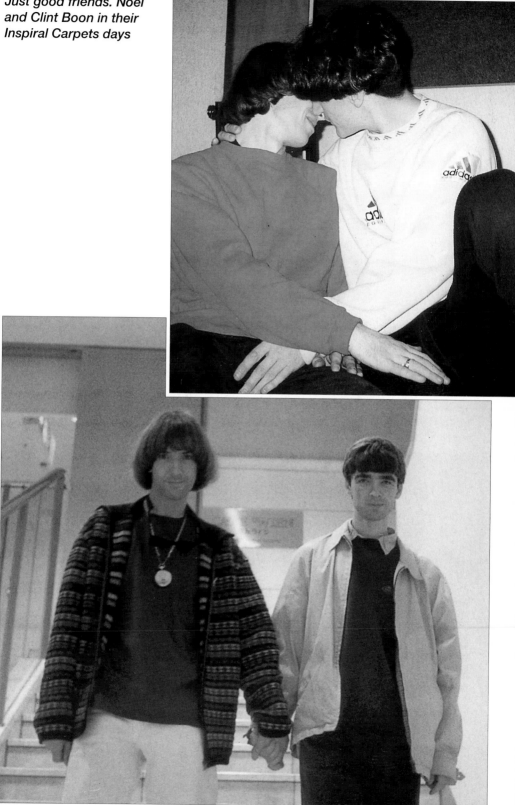

Just good friends. Noel and Clint Boon in their Inspiral Carpets days

Pop star in the making . . .

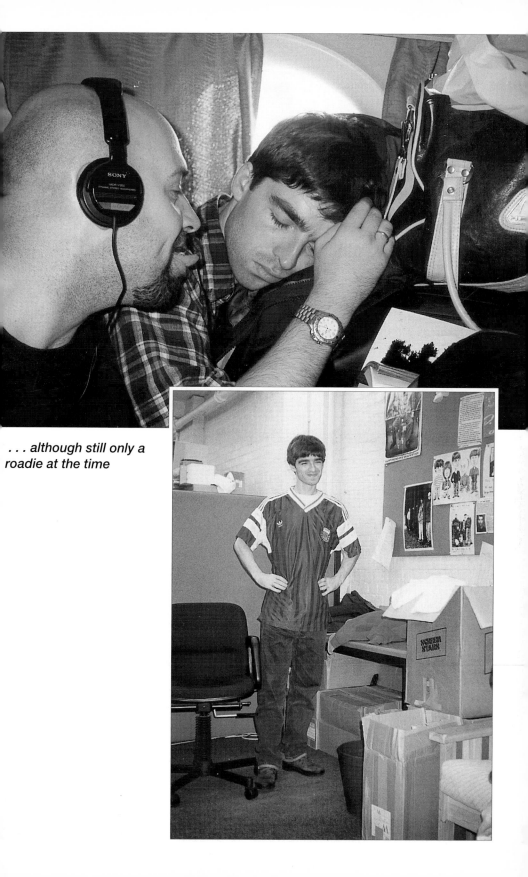

. . . although still only a roadie at the time

Travelling the world with the Inspiral Carpets

*Their own band at last.
Oasis at the Middleton
Hippodrome in 1992*

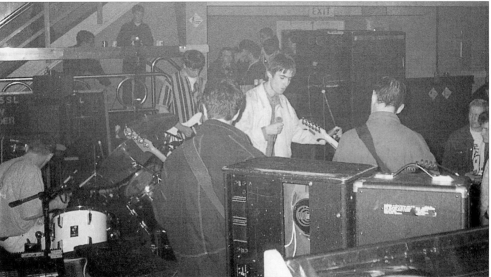

'In The City' festival at the Venue, September 1992

Liam on stage at the Fleece and Firkin, Bristol, 1994

Top left *With one of our kid's heroes, Paul Weller*

Bottom left The White Room

Right *Slumming it at Glastonbury, 1995* (London Features)

Below *A far cry from their Boardwalk days. Earls Court, 1995*

Above *Shy and retiring as always. Mouthing off at the Brits in '96* (London Features)

Top right *The Man City jinx collapses after a game of 'celebrity football'* (London Features)

Bottom right *Playing at Maine Road, 1996*

Top and bottom left
Shopping and singing in
St Louis, USA, in 1996
(Rex Features)

Right *'Are you mad for*
it, Scotland?' Loch
Lomond, 1996 (London
Features)

Below *The greatest rock*
and roll band in the
world play Knebworth,
1996

Right Noel with
girlfriend Meg Matthews
(Rex Features)

Above and left
The loving brothers at
Knebworth (London
Features)

Liam on Noel: 'There's
days he's needed a
slap and I've given him
one'

Noel on Liam: 'If I lived in
America I'd have
blown his head off by
now'

Liam with fiancée Patsy Kensit

assistant across the road to the pub for some Jack Daniels and said, 'D'ye like Rod Stewart?' I said, 'Yeah,' and he said, 'Right, you've got the deal.' We just felt totally comfortable because they were all music fans.

Noel got in touch with Johnny Marr, who'd already primed his own manager, Marcus Russell of Ignition management, on Oasis – and the first steps to stardom were taken.

At the time, Noel was just anxious to get a record out. He believed in his songs and was of the opinion that the big mega deals and the charts would come later. He just wanted someone to put a single out for them and quickly. I think that was his only big stipulation with Alan McGee when he met him. Noel wanted Oasis to get a record out as soon as possible, and then follow it up with another single as quickly as they could, like bands used to in the days of the Jam, releasing up to four singles a year. I don't think he was even contemplating things taking off in the way they did. Our Liam says he was mad for it, mad for the fame and mega success, but Noel just wanted to have the same manager as Johnny Marr and a record out as the first step.

In July 1993, Oasis played their last gig at the Boardwalk, and it was pretty well packed out. It seemed everyone had caught on to the fact that they had landed a deal with Creation Records. There had been a couple of pieces in the *Manchester Evening News* in the past year and *City Life* were now getting interested, mainly due to the live demonstration tape that the band had recorded with the Real People in Liverpool back in May. Chris Sharratt in *City Life* had written a short piece just prior to the gig at the Boardwalk:

I've got to hold my hands up here; saw these live at In The City and again at the Boardwalk. I walked away unconvinced, and maybe a bit pompous about their influences. Then Noel gave me the live tape and I was instantly converted. More power to Creation for getting their finger out whilst everyone else sat on their thumbs, thinking about it. Good luck.

I think just about everyone got a copy of that tape. Our Noel was constantly sending out tapes and faxes, still using Red Alert's office on Deansgate as his private Oasis management office. What was encouraging was that a few local DJs had been playing tracks from it, like Pete Mitchell on his IQ show on Piccadilly Key 103 FM and Terry Christian on Red Rose FM in Lancashire. A lot of people had started to hear Oasis tracks outside the confines of Manchester's incestuous music and media circles.

The usual local bands made good were on the Boardwalk guest list along with the Charlatans, the Real People, the Inspiral Carpets, Simon Moran and some others from SJM promotions where Louise worked, Peter Hook, Johnny Marr, Terry Christian, some journalists, TV and radio people, lads from other bands who were still trying to get a deal and loads of mates from Longsight, Levenshulme and Burnage. More importantly from Noel's point of view, the *NME* were there for the first time. Emma Morgan, a small, quiet, bespectacled girl from Brooklands, just seventeen years of age, who was covering live gigs in Manchester at the time, had heard the Oasis demo on Craig Cash's show on Signal Cheshire and had hustled to get the *NME* to let her review the band's gig. Our Noel was of the opinion that it was about time, but Oasis had only played fifteen gigs in the past two years, and the music press had spent most of those two years with a severe downer on all things Mancunian. Maybe it was part of our Noel's quiet pessimism. Well, you have to remember us Gallagher boys are City fans.

In all the time that my mother and I have been keeping scrapbooks of everything published in English about Oasis, no one, not even the *NME* who she wrote her piece for, have ever given any credit or mention to Emma Morgan for giving Oasis their very first review in the national music press. It was a great write-up:

Shout to the rooftops and dance in the streets – Creation have not gone mad! Lately they've been worrying us sick with the lack of pop product and bevy of rash signings, and the chances were that the latest 'find', Oasis, were just going to be another nail in the 'Where are Primal Scream' band coffin.

But no. Because Manchester's Oasis are a genuinely fine guitar-propelled pop band, with little of the crass baggage such a description suggests. They're not perfect, they might find it hard instinctively to impress, but they still stomp out the kind of terrifyingly memorable tunes that most bands forgot how to make as they blundered around on the periphery of true talent. Sound-wise they're slightly reminiscent of a drugged up (ahem) version of the Stone Roses. It's almost as though everyone's favourite stroppily invisible Mancs have grown up and decided to take it slow this time, in the process swapping loon pants and T-shirts for sensible trousers and M&S pullovers.

Mercifully what they haven't mislaid is the basic brilliant melodic framework, as demonstrated by opener 'Stray Dogs', with a rhythm involving more than three chords and a lyric concerned with driving your mates mad with jealousy because you're getting some bloke's lasagne (hopefully not a metaphor) and they're not. It's impossible not to be drawn in to take a closer listen.

Bizarre shouts of 'Showaddywaddy' from the floor are utterly unfounded. Good. With any luck, so are everyone's fears about the label that brought you the BMX Bandits. Even better, Oasis really are the shoots of vitality in a barren pop land.

I think our Liam must have memorised it by heart, but I'm not sure he understood exactly what she was on about. Liam loves reading about himself, but someone else should tell him not to take it too seriously. Don't read it, weigh it. Whenever he comes home, one of the first things he does when he walks in is to get the scrapbooks out. Recently he rang me up from Barbados and asked me if he and Patsy Kensit had been in the press while they'd been away. I told him, 'Who's interested in you and Patsy?' To be honest, although he's a right pain and totally childish, you always get a laugh out of him, when he's not snorting, bellowing and stamping his feet like a bull in a pen.

If all the people who now say that Noel asked them to manage Oasis, or who have said that they were thinking of managing Oasis got together, they'd probably fill Maine Road. Noel picked a few people's brains, but Noel wanted someone he could trust, who knew the market, was as ambitious as Liam and himself, and had a proven track record. Marcus Russell, a 40-something Welshman and ex-school teacher, realised there was a huge gap in the market for a truly great British rock band and Johnny Marr had convinced him that Oasis were that band.

I first met Marcus Russell later that month when Oasis played at the Hop and Grape bar upstairs at Manchester University, supporting Dodgy. I wasn't impressed, partly on account of his incredibly naff dress sense. He was wearing a tatty jacket and jeans and looked like he was off to sign on the welfare. If this is what managers dress like, no wonder roadies look so scruffy. Anyway, it was a great night. Oasis opened and went down a storm. Dodgy were really good too and I especially liked their song 'Water Under The Bridge'. Liam and I were in agreement that we doubted they'd ever better it. I don't think they have to this day. It's a classic.

As things started to happen for them, Noel and Liam really showed their ambition for the band. They wanted to be the biggest and the best in the world. Even though they fought each other and bitched about each other, they believed in each other's talents. I think Noel looked at Liam and to a certain extent wished he could be him and have that outward confidence and cockiness and, of course, be that age again. Liam really admired our Noel's ability on the guitar and wished he could write songs like him.

As for me, well, I just wished I had a chance to show some talent somewhere and not have to spend my whole life digging ditches for a pittance at the end of the week. Early on, I did rather cheekily suggest I'd give up my job shovelling the good earth to work for them doing their T-shirts, but Liam and Noel let me know in no uncertain terms that I wouldn't be required. I'd worked on the building sites and for Kennedy's Civil Engineering with both Liam and Noel at different times and we hadn't got on too well, so getting involved with the group was always a non-starter. Come to think of it, we were always whingeing and shouting or being off with each other. It drove our mother spare – it still does.

There was a definite buzz at the time. I remember going for a drink with drummer Tony McCarroll and he was a bit apprehensive about the band's future. I reassured him that the band would do really well (although I didn't realise how short a future he'd have with them once the band took off). I know people say stupid things like, 'I knew from the first time I saw them they were going to be massive', but I knew Oasis would be successful because you could see the improvement every time they played, in both their performance and the way the songs were coming together. I don't think musical ability alone takes you to the very top. It's hard to imagine your younger brothers becoming the new Keith Richards and Mick Jagger. They are too real for that. But our Noel, who I always knew was talented, outshone even my expectations with both his songs and superstar demeanour. It was fascinating to me to be able to see them take off; that's why I wanted to be there like the devil on their shoulder. I wanted to witness their metamorphosis from Manchester lads to Rock Stars.

Thanks to Oasis's tie-in with promoters SJM in Manchester, more gigs followed. There were support slots being pencilled in for the late autumn with Liz Phair and the Milltown Brothers at Manchester University, but first they made a triumphant return to Le Bateau club in Liverpool where they again headlined.

The live demonstration tape was winning them fans, and there was suddenly a lot of interest. The band now had management, a record deal and a promoter. The next thing was a record and plans were afoot to get a promo twelve-inch white label out by Christmas, which would be sent out to radio stations. Creation would get their promoters, Anglo-plugging, to deal with Radio One, and Red Alert in Manchester plugged all the local independent and BBC radio stations outside London, plus regional TV stations. Red Alert had a good reputation, especially for breaking new bands. They had plugged all sorts of obscure bands until they made daytime playlists, at a time when Radio One weren't quite so adventurous with new music. They had worked for the Charlatans from the start, KLF, the Sugar Cubes then Bjork, the Shamen, Primal Scream, New Order, East 17, Coolio, Inspiral Carpets, Suede ('Stay Together' was the only Suede single they worked with and the group's biggest hit), the Farm from the beginning, Prince for 'The Most Beautiful Girl In The World', his only UK number one, and numerous other acts. They'd sent out Oasis live demo tapes to various heads of music and a number of record companies, and Noel even had the contract from Creation Records faxed through to Red Alert's office. They stapled it together without even having a sneaky peek, and phoned Noel to tell him to come in and collect it.

Oasis's first break nationally came in August 1993 when they were live on BBC Radio Five's *Hit the North*, playing two or three songs including 'Cigarettes and Alcohol'. It was Red Alert who introduced them to Mark Radcliffe and Marc Riley who presented the show, and then to Rhys Hughes who took over from Radcliffe and Riley when they set up their regular late-night show for Radio One.

In September, the band received a glowing write-up from Terry Christian in *The Word* column in the *Manchester Evening News*. Terry described them as a band that had got it all, a Primal Scream meets the Beatles with a tinge of Stadium Rock thrown in for good measure. In reviewing the tracks of the live demo, one almost prophetic thing he wrote concerned the song 'D'Yer Wanna Be A Spaceman'. In the article he described them as a band with a very big future and compared them to current music press flavour of the month, Evan Dando, saying:

If Evan Dando had penned a song like this, journalists would be writing even more reams proclaiming his genius. Having said that, I wouldn't be surprised if indie music's golden boy covered a delight such as this.

By the following year, Evan Dando had latched on to the band as a celebrity fan and did record a version of 'Live Forever', but decided not to release it. I've got possibly the only copy.

The band had been going for just over two years and still hadn't played a gig in London, except that very early gig at Dartford Polytechnic, if that counts as London. Consequently nobody from London had been to see them live, and the only national review they'd had was Emma Morgan's in the *NME*, plus a brief mention in *NME*'s gossip column which said that when celebrating their signing to Creation by drinking champagne, they started brawling when Liam and Bonehead tried to jump on stage at the Camden Falcon to jam with Whiteout.

The situation was about to change when the band were booked to play at the Canal Cafe Bar on Whitworth Street, Manchester, on 14 September 1993, as part of the second In The City international music seminar. Manchester was buzzing for those four days or so, with music business people from London, New York, Los Angeles, all over, descending on Manchester and bringing in their wake hordes of journalists and the like.

For the Creation Night at the Canal Cafe Bar, the line-up was 18 Wheeler, Oasis and Medalark Eleven (another Manchester band signed to Creation who, in a former incarnation, had had some success as the Bodines). There were probably about 250 people crowded into the place, but it wasn't quite full. There was a good atmosphere and it's where I met Oasis manager, Marcus Russell, for the second time. He was in a buoyant mood. Most of the delegates from the music convention present were people from the industry in Manchester. The only national journalist there was Paul Mathur from *Melody Maker*, who came and introduced himself. Mathur, a tall, bespectacled Scouser, was blown away by the band. I don't know if he'd been tipped off about them by some of his mates in Liverpool, but I hadn't seen him at any gigs before this. He gave Oasis a brilliant review in *Melody Maker* which appeared two weeks later on 25 September, although he got the attendance figures completely wrong. I'm not sure if he realised that Emma Morgan from the *NME* had beaten him to a live review in a bigger paper two months earlier, or that Oasis had been well covered by the local press in Manchester. This might not have seemed a big deal to him, but the *Manchester Evening News* did have over a million and a half readers, figures which even the *NME* would dream about, never mind *Melody Maker*. The piece was headlined 'Desert Brats':

> Creation Records choose to showcase some of their sparkling new signings at exactly the same time as some of the more established crowd-pullers are packing them in on the other side of town, meaning that less than a hundred people turn up to witness a searing show. In years to come, everyone will claim to have been here, but a word of warning, I've got all the ticket stubs. I know who you are.
>
> Oasis are magnificent. I've been exploring their edges for three months now, watching them get ready to slay you, to obsess you, to prove themselves as – get ready for this – the best new band in Britain.
>
> Let's get the sign posts out of the way first. The Stone Roses, Happy Mondays, the Sex Pistols – and oh, about a million others – have all played their part in creating the joy that is Oasis, but it's the way they pull their influences together and invest them with an exuberant menacing freshness that makes them so important. Oasis are the most natural stars I've seen in years.
>
> Singer Liam lopes around the stage with the air of someone who was born to inhabit the space around the mike, guitarist Noel exuding similar ease as he hurls out waves of shimmery, rich sounds. The first song, 'Shakermaker', was apparently written 48 hours before

they came on stage but it feels like they've lived with it for years.

At the time Oasis played the Creation Night, almost four months after the Glasgow gig, they still hadn't actually signed the contract. Noel was shrewd enough to get a manager first, and Oasis could easily have gone elsewhere, with labels like U2's Mother sniffing around and offering to double the advance offered by McGee. It wasn't until October 1993 that Oasis finally signed on the dotted line. I wonder if all the record company scouts present at the Canal Cafe Bar to see the band that had supposedly slipped through their net were aware of that.

Chapter 11

Mad for it

Noel was pleased when the national music press started to sit up and take notice of Oasis at last after two years, but he'd seen it all happen with the Inspiral Carpets. One week you're, to quote the famous T-shirts Noel used to sell for them, 'Cool As Fuck', the next week you're not. Good press doesn't sell records. Even the most impressionable sixteen year old isn't going to go out and spend money on a record just because a music paper likes it, although I'm sure there's the odd goon who does. Where the press helps is in landing bands TV slots and getting them listened to by radio producers. I heard that one music producer on Channel 4's *The Word* would never have the Inspiral Carpets on because *NME* didn't like them, despite the fact that their album was number four in the charts and they'd done umpteen sell-out tours.

Our Noel was aware of this and aware of the fact that bands like the Happy Mondays with their semi-criminal, hardtype image always got better press than the Inspiral Carpets because firstly, they took drugs and talked about it, secondly, the wild image made journalists a bit scared of them and thirdly, most journalists were middle class and couldn't tell a genuine working-class person from a stereotype. To be genuinely working class in their eyes you had to seem a bit criminal, especially if you were from 'up north'.

As far as press image is concerned, you couldn't be seen to like or be friends with anyone deemed uncool. So although Noel had always really admired Clint Boon as a musician, mentor and songwriter, he wouldn't say that to the press or give Clint any credit. He couldn't go round saying he was a huge fan of U2 or of any other thing they thought were non-U, to use the old-fashioned phrase.

I think maybe the worrying about their image became more and more of an obsession as they rode all the accolades to the top. The constant references to having a shady past brought them more into contact with some genuinely shady people in Manchester, which might go some way towards explaining why Noel and Liam now live in London.

After Oasis's big review in *Melody Maker*, they were back gigging again. Oasis supported Liz Phair, the strange American, at the University in Manchester, and got another mention in the gossip column of the *NME*:

> Woman of Rock Liz Phair may not be all she seems. Apparently Ms Walk-on-the-Wild-Side was completely appalled when she had to share a dressing-room with rock-gods-to-be Oasis at Manchester University, not because their feet or breath smell (though they do) but because they look like extras from an Andy Warhol movie and talked like 'New York drug addicts' to boot.
>
> Wow, really? We thought they'd be dressed up like Heidi and into selling the *Watch Tower* in between songs. Ms Phair stalked out leaving her rider for the rock slobs to scoff. Now that's what we call a chick with scruples. Ciao.

The real story that night was that we were all in her dressing-room drinking her beer and being generally rowdy, when she came in and started ranting about how we'd just taken over. Then one of Liam's mates asked her to 'get her tits out for the lads' which we all found highly amusing, such was our state. She wasn't too pleased about that, and then another of Liam's mates asked her if she had any drugs and she just did a double huff, calling us a bunch of low-lives and junkies.

Manchester's old punk rocker, John Robb, got in on the act, writing a short piece about the state of Manchester's music scene, saying the future was Oasis. All good stuff for the band.

That same month, October, they supported the Milltown Brothers at the university again and then set off on a short tour supporting the BMX Bandits. I kept an eye out for any mentions they had in the press, cutting out even the little adverts and sticking them in scrapbooks I bought from the local paper shop. It started getting too much like a full-time job by the middle of 1995, so now our mam does the scrapbook honours. In November, they set off supporting Verve, from Wigan, bottom of the bill to American band Acetone (who were to be supporting Oasis in the States within eighteen months), playing universities and medium-sized clubs.

My brothers, who a year earlier had been as underground as the pipes I buried every day, were starting to be talked about everywhere. I have to confess I was getting a bit sick of conversations with strangers already, and they weren't even out of the starting gate properly yet.

Once the Creation deal was in the bag, my brothers went into overdrive. I couldn't keep up with them. They had a promo twelve-inch of 'Columbia', a favourite at their gigs, due out as a sampler in January, with their first single proper due in the early spring. The more heated the press became, the more obvious it was that there was no one else around. Suede were too self-conscious as a band and were never going to cross over into the big time because they were too quirky. Morrissey's effete image was acceptable because he was a working-class lad and the rest of the Smiths the same. Suede were mere student fodder, although Bernard Butler is a talented guitarist. You're never going to be a big pop star playing slightly left-field rock and roll if some fifteen year old in a council house can't look at you and want to be you. Few fifteen-year-old lads in Manchester would have wanted to be Brett Anderson of Suede. But Oasis had it all. They had the laddishness of the Happy Mondays, the rock and roll poise and coolness of the Stone Roses and a way of touching sensitive parts other bands could not reach, the way the Smiths did. Most encouraging about the deal with Creation from Noel's point of view, though, was Alan McGee. He encouraged Noel, as Noel later acknowledged: 'I get a buzz from giving new songs to Alan McGee, because he actually thinks we're the greatest rock and roll band in the world. He phones me up at four or five in the morning. I'll get out of bed and it's McGee on the other end enthusing, "I'm feeling supersonic, give me a gin and tonic. We're gonna annihilate the world, man." That in a nutshell is why we're with Creation Records, because the president is up at five in the morning reciting the lyrics down the phone.'

The music press were catching on to this and so were audiences. Coming up to Christmas, 4 December 1993, Oasis were playing at Warwick University. I managed to scrounge a lift in the van with Bonehead, Guigsy, Tony and Phil Smith, the band's drum technician. Noel had decided he was fed up with sitting in the van and went down by hire car with Mark Coyle driving. Liam had just moved in with a young lady, for what turned out to be a very short-lived relationship (three weeks to be exact), and said he'd make his own way down on the train.

Warwick University is a modern-style student campus. Once the band had set up, they started looking for Liam. There was no sign of him. The band soundchecked. Where was Liam? There were a few suggestions being voiced: 'He's drunk somewhere', 'He doesn't know how to get off the train', 'He's got the wrong train'. Noel was really tensed up about it because if Liam didn't arrive Noel would have to sing, and it wasn't his job. Eight-thirty, and still no sign of Liam. The dressing room was quiet. Marcus Russell was pacing up and down. The band were due on stage at 9.30. Suddenly, at 8.45,

Liam's head pops around the door, as cool as you like. 'All right?'

Noel was so mad he couldn't hold back, and he grabbed a plastic chair and flung it at the floor in front of Liam. It bounced up with that much force it went right over Liam's head and flew over the stage area and smashed to bits on the dancefloor. 'You dickhead, what time do you call this? Where have you been?' Noel shouted.

A heated argument raged as to who was right and who was wrong, with everyone siding with Noel against Liam. Ill-advisedly, I put my twopenneth in, telling him how stupid he was, and he countered: 'What's it got to do with you?'

After all the shouting, the gig went brilliantly, all that anger and adrenalin fuelling a powerful set.

Liam came home with us in the van. He was in a big sulk about everyone picking on him. He started on me, and I kept telling him what an unprofessional prick he was. Bonehead, Tony, Paul and Phil stayed out of it. This was a classic Gallagher brother argument, neither of us listening to what the other was saying, just repeating the same things at each other over and over. We were both completely drunk. Liam decided we should stop the van and get out by the side of the road and sort our differences out. Bonehead was having none of it, and just put his foot down and got us home to Burnage as fast as he could.

I shouldn't have joined in on our Liam like I did, but I couldn't resist it. Liam will never admit he's wrong, and when he knows he's wrong he's even worse to argue with because he becomes aggressive and starts threatening all and sundry. I wonder who he got that from?

Instant self-worth is what I got, no matter how fleeting, by going to my brothers' gigs. I knew the songs, I knew Liam and Noel, and that suddenly made me someone worth talking to. I'd been a DJ around the Irish clubs a few years earlier, just like our dad, for the same reasons. I'd been one of the three founder members of the Manchester branch of the Republic of Ireland Supporters Club. I'd even spent time following Celtic with another bunch of stalwarts. Most of the money I earned, I spent trying to be a somebody in one group or another. Now I had my brothers to do that for me, so I'd annoy them and wind them up when maybe they had other things on their minds, and I had to bear the verbal brunt. It was much later, when they'd had a couple of chart successes, that our Liam turned round to me and said, 'Pretend you're not my brother.' He could charm the birds off the trees, that boy.

It was an exciting time for Oasis, that whole run up to Christmas. The demo of 'Columbia' was pressed up on a white label and sent out to radio and TV stations. Radio One started playing it on the *Evening Session* and gave Oasis their first Radio One spot before Christmas. The press were starting to rave about them, but one piece, the first review they'd had in the *NME* since Emma Morgan's in July, caused quite a stir. It was written by Johnny Cigarettes who saw the band supporting St Etienne. He slagged them off as being a bunch of refugees from Manchester's 1989 scally baggy scene, and wrote some rather unkind things about our Liam as a frontman. Liam was fairly frothing at the mouth, and his language was choice.

Some time later all the band were in a club in London watching Scottish four-piece guitar band Whiteout, when Bonehead pointed Johnny Cigarettes out to Liam. He was blond, wore glasses and was about 6'6" tall, like some clone bred in an SS breeding vat in Nazi Germany. Bonehead turned to Liam, and said: 'Bloody hell, he's big.' Liam was unperturbed, and replied: 'He won't look that big with a bottle sticking out of his head.' Not one of our Liam's more poetic moments. I imagined the horrific scenario if it had got back to Johnny Cigarettes. He'd probably have laughed about it . . . and that would have been a big mistake.

Johnny Cigarettes was a mile off the mark and too late to be dismissive of a band who were already more than half way there. His bosses at the *NME* must have panicked somewhat; the buzz about Oasis was relentless and they were in danger of missing the boat. The gig Johnny Cigarettes reviewed was on 1 December 1993. The following night Oasis were again supporting St Etienne, this time at the Plaza in Glasgow. Luckily for the *NME*, Calvin Bush was there to put things right. One week after Johnny Cigarettes' hatchet job, the *NME* made amends with a glowing review and a bigger piece this time for Oasis than for the headlining band St Etienne:

> They are frankly incredible. They leave, I gasp and ache; the thought of having to wait a whole ten days before they play here again is already cramping my lifestyle.

Oasis were on their way to the top and still had nothing out on vinyl. With the release of the twelve-inch promo of 'Columbia' imminent and a Radio One session in December, hysteria suddenly struck the music press. There's no bigger nightmare for any self-respecting music journal than a band breaking big and missing out on them – not being able to say, 'You read it here first.' In fact, in the case of Oasis, there was blitz coverage and they were still plodding along doing support slots and improving song by song, gig by gig. It's strange now to look back, especially when people say that Oasis were a band hyped by the national music press, and Radio One refer to Oasis as their band. Back in 1992 there were few people willing to listen apart from Steve Cowell, Penny Anderson and assorted members of the Inspiral Carpets, who knew how talented Noel was and plugged the band as much as they could. As the Salford punk poet John Cooper Clarke once said of his own modest rise from playing working men's clubs to headlining 2000 capacity venues and releasing albums for CBS: 'I did it all the hard way and, long term, the hard way is the smart way.'

Oasis hit the headlines in the music press again for their first gig abroad – mainly because they never got to do it. They were due to play in Amsterdam at the Sleep In Arena with Verve. They were excited about it. It was Liam's first-ever trip outside the country and he was 'mad for it', to use his own vernacular.

The story is well documented. The boats going to the Hook of Holland have a disco on board and a bar open all night. The band were drinking during the eight-hour ferry trip, and Guigsy and Bonehead were singled out and accused of passing a fake £50 note over the bar. Despite protests, they were approached by the security people and a fight broke out. The sound of any fight or argument immediately attracts our Liam, who tried to calm things down by taking a swing at one of the boat's crew. They all ended up involved in a drunken brawl and were arrested and put in the brig. They were deported the next day – all of them, that is, except Noel who was sleeping in his cabin totally unaware of what was going on. He got off at the Hook of Holland and was left waiting for them at the port not realising they'd been shipped off back to England. He was more than just annoyed. They'd started living up to the reputation the press had given them, but it meant the gig was cancelled. Noel might find it amusing now, but at the time I think all he could see was the group throwing it all away before they'd even got their first record out. I know he blamed Liam and must have been thinking it was Warwick University all over again, only much worse. He felt let down so he fined each band member £500, thinking that the only way to stop that behaviour was to hit them where it hurt – in the pocket. That money actually went towards furnishing his new flat. Well, he was always the pragmatist. The band did calm down somewhat, for about a week and a half at least.

The first single was supposed to be their live favourite 'Bring It On Down' but according to Noel things didn't go as planned in the studio:

We were in Pink Museum studios in Liverpool, recording 'Bring It On Down' and a couple of old songs for the B-side. It was hell. We were falling asleep playing them and I was thinking, These are crap. I just threw a bit of a tantrum and said we should scrap the lot, and that I was going to write two new songs. That's when I wrote 'Take Me Away' and 'Supersonic'. In fact if you listen to 'Take

Me Away', it lasts four minutes 35 seconds and that's exactly how long it took me to write it. I rang Alan McGee and he asked if I'd finished and done our B-sides, so I played him 'Supersonic' down the phone. He couldn't believe I'd written it in a day and threatened to sack every other artist on the label.

This is Noel and he's prone to exaggeration, but he's mighty prolific as everyone was to find out in the next two or three years.

On 14 March came Oasis's press-the-flesh gig at a big Sony 1994 launch party at Gleneagles in Scotland. The bash was held in the very swanky hotel next to the famous golf course. It was full of champagne-swilling corporate types. Their attitude to Oasis was, 'Go on then, impress us', although they had actually already signed for Sony in the States, before they had signed for Creation. The band did just that and the Sony executives were more than pleased with their new signings.

It was a matter of six to eight weeks before the band's first single was to be released. They were desperate for a TV slot to go with it, but the only major pop show, Channel 4's *The Word*, was finishing its run for that season on 18 March. The Oasis single wasn't due out until 11 April. Terry Christian, the show's presenter, had been to see the band a couple of times and had given them a good write-up in the *Manchester Evening News*. He had also assured Noel he'd do what he could to get them on, but our Noel wanted to make sure. While they were in London, he got the band down to the studios a few weeks before the end of the run to see Terry and persuade the music bookers they were worth a slot.

Sure enough, on 18 March 1994 they were included in the band line-up for the final show. Joining Oasis were Rochdale-based Asian hip hop group the Kaliphz and top American rock band Soul Asylum, whose lead guitarist was dating Wynona Ryder, the film star, who was also down at Teddington Studios that day.

I have to admit that I was really excited at the prospect of my two brothers and Oasis appearing on *The Word*, a late-night Friday show, which was controversial and got slated by the press, but that everyone seemed to watch. It was, to use that old Hollywood critics' phrase, a show that 'only the public liked', but with around two and a half million viewers nearly all aged between 16 and 34, the advertisers and record companies liked it, too.

I think about a third of the audience that night had travelled down from Manchester. It was fairly rowdy in the studio and a couple of lads got thrown out. After about eleven hours of setting up, soundchecking and rehearsing, Oasis's performance was magnificent, eclipsing the much raved about Soul Asylum whose album had been number one in the American charts for weeks. Terry's guest that night was Sir Bob Geldof who was wearing a strange yellow tartan suit. He said, with some vigour, that Oasis were great. Yes, Oasis got the thumbs up from Sir Bob and he isn't the type of person to beat around the bush when giving an opinion.

After the show, we all piled into the backstage bar area where there were about 200 people having an end-of-show party. We stayed there for a couple of hours drinking with all these different Mancs and Digsy and all the lads out of Smaller, who'd come down as well. Liam was off his face. He'd been walking around all night pretending he was a Scouser and had spoken to Paula Yates for the first time. I don't think she'd have remembered him that night. There was a rumour that Wynona Ryder would be at the bar after the gig, but we didn't spot her. Nowadays Liam and Noel hob nob with her ex-fiancé, Johnny Depp, and his girlfriend, supermodel Kate Moss. However, that night our Liam had his eye on a girl from Manchester who was enjoying a drink after the show – I *should* say she had her eye on him as well. Liam's mate Darryl came over saying, 'Hey Liam, there's a girl over there who's mad for you.' Liam, shy hesitant guy that he is, was straight over.

My mam watched the whole thing on the television at home

and she videoed it to watch again later. She used to watch the Inspiral Carpets on TV all the time, hoping for a glimpse of Noel. But on that particular Friday night she had two of her beloved sons playing in their own band in front of a TV audience of two and a half million people. She cried her eyes out, she just couldn't help it; she felt so proud and as they'd been away touring a lot she realised how much she missed them.

I loved those kind of nights – there was something magical and special about them. I suppose for some people life is always like that, but for a lad who spent his eighteenth birthday night in a freezing cold park with two bottles of cider and thought he'd had a great time, it was special. Yes of course I wanted to join my brothers at as many of those kinds of dos as I could. I've had some good times in my life, but it was only through travelling around with my brothers that I knew anything about hotels and room service and all-night bars, and all the girls who would hang around them. They got paid for doing something they loved. Getting up for work to me became worse than ever, thanks to their success and lifestyle.

After their appearance on *The Word*, everything seemed to go smoother for Oasis. The crowds at all their gigs almost trebled and they began to get the real star treatment at all the venues they played at. It was a case of constant gigging right up to and through the release of 'Supersonic'. Noel found it all highly amusing – one TV appearance and a few press write-ups and everyone was shouting hype:

It's funny; we'd done two and a half years trying to keep a band afloat with no money and then you get all these sad, bitter Manchester musicians coming up saying, 'You lucky bastards,' and trying to give us advice. I'd be thinking, Yeah, but listen mate, what can you possibly say to me? You're on the dole. You blew it. People would say, 'What about the hype?' or, 'Does too much press worry you?' I mean, up until just after the first single and going on *The Word*, we'd had two national music press interviews – two! That's not hype. I mean, we'd had live reviews and it's not our fault if the person reviewing the gig raves about it, that's up to them. The thing about the press is that they don't want to like another band from Manchester. To me, it's really getting their backs up, thinking, Oh no, not them Mancs . . . here we go . . . again! But we've won them over, probably because they know we don't give a shit anyway. We're not bothered. The thing with the press is you can't believe the good or the bad. One week they're saying we're the greatest band since the Stone Roses, the next they're saying we're mods because we wear Adidas trainers. Mind you, one member of the band *does* believe what he reads in the press.

Oasis started their first proper UK tour as the support band to Whiteout. Whiteout had also been on *The Word* earlier in the same series, but it had come too soon for them. Playing live on *The Word* just made people think they were being hyped, as their performance wasn't very good. Consequently, Oasis ended up headlining half way through the tour with Whiteout supporting them. All the press who'd been holding back on Oasis now started muscling in too. Whether it was *Q* magazine, *Vox*, *Select*, *Smash Hits*, *Melody Maker*, or the *NME*, you couldn't open the paper without seeing Noel and Liam staring out at you. It was like a runaway train. One review, Ted Kessler's in the *NME*, turned out to be quite amusing in retrospect. It was a review of Oasis's gig at the famous 100 Club in London on 24 March. Mr Kessler thought Oasis had a very bright future, stating '. . . If Liam Gallagher stands up straight every now and then, he'll be on *Top of the Pops* before Christmas.' As fate would have it, it didn't even take that long.

When 'Supersonic' was released, we weren't sure what to expect. All the specialist shows on the independent radio stations were playing it, as were the nighttime shows on Radio One. The band had certainly gigged enough, but it was very different from what had been charting at that time.

I remember sitting at the kitchen table with my mother. It was tense, listening to the brand new national top 40 pop chart rundown on BBC Radio One that night, 17 April 1994. We had an inkling that the record might go into the top 40 but we weren't quite sure whether Oasis had made it. We were both nervous but after numbers 35, 34, 33 and 32, we even dared to think it might have gone straight into the top 30, no mean feat for any band with their debut single. Then the DJ announced that Oasis had gone straight in at number 31. My mam's face just lit up. She was so thrilled that her two boys had at last achieved what they'd worked so hard for. My mam, who suffers from arthritis after all those years of running around after us, got up and made herself a cup of tea to celebrate.

'Supersonic' peaked in the national chart at number 31, but made the number one slot in the independent charts (although with Sony's money behind them, they were hardly independent). Then they set off on their second UK tour to such exotic locations as Hull, Coventry, Portsmouth, Newport, Derby, Leicester, Northampton, Chelmsford, Cambridge, Sheffield and London. There were even grimmer places than Noel and I had travelled to when we followed Manchester City away in the Second Division nearly ten years earlier.

Until 'Supersonic' charted, fans hadn't been a problem, but with their appearance on *The Word*, all the photo spreads of our Liam in *Smash Hits* and the press articles, the band were starting to get mobbed. I'd seen our Noel pushed all the way across a room by hoardes of screaming girl fans, until he was almost flattened into the wallpaper. They would all talk at him at once, ask weird questions, and then carry on talking over him when he tried to reply. They didn't listen to him, they just wanted to be noticed.

It wasn't too long before my brothers' magic rubbed off on me. It seems like for the past three years I've had people stopping me in the street, especially in Manchester, saying, 'You're Noel and Liam's brother, aren't you?' At first it was flattering and I quite enjoyed it, but then I noticed the questions all sounded like a tape loop: 'How are you, Paul? How are Noel and Liam doing? Where are they? What are they doing? When are they coming back? Where do they go out for a drink? Are they millionaires? Do they give you loads of money? Are you rich? Is it true you're moving house? Is such and such a thing in the papers true? You're really lucky having brothers like them.'

Do you think so?

Sometimes I must confess I feel like saying, 'Get a life, you sad bastards,' but usually I try to answer questions pleasantly. I personally think that both my mother and I would get a lot less bother from Oasis fans if they set up an official fan club. It's usually the really young ones who hang around outside our mam's house and pester us with stupid questions. I have, in fact, offered to help sort a fan club out for them (it would have been better than digging holes for a living and good PR for them), but they weren't keen on the idea at all.

Liam was beginning to find it all a bit too much. Noel had travelled everywhere and knew the ropes, and he understood about interviews and publicity and just how totally gruelling touring is. Early on in the tour, Liam found himself doing the interviews. He didn't mind at first, but it started to 'do his head in', as the callow youth himself may have put it. I know Liam had never worked so hard in his life. He made a few gaffes doing local radio interviews, some of which, luckily for Oasis, never got aired. In a famous *NME* interview, Liam gave a journalist a first-hand, eyewitness account of a fight between him and Noel. He explained later:

> We had the first big interview we'd ever done with the *NME*. Our kid started putting me down like I was this big, so I just told him, 'Here y'are, someone's asked me a question, you chill out and let me answer.' Anyway, he just kept on and on, getting me at it, so we had a fight and the press got on to it. Now the press think we're these bad lads up for a fight and we're not. We're just around to play gigs and do music.

Finally, at the Creation Undrugged concert at the Royal Albert Hall, Liam was just totally done in. That night was a rest compared to Oasis's previous touring schedule. They were one of several Creation acts on. They only had to perform three songs, 'Shakermaker', 'Live Forever' and 'Whatever', but Liam complained of a sore throat. Our Noel wasn't having that. He didn't believe Liam but found himself taking over the vocals that night for the first time ever, doing more than a decent job. It helped him decide to sing more often live, although he had sung on various records including 'Take Me Away', the B-side of 'Supersonic'. Liam didn't help at all by turning up at the Albert Hall on the night, heckling Noel and shouting abuse at him. He hates not being noticed, Liam, and he'd inadvertently pushed Noel into getting a taste for singing and performing acoustically live.

After the Albert Hall, it was back on the road doing gigs in Norwich Arts Centre and the London Marquee before a triumphant homecoming gig to over 1000 people at Manchester University. It had been six months since their last gig in Manchester, when they played as a support slot to Verve back in December '93. They'd played 41 concerts across the country in that time, and Manchester was at last ready for them. Oasis were unusual in that way. They struggled early on to build a following in Manchester, maybe because they had hyped themselves to various people in the press and, earlier on, weren't really good enough to live up to it, so the word of mouth was bad. They had kind of crept up on the outside; dark horses in the race to fill the yawning chasm left by the Stone Roses.

The set was sounding really good by now, though, with the old songs sounding better and some impressive new ones. The band's next single, 'Shakermaker', was scheduled for release on 20 June and had already been played on the local stations and Radio One weren't too far behind. There was no doubt in my mind that it was going to get them on *Top of the Pops*. Noel explained:

I'm obsessed with the guitar, I always have been. I've got a 1960s Les Paul Gibson that I bought from Johnny Marr, but when I write I normally do it on my acoustic. To me it's not a great song if it doesn't work on an acoustic. To write a tune, I normally just bash a few chords that fit together, have a melody in my head, find a starting point and then hum the melody. That dictates where the music goes and vice-versa, and then I get the shapes of the words. I just play it over and over. The lyrics I find a lot more difficult. I usually lock myself in a room with a bottle of gin and 20 cigarettes, get drunk and write the words. I don't write songs with messages as such, or a song about any one particular thing, but there are some lines in each song that I'm proud of.

Just how big Oasis had got by this time was made clear when people in the audience at that Manchester University gig started to sing along to 'Supersonic' and 'Shakermaker' and seemed to be going wild everywhere. I don't think it was a happy homecoming for Noel, though, as it was the night he finally split up with Louise Jones after going out with her for six years. They'd split up before, but always got back together again. He didn't talk about it, but I know he was feeling dazed and confused. He decided to move away from Manchester permanently.

Noel has always been moody and he knows it's not his most endearing trait. He's an obsessive and I believe that he was always too willing to think that people disliked him. A lot of that has to come down to our father and how Noel rebelled against him. Sometimes he just lets go of people, and stands back from them saying, 'Go on, you don't really like me anyway, so go to hell.' He became especially self-conscious about finishing with Louise because they had a lot of friends in common. To the outside world Louise may have seemed to be the injured party, dumped by the budding pop star. Noel might have thought that most of their mutual friends in Manchester were taking her side, but that isn't really the case. Of course they supported her, but Noel felt embarrassed and guilty about it, thinking again that no one liked him. If people finish, it's sad, but it's their business and their pain to deal with. The majority of people realised that.

I know my mam was quite upset at the time, because Louise had become like a daughter to her, and until recently there was a huge photo of Louise on top of our TV at home. It was only removed once our Noel had pointed out to my mother how nice his girlfriend, Meg, is and that it made her uncomfortable when she came round. So now Louise is in the drawer and Meg's photo adorns the top of our TV. Louise still rings my mam occasionally for a chat and I'm sure she always will.

Liam was having his own problems with his friends coming to terms with his fame:

When I go home I get these lads coming up saying, 'Your band's top, it's just a ball of hype.' I say, 'What do you mean? Hang on, you're only gutted because the press aren't writing about your band.' The reason we're in every paper is because there's something to write about, we're playing the game and we're honest and we've got the best songs . . . and that's why we're in everyone's face.

Before the release of 'Shakermaker', Oasis had a chance to warm up for their festival debut at Glastonbury by playing at Avenham Park, Preston, as part of the Heineken Big Top free music weekend. Oasis played second on the bill to the Boo Radleys, who as it turned out were huge fans of Oasis and were reluctant to headline the concert and let Oasis go on before them. The two bands did a long and exhausting signing session with over 1000 people queuing for autographs. Liam even signed somebody's trainers. Oasis are good with their fans like that, but they have been getting mobbed and our Liam's obsession with John Lennon has made him very wary. Their tour manager, Margaret Mouzakatis, turned round to me that day and said, 'Have you seen how big your brothers are now?'

There must have been 8000 people in the park, most of them fairly rowdy. Half way through the band's second song they had to stop when some idiot in the crowd threw a bottle at Noel. Once things had calmed down, they belted out an almost immaculate set, finishing off with 'I Am The Walrus'. They were more than living up to their hype. They were going into orbit. I remember Martin Carr of the Boo Radleys walking around the side of the stage area, shaking his head and saying, 'How on earth can we follow that?'

After gigs in Glasgow and a hop over to play a famous one-time strip joint, Erotika, in Paris, it was time for the band to get ready for the release of 'Shakermaker' and the Glastonbury Festival the following weekend.

'Shakermaker', with its reference to Mr Sifter's record shop, had been getting hammered to death on all the radio stations. It came out on Monday 20 June. On 22 June, Oasis were recording a live version for a new and deservedly short-lived Channel 4 show called *Naked City*. Noel was being interviewed, trying hard to do an impression of Shaun Ryder of the Happy Mondays. I could see how drunk and edgy he was – he certainly wasn't being himself now that he was a pop star. But overall I was impressed with the way he came across. In the early days, Noel worried more about interviews than writing the songs and performing. He did at first give Liam that task, but Liam just says the first thing that comes into his head and sometimes that can be explosive and career-threatening. On *Naked City*, Noel was fairly amusing, wittily replying to some fairly *Smash Hits*-style questions: *Interviewer* – 'What would you do if you thought you were being too famous?' *Noel* – 'I'd probably go out and buy a chocolate brown Rolls Royce and my own hotel room so I could trash it.'

On Saturday, 25 June I travelled down to Glastonbury to see my brothers play the following day. The hotel where Oasis and their entourage were staying was playing host to a town criers' convention. Far from being taken over by pop stars playing the festival, it was full of portly fellows who sounded like they could bring the roof down when they were just ordering a few lagers at the bar.

Glastonbury was a real culture shock to me, full of hippy and crusty types, veggie burger stands and local hawkers and sellers. Every July in this beautiful part of the country, with the distant hills and sheep grazing quietly, these locals who sell cans of Coke and bits of cardboard for you to sit on (in case the ground's damp and it plays havoc with your Farmer Giles), go from fleecing sheep to fleecing festival-goers. A quid for a can of Coke – you've got to be joking!

Liam hadn't returned to the hotel on the Saturday night which put everyone on a bit of a downer. This was Sunday; the new charts would be announced between five and seven on Radio One, they were playing in front of the biggest crowd ever, and our Liam wasn't anywhere to be found.

It was a carnival atmosphere on the site. There must have been over 50,000 people milling around the place, over half of them caned out of their brains on booze and drugs. The place was crawling with mangy-looking dogs, posh white youths with dreadlocks and joints the size of hot dogs, people shouting and arguing and student types dressed to look like *Big Issue* sellers with small scraggy dogs on bits of string. Loud music, dogs barking, lost kids crying, plain clothes policemen – it was like our house when I was about fourteen.

I was in fine fettle, but the rest of the band were still fretting – Liam still hadn't turned up. Search parties were dispatched to find him and our Noel was feeling particularly moody. Finally, about an hour before they were due on, Liam showed up, bad-tempered and defensive about where he'd been and wearing the same clothes he'd had on for the past two days. I'd learnt my lesson at the Warwick University gig and stayed out of it while he was given a verbal dressing down, which he wasn't going to accept without a few choice insults of his own. I just thought, It's a great day, everything is going fine for them, yet they must be two of the moodiest people here.'

But Oasis were really up for this one. This was their FA Cup final. I estimate there were 5000 people watching them play, dancing around (even to 'Live Forever'), sitting on each other's shoulders, waving plastic beer, Coke and water bottles in the air above their heads. I felt really proud of my brothers, especially when we heard later that 'Shakermaker' had just gone straight into that week's chart at number eleven.

After the gig, everyone was buzzing. I spotted the Inspiral Carpets – they were due to play on the main stage later that day. The lead singer, Tom, Clint, Graham, Noddy and Martin were hanging around next to their luxury tour bus with its built-in video player and all mod cons. They looked very well, sporting tans from their recent Italian tour. As I chewed the fat with the lads from the Inspirals, I could feel my brothers' eyes burning holes in my back, as they and other members of the Oasis crew hung around their hired mini-bus.

When I went back to Noel and Liam, they said, 'What are you talking to them for?'

I thought it was really childish and said so. I don't know why Noel was bothered. He was doing all right. Oasis's single was number eleven in the chart and the Inspirals were very pleased for him. Maybe it was the fact they had a flash tour bus and were playing on the main stage, while Oasis had a mini-bus and had just played on Glastonbury's second stage. I knew Noel had fallen out with them, but that was a few years ago and life's too short. Liam made me laugh. After gobbing off to me about talking to them, he went over for a chat and even posed for a photo with them for an *NME* photographer. But then that's all part of rock and roll.

Oasis finally made their *Top of the Pops* appearance. History had been made and they'd make some more, but it was only 1994 and they were still small-time, though they didn't act it.

In July they made their first trip to the States to play Wetlands in New York City as part of New York's international music seminar. The gig went down well with various luminaries in the audience including Soya, the lead singer with Echobelly. Our Liam wasn't impressed with how unstylishly the American fans dressed – sort of heavy metal cyber punk

c. 1982 meets flannel-shirted lumberjack. Neither did he like the way they moshed about and indulged in strange things like stage diving. It's that whole heavy metal scene in America – the Harley Davidsons, the wide open roads, the fact that musically it will always be 1972, harking back to the days of Led Zeppelin, Deep Purple, Black Sabbath and all that type of stuff.

After the concert at Wetlands, Oasis stuck around in New York to film the video for their next single, 'Live Forever', in Central Park. It's an unusual video. In it, the band bury Tony McCarroll the drummer. I wonder if he knew that within a year he would be buried again, and this time for good as far as playing with Oasis went.

Their next big fun away day was at Glasgow's T In The Park, my favourite outdoor summer festival in Britain. The festival actually takes place in Strathclyde Park near Hamilton, about fifteen miles south of Glasgow, and it was a major haul to get there.

I travelled up with the band in the mini-bus, driven by ex-Stone Roses roadie, Al Smith. Al was a top geezer, a damn fine fellow, but all those years with the Stone Roses had destroyed or pickled a few of his brain cells. We were about 30 miles south of Glasgow when he decided to fill the tank up at a garage. Now he either wasn't paying attention or genuinely didn't know, but he filled the tank with unleaded petrol. About 200 yards further down the road, the engine spluttered and died. Icy stares bore into the back of Al's neck. Noel was furious and said so.

Al's years of training on the road took over as he sprang into action by shrugging his shoulders resignedly and skinning up a large joint. Well, what could anyone say to that? We called the AA who said we could rely on them to be there some time in the next three hours. It was a lovely summer's day, so we all piled out of the broken van, which we'd pushed on to the hard shoulder, and started playing frisbee across the dual carriageway, dodging the traffic as it sped by. That's marijuana for you.

We were laughing our heads off, when the frisbee suddenly got stuck in a sign on the central reservation. Our Noel, competitive to the last, dodged in and out of the speeding cars to retrieve the plastic disc and continue the game. Mark Coyle commented wryly on Noel's imperviousness to the danger: 'There goes the future of rock and roll. I hope he doesn't get run over.'

It was two hours before the AA arrived and sorted out our vehicle, syphoning off the unsuitable fuel and replacing it with the correct stuff. We spent a good Saturday night in the hotel and laughed about Al's dopey driving and the curse of self-service gas stations.

Oasis were playing on Sunday on the same bill as D.Ream, House Of Pain, Whiteout, Thrum, One Dove, Mike Peters (formerly of the Alarm), and Tiny Monroe. Oasis were third on the bill. It was without a doubt Oasis's gig of the year so far. They weren't playing on the main stage, but in a tent with a capacity of around 6000. By the time Oasis came on there were 10,000 people trying to cram in and many more outside.

Maybe it was the Celt in them, or the fact that they were working-class northern boys, but the Glasgow crowd welcomed them like they were local heroes, cheering when Liam started playing football on stage. I was wedged at the side of the stage, endeavouring not to get crushed by the throng of screaming girls pressing ever closer: 'Liam, Liam.'

The crowd were mental, singing along to *every* song – the first time it had ever happened. It was that Celtic blood getting on the same wavelength and it was truly inspiring. When Liam and Noel came off they were on cloud nine, saying it was the best gig they'd ever played.

After Oasis's set, I met Alan McGee and his business partner, Dick Green, in the beer tent. We talked about the forthcoming debut album, *Definitely Maybe*, which they hadn't heard as yet. It had taken longer than anticipated to record – almost eight weeks in various studios and then more for mix downs. *Definitely Maybe* was originally going to be produced by Dave Bachelor, who'd been the front-of-house sound man for the Inspiral Carpets. Dave had worked with and produced several bands up in his native Scotland in the late seventies, including the Sensational Alex Harvey Band and Richard Jobson's group, the Skids. Noel wasn't pleased with the sound he was getting. Everything was too clean and there was too much separation on the instruments; it wasn't very rock and roll. So together with Mark Coyle he took over the production of the album himself. They'd recorded the whole album twice and scrapped it, so when it all started to come together I think it was a big relief for Noel and an even bigger one for Alan McGee. I assured both Alan and Dick that when *Definitely Maybe* came out it would be huge – but how huge I had no idea.

Chapter 12

Oasismania

Fame, like the river, is narrowest where it is bred, and broadest afar off.

William Davenant

I t was getting too big, too fast. Oasis's success was phenomenal. They'd released two singles, neither of which had made the top ten, yet they could have sold out the venues on their fourth tour five and six times over. All the press stories of backstage punch-ups and trashing hotel rooms and their appearance back in June on the *Naked City* TV show had hyped up this image of the fighting Gallaghers. My brothers can be spiky and aggressive, especially Liam, but I heard many a person say when they saw them, 'They're not very big, are they?' At the Newcastle Riverside club on 9 August, this must have gone through the mind of some moronic Geordie, who after one too many Newcastle Brown Ales, jumped up on stage and punched Noel in the face with his sovereign ring, cutting our Noel around the eye and leaving him with a nasty bruise. The gig had only just started and Oasis had only played two numbers. Noel retaliated by kicking the guy in the head and swinging his guitar at him, while Liam went into overdrive, frothing at the mouth and steaming into the guy ferociously, eventually being dragged off. Noel was bleeding and shaken and the crowd weren't pleased when the gig was abandoned, throwing bottles at the group and later when they were leaving the venue attacking the tour bus and smashing all its windows in . . .

It was this incident that made the group's management realise that they were a big name band now, even if they weren't yet in the top ten. They were the group everyone wanted to see. After some discussion the band's security was immediately stepped up by bringing in Ian Robertson, an ex-army man and an old friend of the band's manager, Marcus Russell.

Ian Robertson (Robbo, as he was known) thought he was the group's manager as well as minder and took it upon himself to keep a wary eye on all of them. I think he tried to keep them all regimented and Liam in particular felt it an intrusion when Robbo would try ordering him about like he was one of his squaddies from his army days. Liam isn't the sort of person who likes being bossed around by anyone, and Robbo was constantly keeping Liam in check, trying to tell him when to go to bed, who with, when to get up and being quite forceful about it. I think Robbo treated it as a battle of wills, which is all very well, but that isn't what he was paid to do. Liam hated him after several incidents including being physically dragged out of bed one morning when he was entertaining, and pushed up against the wall with no clothes on.

The first gig when Robbo was looking after security was at the Irish Centre in Leeds, which went off without a hitch, despite being the night after the incident at Newcastle. Our Noel was still sporting a rather ugly bruise on his face, and I think the fact the band hadn't cancelled the show brought some extra applause and cheers from the audience.

The band waited all that week while gigging, excited to find out how their new single, 'Live Forever', would do in the charts.

Number ten with a bullet, or however they put it. 'Live

Forever' went straight in the charts that week, but deserved to be a number one single. There'd been nothing quite like it in the chart for a long time. I felt especially proud and was now quite certain that when *Definitely Maybe* came out it would top the album charts. That must have been what most of the band's fans were hanging on for, otherwise 'Live Forever' would definitely have been a number one single.

On our way to Wulfrun Hall in Wolverhampton (the heart of the black country where they talk with a funny accent and support a crap football team), we took the scenic route from Leeds thanks to Ben the driver's strange sense of direction. Al Smith had just left to go back to the Stone Roses and their unleaded petrol. Ben was OK when it came to fuel, but got stuck in heavy traffic near Tamworth. Liam, patient as ever, was bored and so decided to punch Bonehead, because Bonehead's a Manchester United fan. Of course, everyone joined in and then jumped on Tony McCarrcll for the same reason.

On arriving in Wolverhampton, Liam decided he was a huge pop star. Ian Robertson's new security arrangements for the band meant that they would sneak into the venue around the side entrance. There was a huge crowd waiting out front for the band and good old Liam was most put out that the band should sneak in unseen: 'You lot can do what you want, but they're my fans, and they want to see me, and so I'm walking in the front way.'

Thus a major and rather childish argument started – the kind of argument that's right up our Liam's street. Behave illogically to begin with, try to justify it, and when you realise you can't without sounding like a prat, start whining and whingeing, then get angry and threatening.

There was a fight in the Wulfrun Hall that night, but this time in the crowd, unusual for an Oasis concert. Liam and Noel, my two beloved brothers who are no strangers to physical altercations themselves, were quite disgusted with it.

The enthusiasm of Oasis's loyal fans was starting to become overwhelming by this time and they also had a bevvy of groupies, press and weirdo types tracking them down to their hotels. To counter this constant invasion of privacy, for the gig at Nottingham's Rock City on 15 August, Oasis checked in under aliases for the first time. They were well on their way to becoming the biggest band in Britain.

Rock City was a 1500 capacity venue and was a real sweatbox. It was hard to see the band, though the sound was great. Wandering through the crowd to quench my thirst at the bar, I bumped into this lad from Windsor called Nigel Hallett. He was following Oasis around on as many tour dates as possible and offered to give me a lift to London for their Forum gig the next night.

The Forum was absolutely heaving with people, but the problem with the London venues by this time was that Oasis had become a 'socialite' band, so all these terribly nice people, the exact opposite of Oasis's scally roots, were turning up just because Oasis were the band to go to see.

The day following the Forum, Oasis made their second appearance on *Top of the Pops* playing 'Live Forever'. It was their third top 40 single and third indie number one.

Still in London on Thursday, 18 August, they played the Astoria. It holds around 2000 people and I think 1800 of them were on the guest list. 'Oh, I just had to come, I mean they're so cool and, well, northern, aren't they?' I hate those big venues full of people just jumping on the bandwagon. The support at the Astoria that night came from Sixty Foot Dolls and Ocean Colour Scene, and you could tell it wasn't a music crowd by the way they were virtually ignored all the way through their sets.

Oasis had already done a fair day's work before they set foot on that stage at the Astoria. Earlier in the day they'd been doing an MTV acoustic set of 'Live Forever' and 'Whatever', with Bonehead on piano, Noel on guitar and vocals, and Liam on vocals. That day, with the amount of work and associated PR, and the sloaney types at the gig, I realised that Oasis had been adopted by the establishment. The guest list places once saved for their old buddies from Manchester would in future get swallowed up more and more by the people who worked for them in London, who'd rather their friends went on any guest list than old friends of the band.

Oasis were in overdrive again. They would gig any time, any place, anywhere. They planned a video shoot on 21 August at the Borderline club in London for the 'Cigarettes And Alcohol' single. When they arrived there they found 500 fans waiting around outside, so they turned it into a free gig.

Following the video shoot they were off again, this time to Holland and the Lowlands festival, where they played another tent gig to over 7000 people. They still had a few smaller venues booked in on their tour; places in deepest darkest Britain that none of the band had heard of. 'Buckley? Where's Buckley?' was a familiar cry from the band looking down their itenerary. The band were in buoyant mood. Their debut album was ready to come out and all the lead up to it told you it was heading straight in at number one.

It was at the Buckley Tivoli gig (in North Wales) that I first came into contact with Evan Dando, geeky rock god and lead singer and songwriter with the Lemonheads. Evan was hanging out with Oasis, turning up at their various gigs around Britain, including the band's album launch at the Virgin Megastore in London, where he'd played a surprise acoustic set as a warm up, even though he was well out of it thanks to plenty of backstage hospitality. He carried it off like a true professional and the crowd were very pleasantly surprised at having such an honour bestowed on them, all for a £6 ticket. When Oasis came on stage, it was blistering and powerful stuff. Somebody in the crowd flung a bottle at our Liam, who remonstrated by shouting, 'Leave it out, I'm not a soddin' coconut on a stall.'

Buckley was a seething mass of bodies. All the girls, as ever, pressed to the front of the stage gawping at Liam, who when singing 'Live Forever' changed the words: 'I think you're the same as me, take two sugars in your tea.' I think he did it as a dig at our Noel. Before the launch at Virgin Megastore, Liam had been arguing about Noel's choice of songs to perform acoustically. Agitatedly pacing around inside the dressing room, Liam was trying as ever to get Guigsy, Bonehead and Tony to back him up in his argument with Noel: 'You can't do 'Digsy's Dinner' acoustically as well. You're going to be a dick trying to do loads of songs that won't work right.' Noel just ignored it. Liam wouldn't leave it though. 'All right then, do 'Sad Song' last. Then you can play your little game.'

Liam does genuinely get a bit miffed when Noel takes over on the vocal duties.

After the launch, Evan Dando, by now totally off his trolley on gratis beer, went running out on to the roof of the building with his guitar and proceeded to perform an acoustic set to the throng of girls hanging around for him and the Oasis boys in the car park below. Evan Dando's a cool mad rad guy who I'd meet again and again over the next couple of years, but I think he found it difficult understanding our Mancunian sense of humour. As an American, he never could quite get to grips with taking the piss as an art form. For that you need a much better sense of irony, and Americans are too open about their feelings (at least on Oprah Winfrey) to understand.

It was like Beatlemania in Dublin, Oasis's first Irish gig, and the local press went to town on all the band's Irish connections. Bonehead's parents were from Mayo, and Tony McCarroll and Paul McGuigan's people were from Northern Ireland as well as the Gallagher boys with roots in Meath and Mayo.

I decided to make my own way to Dublin on the plane. I didn't fancy a ferry crossing with the grump twins, and I couldn't get on with the band's tour manager, Margaret Mouzakatis. She struck me as someone with an attitude problem on a power trip.

I met up in Dublin with some mates and with a bit of messing around I got eight of us into the venue, which was again heaving. Unlike the London dates this concert was full of genuine fans and it made a big difference to the atmosphere. I'd spent loads of weekends on the booze in Dublin and I think for people from Manchester and Liverpool at least, it feels like a second home. I felt sorry for all the kids who couldn't get in – real fans – and I wish I'd had some tickets left to give them. Those were the people deserving of a place on the guest list to see Oasis, not some jumped-up public school twat from some PR company with a tossy name and a horsey girlfriend.

Those young Irish fans took the biscuit. They were cheeky and down to earth, but music mad. One fan told me, 'Oasis are *our* Beatles, not U2.' It was like a homecoming for the Manchester Irish. Now, apparently, one in two Irish house-holds own an Oasis album. Outside after the gig, Liam and Noel were literally mobbed, while I stood to one side to let them get on with it. This was my brothers' time; they deserved to wallow in their fame and enjoy it. I watched, amused, as one desperate young lad pleaded with Liam: 'Liam, have you anything you can give me as a souvenir; anything in your pocket at all, even a piece of paper or a bus ticket? Anything would be grand, sure it would.'

Liam self-consciously fumbled around in his pockets, pul-led out a 2p piece and handed it over to the young lad, who ran off holding it up as if it was a pot of gold from over the rainbow. Liam had blessed his life with that one gesture and that's the best 2p Liam's ever spent.

There was no after-show party that night as Oasis were travelling at first light to Belfast, and the Dublin Tivoli gig didn't finish until around two o'clock. Evan Dando couldn't make his mind up what to do. 'Hey guys, I don't know what to do. I might just find a place to sleep on the streets.' Everyone else was in agreement: 'You must be bonkers, Evan. This is Dublin not some sleepy village. You'll wake up tomorrow with nothing left. You'll get robbed blind if you kip here.' Evan seemed insistent: 'No, Dublin's cool, man, I'll just stay here.'

Noel, who was waiting to leave in the van, just stuck his head out the door and signalled to the roadies. 'Put him in the van with us will you, or we'll be here all night.'

As Evan and Oasis headed for their hotel, we all headed off to my mate's house in Ballyfermot near Kilmainham prison, where some of the locals even paint the pavement green, white and gold. I chuckled and wondered how Mr Dando would have got on sleeping rough around there.

A couple of nights later, Oasis played at the Hacienda in Manchester. A lot had changed since they last played in Manchester. The tickets sold out in a couple of hours.

After the In The City week, Oasis headed off to Japan and then on to their first American tour. I'd been laid off – it often happens that way in the winter when you're self-employed on contract work, so I went down to the dole office to sign on for my fortnightly welfare cheque. I followed the tour with interest via the music press. I read about them cancelling gigs and Noel and Liam arguing, until finally our Noel just skipped off and left them and spent a week or more in Las Vegas gambling, trying to sort his head out.

I think the strain of the constant touring and the sheer amount of gigs still to play, was telling on the band. Noel had seen it and done it all before with the Inspiral Carpets and I've no doubt that most of the arguments stemmed from the fact that it was the first time the others, and particularly our Liam, had ever been to the States. I think they wanted a mini holiday. Noel would have objected to this, eager as ever to get on, but realising it wasn't working and the band couldn't perform that well if they were all tired and disgruntled, he probably just thought he'd let them take the blame for all the cancelled gigs and skipped off on his own. It saved him from backing down from his position of 'the show must go on', but also showed the rest of the group he was annoyed. In fact, he skipped off with the band's $800 float for a lost week probably spent sitting in a hotel watching TV and writing another 23 albums' worth of songs. Noel returned for a big showdown meeting with the group. Tim Abbott flew over from London to act as intermediary. Noel and the band made it up, and the Oasis show was on the road again.

Oasis were causing a minor stir in the States, certainly among critics and the business side. Even the national daily, *USA Today*, had a cover story on the group, despite the fact that they weren't playing big venues with the average audience being 350 people or so. Lewis Largent, MTV's Vice President of music, said of Oasis: 'It's a little early to talk about a British invasion, but this is the first great band to come out of England in a long time.' The *USA Today* article said:

Here comes the biggest British rock band since the Beatles. Yeah, yeah, yeah. In recent years, England's major musical export has been hype. Lauded bands like James, Blur and Suede wowed crowds in the UK while barely denting the grunge-obsessed charts and minds of American rock fans in the nineties. The closest thing to a smashing British success here are Green Day, the English-punk soundalikes from California.

But now Oasis is on the horizon. Fresh from conquering the charts in England the British quintet has leapt the pond in hopes of Stateside success. And they just might get it, bucking the US fate of British titans like Depeche Mode, Morrissey and the Cure.

The band's acclaimed *Definitely Maybe*, Britain's biggest-selling debut album ever, has seduced MTV and radio and is inching up Billboard's chart. With its tuneful rock and devilish air, Oasis is considered a frontrunner in an anticipated replay of the 60s British Invasion.

I was sitting at home one day when the phone went: 'Hello. Is that Paul? It's Nigel here, Nigel Hallett from Windsor. We met at Rock City in Nottingham. Look, I know it's cheeky, but are you going to see Oasis in New York on 28 October?' I told him I'd love to, but that I was on the dole and couldn't afford it. He continued: 'The thing is we can't really go without you as we haven't got any tickets, so if you reckon you can get us into the gig, we'll pay for your flight.'

Well, that was an offer I couldn't refuse. I'd never been to the States. In fact the only times I'd ever been abroad were on a skiing trip to Andorra with some mates, and to watch the Republic of Ireland in Poland, a coach trip from hell for a

European Championship match. New York is one of those places everyone dreams of visiting once in a lifetime. I could hardly believe my luck. Noel had said that if I managed to get to any gigs in America he'd sort us out somewhere to stay, so everything looked sweet for my four-day round trip.

I cashed my giro which totalled about £90, borrowed £30 off my mam and headed for Windsor. The next day, 28 October, Nigel, two of his mates and myself set out for New York via Heathrow.

Straightaway after landing, we made our way by cab with all our bags to Maxwell's Bar in Hoboken, New Jersey. Hoboken is famous for being the birth place of Frank Sinatra, but tonight it would be a band from Burnage in Manchester who'd be providing the musical entertainment. We arrived at Maxwell's a good few hours before the gig, so we had no problems getting in. Noel and Liam were quite surprised to see me. Maxwell's was just a small bar which only held about 200 people and it filled up as the night wore on. I had to keep pinching myself to prove that this was real – that I was in New York and about to see my brothers perform live to an American crowd.

Oasis were like a finely tuned car, the way they seemed to cruise effortlessly into top gear on stage. I could tell they'd been playing constantly, well over a hundred gigs now, and over half of them in less than six months. For the first time ever, they dedicated a song to me on stage, Liam grabbing the microphone and saying, 'This one's dedicated to our kid who's just flown in from Manchester.' Noel leaned to the microphone for his sly dig. 'We're not playing "Lip Up fatty", are we?' It's a good job he was on stage at that time, because if I could have got my hands on him he'd have been tuning that guitar of his with his sphincter muscles for the next week. 'Anyway, this one's for our kid who's over at the bar: "Cigarettes And Alcohol".'

I'd be lying if I said I wasn't really chuffed about that. It's the only time they've ever dedicated a song to me and I'll treasure it.

After the gig, Nigel and his mates went off to Catskill to stay with a couple of friends who had a house there. I thanked them for the plane ticket and arranged to meet them on the way back. I went to get on the band's bus for a lift to New York and the tour manager wouldn't let me on.

'No, you can't come on the bus. This is our home.'

There I was 3000 miles from home with about £90 in English money in my pocket, no idea of where to stay, and she wouldn't let me on the tour bus for a lift. Tony McCarroll came to the rescue: 'Why aren't you coming on the bus?' I told him the tour manager wouldn't let me, and he just dismissed her, with, 'Just get on. Ignore her, she's off her head.'

She gave me a steely look, and I could hear her moaning on to Marcus Russell. 'This bus is our home, and we don't really have room for him. Nobody told me he was coming.' Marcus just sighed and said, 'What's the problem? It's only Bod, he's Noel and Liam's brother.'

We got back to the Macklowe Hotel and hit the bar with a vengeance. Tony McCarroll said I could stay in his and Bonehead's room that night. I was knackered but couldn't sleep, so I stayed in the bar drinking until exhaustion kicked in and forced me to bed.

The next day Oasis were playing Wetlands in New York, a much larger venue than Maxwells. I slept in late and then travelled down with the band for their soundcheck at four o'clock in the afternoon. There were about 500 or so people at the gig including a lot of ex-patriate British, a whole bunch of Chelsea fans who were fairly obnoxious, several record company types, Paul Mathur from *Melody Maker* who was standing on his own in a corner with his jotter out like a trainspotter waiting for an InterCity 125, a bevvy of beautiful rock chicks, Bonehead's brother Martin who lived in Los Angeles and had flown across especially for the gig, Evan Dando and some American journalists.

After the gig, we went to a party hosted by a well-to-do American woman who is involved in running the world famous Wilhelmina modelling agency in New York. The party was held in her loft apartment from which you could gaze across the alluring New York skyline. It was like something out of a movie. The booze was flowing freely and I ended up drinking myself under the table and promptly falling asleep there. I wasn't the only one, I hasten to add. It was a good party. I awoke around nine o'clock the next morning, feeling rough as hell, and made my way back to the hotel to collect my stuff. As I arrived the band were packing up to go. Unfortunately I was now so skint that church mice were stopping me in the street and giving me their loose change. I was as broke as the ten commandments.

As I worried about my almost non-existent finances and toyed with the idea of sleeping in a shop doorway, our Noel suddenly pulled out a wad of money. 'You need any dough?'

He just handed me the bundle. There was about $300. I was rich. Then Liam came over to me. He was being nice, so something was obviously up. 'Hey Bod, can you do us a favour?' I was suspicious, but said yes.

'Can you take a bag with a few things in it back to our house in Manchester with you?' I said that would be no problem. However, I started sweating a bit at this juncture. I'd seen *Midnight Express* and wondered what Liam wanted me to take back. Would I end up surrounded by armed guards and Alsatian sniffer dogs at Newark airport suffering the rubber glove treatment and facing a dim future sharing a cell with a musclebound bisexual on Ryker's Island?

Liam gave me the suitcase. It was the oldest, most battered bag I'd ever seen. He'd nicked better ones off me and given, or sold, them to his mates when he was fourteen. It weighed a ton, the handles were coming loose and it didn't have any wheels on it. 'Bloody hell,' I gasped, 'what have you got in here?' 'Oh, just a few trainers and shoes and things,' Liam replied.

Later I took a peek; there were about 25 pairs of brand new trainers and an electronic Japanese World Cup '94 souvenir that lit up and played 'Olé, Olé, Olé, Olé, Olé, Olé'. Very amusing.

I had a couple of days sightseeing in New York. On the day I was leaving I'd arranged to see David Massey, the Vice President of Epic Records A & R, a division of Sony, who'd signed Oasis for America. David is originally from Bristol and had been living and working in the USA for ten years. We chatted about music and I was struck by how enthusiastic he still was after all his years of working his way to the top in what is, after all, a very cynical business. David makes me laugh. He looks and sounds like a real corporate bod, but get him talking about music and he enthuses like a fan. I agreed to send him tapes of any decent bands I came across in the UK. As I was getting ready to leave, he asked me how I was getting to the airport. He said just to ring him when I was ready to go and he'd send a car to wherever I was, to pick me up and take me there. He was as good as his word and sent a big black stretch limo. I felt terrific riding in it.

I didn't feel so terrific dragging Liam's heavy suitcase to the check-in area. These training shoes have been breeding overnight, I thought. While armed, uniformed, airport police watched, I had to pass it through an X-ray machine. Suddenly this siren in the bag goes off – 'Olé Olé Olé Olé Olé Olé'. The security police reached for their weapons and I thought, Oh, no. I opened the bag trying to explain that it was just an electronic toy our Liam had bought.

'Are these all *your* training shoes?' I was asked. I tried to explain why I was carrying so many pairs of trainers: 'Er no, officer. I'm taking them back for my brothers who've been on tour here and they've run out of room.'

Eventually they let me check the bag in and I met up with Nigel and his mates in the departure lounge. They looked quite miserable. It turned out the girl they knew in Catskill who had promised to put them up, had gone away for the weekend, so they ended up spending all their money on motel accommodation. Meanwhile I was going home with more money than I'd had when I arrived. The beers were on me.

I made it back to Manchester with the bag. Many of its still unworn contents now lurk in Liam's Imelda Marcos-like wardrobe. When he goes back to Manchester, he'll go up to his room and open that wardrobe to commune with his belongings, read a roll call to himself, checking that each item is present and correct, shut the door and leave them again until the next time.

Liam was a bit nonplussed by America. He couldn't get used to how quiet and dull a lot of the bigger cities were, with the exceptions of New York, Chicago and LA. There weren't many decent nightclubs to go to – drinking and clubbing aren't really the main leisure activities over there. He was also a little out of sorts because one night, when leaving a club with Bonehead, a car full of guys drove past nearly running over Liam's foot. Liam started shaking his fist and shouting abuse at them. The car stopped and Liam was about to go for the guy who got out, when he pulled out a gun. Liam was still shouting abuse when Bonehead intervened, dragging him out of harm's way.

1994 had been a great year. Noel's philosophy of putting out at least a single every three months had worked. He'd liked that about the Jam. He'd admired the way the Smiths always seemed to put really good songs on the flip side, so every Oasis CD had four songs on it, all of them good enough to be A-sides. *Definitely Maybe* had become the fastest-selling debut album of all time in Britain and Noel was more than pleased:

> We can't predict the future. It's not up to us. All we can do is write and record and if people buy the records, then we'll be part of 1995's pop history. Hopefully we'll still be going in the year 2000. But as for 1994 – this is our year without a doubt; no one can touch us this year, we're on a roll.

The next American tour, in 1995, was to place Oasis firmly in that nation's rock and roll hierarchy. They are aware that for a group to be worth its salt, it has to be successful in America. So far, after peaking in the American album charts at number four with *What's the Story Morning Glory*, and clocking up sales of almost four million, they are just one hit single and a tour away from cracking the place wide open. The reviews in America for Oasis have been cautious but optimistic. They have an edge, they aren't effete or pretentious, and the songs are direct and anthemic. America likes songs that sound good played on a car stereo, that conjure up images of space and a dream. Any band who wants to be able to adapt material for the American market needs to travel there. *Definitely Maybe* was perhaps too British and too raw to be a huge commercial success in the States, but *What's the Story*, with its mixture of ballad-type songs like 'Wonderwall' and 'Don't Look Back In Anger', and the hugely anthemic 'Champagne Supernova' are exactly what the public wants. When *What's the Story* came out in Britain, the initial reviews weren't that kind. It took some critics several months to realise that *What's the Story* is a better album than *Definitely Maybe*; but what's the betting that their American fans will soon own copies of both?

America is the number one priority for Oasis now; it has to be. You can't crack American open with just hype, attitude and the influence of the press. Ultimately, in America you'll be judged purely on the strength of your records and gigs. The American fans took to Oasis quickly. All their songs have universal themes – being free, being positive, making things happen. That's their view of the way life is. Opportunities don't come every day so when they do, seize them. That's why those ordinary working-class kids in Britain love them, too. They aren't a band for intellectuals or students to muse over. They are in your face, warts and all. Remember it wasn't that long ago that the various band members were trowelling concrete and digging holes for a living, and they've made it. That's a powerful message to deliver.

Chapter 13

Superstars and runners-up

G igs, more gigs, singles. 'Cigarettes And Alcohol' hit the spot, reaching number seven in October, and 'Whatever' charted in Christmas week, 1994. That song oozed class, and Noel could have saved a few bob on session musicians if our Liam had kept up those violin lessons. 'Whatever' was a turning point for Oasis; with that song they proved they weren't just flavour of the month but that they had ideas and were musically ambitious. Despite all the plaudits for their debut album, *Definitely Maybe*, Oasis could and would do better.

'Some Might Say' sailed into the number one spot in April 1995, although it only remained there for one week. It was quite funny how the press covered Oasis's first number one. They concentrated on the big name stars spotted at the group's gigs on their second American tour – Ringo Starr, Janet Jackson, the Edge, Bono and Adam Clayton. They were becoming tabloid fodder. Every day I'd read stories, like our Liam saying he'd tried taking heroin when he was fifteen.

At the time, a number of British guitar bands had been desperately trying to break into the USA. Suede had been hyped up and gone to the States with the tag of best new British band only to end up supporting the Cranberries from

Limerick in Ireland who proceeded to sell six million albums in the States. Oasis not only had hype, but a knack for writing anthemic stadium-type poppy rock songs. They looked likely contenders. The Stone Roses had created a buzz, the Charlatans had sold over half a million albums in the States back in 1990 without too much heavy touring, and Oasis were prepared to go for it. Any wannabe pop stars out there who think Oasis had it easy, just take a look at the punishing gigging schedules over the past two years, the niggles, the total exhaustion, the frayed tempers, the incessant travelling, and the constant pestering. Yes, it's that easy.

In Britain, Blur had established a firm fan base and it had taken them the best part of four years to fill the vacuum of Britain's number one band. The music press already had an inkling that Oasis were heading to be that number one band. Blur had swept the board at the Brit Awards for 1994, Britain's version of the Grammies, and Oasis had won a Brit for best newcomers, but preceding that, in the *NME*'s Brat Awards – in the main voted for by the magazine's readers – Oasis and Blur won just about everything, and the evening belonged to Oasis. As the awards were announced Oasis went up several times. First award was for Best New Band.

> Liam: 'Thank you very much. It's a good job Shed 7 didn't win it.' (with a cheeky grin)
> Noel: 'I think there's enough said there. Thanks a lot.'

The best single voted for by the readers went to Oasis for 'Live Forever'.

> Liam: 'I'm just glad Elastica didn't win it.'

After the awards, drunk and heady, Noel and Liam were in great spirits and being interviewed by various people.

> Interviewer: 'What did you think of it tonight?'
> Liam: 'Boring.' (but with a smirk on his face)

> Noel: 'I thought we should have won more.'
> Liam: 'Yeah, we should have been voted Best Rap Artist.'
> Noel: 'Our kid [indicating a smiling, drunken Liam] should have been voted best band because he's got seven different personalities and he's got a top brass section.'

Even later the same evening, Noel was interviewed by a very studenty overly precious and agitated Donna, from the group Elastica.

> Donna: 'How do Oasis feel about winning the amount of awards they won?'
> Noel: 'Quite pleased.'
> Donna (now agitated): 'Is that all?'
> Noel: 'Well, they were voted for by the kids and that's all that counts to us. It's the fans that decide whether your records are worth buying so, yeah, I'm pleased with the ones they voted for.'
> Donna (almost pleading): 'And what about the *NME* writers. Aren't they important?'
> Noel: 'Well, it was no contest really. Who else was going to win them?'
> Donna: 'And what about Liam slagging off other bands?' (Donna's band, Elastica, for example.)
> Noel (ready to laugh his head off, but biting his lip): 'No, that's wrong. You can't come here and slag other bands off. It's about creating something British. For us personally, 1994 has been the best year; 1995 will be better and in 1996 we'll take over. It's about America now and we'll go there and make it happen for the other dozen or so good songwriting bands out there. I think my band in particular is the best band in the country and my message to America is that we're coming; we're coming to take your children.'

As sales of *Definitely Maybe* hit the one million mark in the UK and with a number one single under their belt, Oasis looked set to steal Blur's short-lived reign as the top British band in America. So the British press had a field day when Blur and Oasis released two singles head to head in August 1995.

I was never a big fan of Blur. They had a few decent songs, did a few good gigs, but they always reminded me of an ill-thought-out Steve Harley and Cockney Rebels (except Steve Harley genuinely was a Cockney). I know Liam bought a Blur single as early as 1991, and Noel was quite impressed when he went to see them at the Academy in Manchester back in 1992, telling the members of the Inspiral Carpets that he'd been to see this great band who had a brilliant frontman.

I think the whole Blur versus Oasis scam was more to do with Blur than Oasis. Blur needed to crack the States, but to be taken seriously as contenders they had to go over there as the number one band in Britain. The whole thing ended up growing out of all proportion, until there actually was genuine animosity between the two bands. The British press loved it. Northern working-class lads versus southern middle-class boys from the home counties. They played on everybody's prejudices.

Britain as a country is tribal enough. Maybe it's the mixture of indigenous races – Celt, Saxon, Anglo, Dane and Norwegian. The truth is it's racist and as our Liam once pointed out, regionalist. The English don't like the Scots, the Welsh hate the English, people down south hate people from the north. Yes, they're all generalisations, but anyone who's British and being honest would have to accept that viewpoint. It might not be politically correct, but you'd agree if you had followed football home and away like I have. People hide behind it, but class prejudice, regionalism, and all the old gut reactions were brought into play in that Oasis versus Blur battle. Blur won hands down, with 'Country House' going straight in at number one and Oasis's 'Roll With It' going straight in at number two. I upset our Noel just before it was released by saying I didn't rate 'Roll With it' in comparison with 'Whatever', 'Some Might Say', 'Live Forever' or in fact any of the band's previous singles. The irony is that although it only got to number two, 'Roll With It' outsold 'Some Might Say', which had been a number one hit, by about two to one in its first week of release. So the losers of the so-called battle of Britpop cried all the way to the bank.

The press, as usual, made a meal of it. What was the big news last August? Mass graves, ethnic cleansing and kids being blown up by mortars in Bosnia; civil war in the Chechen Republic? No, who's going to win in the battle of Britpop between Blur and Oasis. I must admit, even my mother and I got caught up in the hype. We always do. This will embarrass our Noel and Liam, but it's true. Every time an Oasis record came out, my mother and I would buy about ten copies each, all from chart return shops. We'd send them to relatives in Ireland or give them to neighbours. Peter Sifter grabbed me on the street one day and said, 'How come you don't buy your records at my shop any more?' I had to tell him, 'Peter, Mr Sifter's isn't a chart return shop.'

In the end the battle of Britpop was won by Blur, but so far it looks as if Oasis have won the war. It all seems a bit stupid now and I'm certain both bands find a lot of it highly embarrassing. The insults flew, with our Noel at one point being quoted in an *Observer* article as saying that he hoped Blur's Alex James and Damon Albarn die of AIDS. Obviously our Noel's sense of humour wasn't having one of its better days, and neither was our mam's when she read his remark. The biggest bullshit story of all, though, was a headline in the *Daily Mirror* entitled 'Oasis Mum is a Blur Fan'. The story was even more incredible:

> Oasis stars Liam and Noel Gallagher lost the battle of the bands to reach number one – then discovered their mum is a huge fan of rivals Blur.
> Peggy, 50, reckons Blur's chart-topping single 'Country House' – which left Oasis in second spot – is great.

She says, 'It's a very catchy tune. Blur are a good group and you can tap your feet to the song.'

I sometimes wonder where they get it all from.

Noel had to do something about his AIDS remark. He was probably just being caustically flippant, but things written down have a way of looking much worse than they sound when uttered. So Noel wrote an open letter of apology:

I would like to apologise to all concerned who took offence at my comments about Damon Albarn and Alex James in an *Observer* article printed last Sunday.

The off-the-cuff remark was made last month at the height of a war of words between both bands, and it must have been the 50th time during that interview that I was pressed to give an opinion on Blur. As soon as I said it, I realised it was an insensitive thing to say as AIDS is no joking matter, and I immediately retracted the comment, but was horrified to pick up the *Observer* and find the journalist concerned chose to run with it.

Anyone who knows me will confirm that I've always been sympathetic towards the plight of HIV carriers and AIDS sufferers, as well as being supportive of the challenge to raise awareness about AIDS and HIV.

Although not being a fan of their music, I wish both Damon and Alex a long and happy life.

Looking back now at that whole Blur versus Oasis battle for the number one spot, I find it ridiculous how Noel and Liam were so absolutely gutted at losing. Blur were selling their single a quid cheaper, barcodes got messed up on the Oasis single so a lot of sales didn't register, and at the end of the day Blur had the weight of EMI's marketing department behind them.

Oasis and Blur are like chalk and cheese as people. Blur are typical art house student material, when all is said and done; your genuine amateur intelligentsia. They'd been trying to jump on every bandwagon going since the whole baggy thing came out of Manchester in 1989, and they missed the point then, too.

Liam loves a bit of aggro in his life and tried to wind Damon up some time later by going over to his girlfriend, Justine Frischmann of Elastica, and chatting her up. He propositioned her and declared his undying love for her – all with a straight face of course – on MTV.

It's all quite amusing in retrospect, especially as Oasis have now proved that they were always the only band with any relevance around at that time.

Chapter 14

Legends of our time

Nineteen-ninety-five was a whirlwind year for Oasis. They slogged their guts out across the world. It wasn't like touring, more like a gradual process of attrition. Tony McCarroll was the first casualty in the band. I always liked Tony. I'd known him for years from around the Irish clubs, but he and Noel just never got on. I think Tony guessed that the writing was on the wall from the start. Maybe Noel always intended replacing him. It wasn't long after 'Supersonic' came out, and Oasis were still rehearsing at the Boardwalk in Manchester, that Tony turned up to rehearse one day and found that our Noel had set up his drum kit on the street outside. To be sacked from a band who you know are going to be as big as the Beatles must hurt, especially as Tony had been there from the days of the Rain, before even our Liam joined. Now he might spend his whole life being pointed out as 'that bloke who used to be the drummer with Oasis'. Noel may have had his plans, but it was Tony's falling out with Liam that ultimately led to his demise in the band, because Noel could easily get rid of Tony, once Liam was in agreement. But back in August 1994, Noel's attitude was slightly different:

As it's my band and I'm the writer, I tend to be pretty stubborn. When people interview Liam, because he's not a writer, he can't talk about the music. All he can talk about is himself, how many birds he's had and how many tables he's thrown across the bar. But after we fight, we're the two sorriest people you've ever seen.

If our drummer left, I'd be happy because he's just not very good. He needs to practise more. But if he did leave that would be the end of Oasis. It's all five of us or nothing.

However, Noel changed his mind and used his Paul Weller connection to bring in Alan White on drums, the brother of the drummer in Weller's band. Alan White helped beef up the sound, but Liam couldn't (and still can't) get over the guy's dress sense. Liam is very offended by the fact that all these London boys seem to wear their trousers at half mast to show off their shoes and socks. It bugs him like mad. Alan White would have his eyes opened by a few things before he'd be initiated properly into this group of Mancunians.

We were all concerned when Paul McGuigan claimed exhaustion and temporarily quit the band. Guigsy is quite happy with the money he's made and really just wants to settle down. All the touring has taken its toll on him and I know that Bonehead, Liam and Noel would not be surprised if he decided to call it a day. However, when he collapsed with nervous exhaustion just before their *What's the Story Morning Glory* tour, it left the band searching desperately for a bass player. Guigsy was in a bad way and the doctor recommended a six-month break from the band to recover.

His replacement was Scott McLeod who'd formerly played in the Ya Yas, who Oasis had supported and played a few gigs with in their early days. Scott must have felt like he'd been transported to a different planet, going from playing to about 100 people in Manchester to suddenly playing big gigs in front of up to 4000 people with all the attendant security and wearying travel. He couldn't adapt – but the worst thing was the way he just went, leaving the band high and dry, flying back to Manchester on the eve of Oasis's big TV debut in America on the David Letterman show. It set Oasis back in a way. *What's the Story Morning Glory* had just sold 250,000 copies in its first week of release Stateside and the ensuing tour was to culminate in two sell-out shows at London's Earls Court in front of 40,000 people.

All Scott McLeod has ever said about the whole thing is that he just couldn't handle it. It was too big a deal for him. A week after he walked out he told the *Manchester Evening News* that he'd left because he preferred to be with Saint Jack, the band he'd just formed in Manchester with his old school friend Matthew Cottee on guitar and vocals, Noel Jameson and Mike Fonda. As things went, Guigsy made a swift recovery, rejoined the band and saved the day for Oasis.

What's the Story Morning Glory was huge; the biggest-selling album in Britain since Michael Jackson's *Bad* and U2's *Rattle and Hum*, eclipsing even the excellence of *Definitely Maybe*. My mam went to the launch party. Noel's girlfriend, Meg, secretly arranged for our mam to go down, sorting her out her train ticket and a car to pick her up at Euston station. It was quite a day out for my mam, who had never in her life been down to London. She was so excited. Of course, Noel and Liam were really shocked when our mam turned up at the bash at the Virgin Megastore in London. Liam got quite emotional: 'There are tears in my eyes, Mam. If it hadn't been for you, we wouldn't be here now.' Not exactly a revelation, but then he always was a bit slow in his biology class at school.

London was buzzing for the two biggest-ever indoor concerts in Europe on 4 and 5 November 1995. The press couldn't wait. Every ligger and his mate came out of the woodwork for that one. Our Liam had been home just before it. As usual, with every one of his old mates he bumped into he'd have a conversation like this:

'All right?'

'All right, Liam?'

'Do you fancy coming to see us at Earls Court?'

'Yeah, brilliant. Will you send us a ticket?'

'Just see our Bod, he'll sort you out.'

After a month of his mates pestering me, I got on the phone to Ignition Management.

'It's Paul Gallagher here. Could you sort us out another eight tickets for Earls Court, Alec?'

'Eight? Who are they for?'

'Our Liam's mates.'

'You're such a ligger. Who are they *really* for?'

A ligger – what an insult! To be fair to our Liam, he did go mad at Alec who works at the management company.

As Oasis have got bigger and bigger, the free tickets and guest passes disappear to curry favour with various socialites in London. All their hangers-on and their mates expect free tickets; it's the price of belonging to their club. Meanwhile I get icy glares and get blamed by Liam's old mates because their tickets and passes never materialise.

I don't even want to talk about Maine Road. I couldn't believe how many people travelled up from London for those two gigs, crowding into every VIP area at the ground, while all the people who had really helped Oasis out in the early days, like those who'd been responsible for all Oasis's regional radio and TV promotions up to the second album, had to scrounge a few tickets off the promoters SJM. That was a real sheep and goats gig.

Oasis are very newsworthy, especially thanks to our Noel's stories. What's the old saying? When the truth contradicts the legend, print the legend. Because everywhere Oasis go, the press follow, and all the second and third tier celebrities who are publicity junkies follow in their wake. So, Paul Hewitt and all you people in Manchester who can't get free tickets for Oasis when they are playing to 80,000 at Maine Road, but who were always on the guest list when they played to 60 people at the Boardwalk, you know who to blame. Just open up the photo supplement at the front of the *Sunday Mirror* or

News of the World magazines – that's who's been getting your ticket allocation.

All the press that has been gathering around the band, from Liam's early bedroom escapades, to their views on life, other bands and why they are so great, has become a major and worrying preoccupation for my brothers. Which one of them is actually going to buy my mam a house? Will it be the £80,000 house in Ireland or the £145,000 house in Stockport? Is it to be a castle or even the council house she's quite happy living in which would be a snip at £20,000? My mother and I keep up-to-date scrapbooks made up of articles from Britain, Ireland, the US and Canada, and one of the first things Noel and Liam ask when they get home is, 'Where are the scrapbooks?' Then they sit reading about themselves.

I think it's healthy that Liam and Noel have a rivalry. Noel buys himself a big house reported to cost around a million quid, so our Liam reckons he'll buy one soon for a million and a half. That's what I love about my brothers – they've got class.

Oasis swept the board in terms of nominations at the Brit Awards 1996, with Best Album for *What's the Story*, Best Video for *Wonderwall* and Best Group. Nobody else could touch them, and I found all their antics, though somewhat lacking in modesty, very amusing. Noel basically said that compared to Oasis, everything else in Britain is pretty much dreadful, and I couldn't disagree with him.

The Mercury music prize was well deserved and I couldn't see anybody else winning it when *Definitely Maybe* scooped the award for Best Album. I expect them to do a double by winning it this year for *What's the Story Morning Glory*. It will be no contest.

As for the Ivor Novello award for Best Songwriter, our Noel had to share it with those blokes out of Blur, so he refused to accept it. I should think so. After all, besides being a songwriter, Ivor Novello was a top scally. He caused a massive scandal and was put in prison for buying black market petrol during the war, so I'm sure he would have wanted our Noel to be the sole recipient.

Our Liam could have done with being a bit more discreet as far as his *affaires de coeur* went. I mean, he spins two different French girls the same line ('Fancy a holiday in the south of France?'), sneaks off to the toilet for some intimate fumbling, and then ignores them. They are so overwhelmed by his smooth technique, they both sell their stories and bathe in the subsequent publicity and say, 'He was so romantic.' Now I'm a great believer in passion overflowing and an optimist when it comes to relationships, but I'd hardly describe a quickie in the bog with a relative stranger as romantic, not even in Longsight.

Of course, the *News of the World* and the various Sunday tabloids had great fun with our Liam over that one. They had a laugh with Noel, too, and his 'Cocaine on my cornflakes' confessions. My mother and I were subjected to a constant parade of tabloid hacks doorstepping us and then having the cheek to make quotes up and attribute them to my mam. The classic was an old interview my mother had consented to give to Rosemary Barrett of the *Manchester Evening News*. The *Daily Mirror* bought the interview but tagged on a few imaginative remarks that my mother supposedly said about Liam and the above-mentioned French girls:

> I was most disgusted when I read about Liam going in the toilet with that girl, so I said to him, 'Liam, if you're going to do that, at least take the girl up to your room.'

Our mam is a great woman and quite broadminded, but she would never in a million years say such a thing. She wouldn't want to comment on casual flings or know anything about them. After this lie was printed my mother even received hate mail accusing her of making the Irish community look bad.

At 9.30 a.m. just before the Earls Court concerts in November 1995, on a small street in a leafy council estate in Burnage, there was a knock on the door.

'Oh hi, I'm from *GMTV*, ITV's breakfast show. Would it be possible to interview you and your mother about your brothers and their forthcoming concerts?'

'Hi, posh and fairly attractive female from GMTV. No. See you.'

'Oh please. We'd only be a minute or so.'

'No, sorry love.'

'We've just travelled 200 miles from London. Just two minutes.'

'Oh, you poorly paid TV people have just travelled over 200 miles from London. Listen, I don't care if you've travelled from Timbucktu. If you don't go through the proper channels you're not having an interview. Bye.'

Another morning, feeling bedraggled and hassled, and at a low ebb, I'd just signed on at the local Unemployment Benefit Office, and then I heard:

'Mr Paul Gallagher?'

'Yes?' I turned around, dazed, still clutching my benefit card, to be confronted by a reporter and a photographer.

'We are from the *Sun*. Have you just been to sign on?'

The camera was clicking and whirring, like the confusion in my brain.

'Do your brothers give you any money because you're on the dole?' Whirr, click.

'Look this way, Mr Gallagher.'

'What? Money? Oh yeah, our Liam gave us £150,000 two weeks ago, and our Noel gave us about £200,000 the week before that.'

'Now come on, Paul, don't take the piss.'

'You started it.'

Privacy, I remember that. That was the time when complete strangers didn't come around mithering us.

On a warm sunny day on the estate, a gaggle of teenaged girls from Dublin could be heard.

'Hello Paul, is Liam there?'

'No, he doesn't live here any more. How did you find out where we lived?'

'Oh, some lads down the road told us. We had to pay them fifteen pounds for the address, though. Can we have a photo with ya?' Fifteen quid? Bloody scallies.

'Go on, make it snappy.'

The letters are the strangest. My mam used to answer the genuine ones but there are some weird ones.

My brothers are very good at making pop music, but surely there are bigger stories in the world – exposés on genuine human suffering, primary schools on council estates where dysentery is rife, poverty, armed drug gangs in inner cities, ethnic cleansing in the Balkans. This was the real news, not Liam's latest domestic argument with Patsy. I understand that people who work for the tabloids are just doing a job, but haven't they got wives, families or girlfriends? Would they like to be constantly hounded? It's not really journalism. To me, Kate Adie reporting from a distant war zone is journalism, not adults acting like pre-pubescents and coming up with headlines like 'Freddie Starr ate my hamster'.

Liam has suckered the press a few times. One press headline concerning our Liam was 'Oasis Liam to wed':

Oasis frontman Liam Gallagher is to wed his secret girlfriend. He popped the question to long-time lover Francesca Cutler backstage at the Glastonbury Festival. The 25-year-old brunette said yes, despite his reputation as a rock and roll womaniser. She says, 'It's true. We are getting married. Liam asked me out of the blue. I know he goes out with other girls but it doesn't bother me.'

He was typically modest about the match saying, 'I've got 35 cherubs on one shoulder and 49 on the other. But I've picked one for good.' Now the couple plan a traditional white wedding.

I think my favourite bit was, 'He was typically modest'. But the press are always doing it to us so it's good to give them a taste of it, too.

You get all these weirdos selling completely untrue stories to the press about Noel and Liam. One said that Liam used to scratch the cars of Manchester United players when he worked at a car valeting place, particularly the cars belonging to Ryan Giggs and French international Eric Cantona. It's all absolute bull. In fact, Liam thinks Eric Cantona's a top geezer.

Fans have been, and continue to be, a nuisance outside our house. Most of them are OK, but you worry about some, especially the young teenage girls who travel all the way from France, Japan and Italy and then expect us to act like an attraction at Disney World. I hope most of them have got the message that neither Noel nor Liam live at this address any more.

As recently as July 1996 the press were at it again. I was at the T In The Park music festival in Glasgow. A reporter asked me what I thought of Nowaysis, the Oasis covers band. I was annoyed to see them given a prime spot on the bill just for playing Oasis covers, when original bands like Audioweb were shoved on in bad time slots. I said they were all right for a pub gig, but as far as the real future of music goes, they are shit. The following day's headline was 'Older brother hates Oasis'.

For me, the worst invasion of privacy by the press came when Oasis played two nights at the Point in Dublin on 22 and 23 March 1995. This was going to be something very special and yet so easily spoiled.

Chapter 15

Bringing it all back home

The fans in Ireland were desperate to see Oasis again and they got their chance at Slane Castle where Oasis played second on the bill to REM, officially the biggest band in the world. My mother came over for this one and a gaggle of my cousins and an auntie from the Gallagher side of the family came down from Duleek and Drogheda to witness the proceedings. It was a highly charged atmosphere marred by tragedy when two people drowned in the River Boyne that weekend near the site.

Liam seemed to have murder on his mind backstage. The crowd during the concert had been crushing forward and were told twice by Noel and Liam to back away, then they rushed forward again. Some bright spark threw a rock at Liam's head which just missed and embedded itself in one of the band's speakers on stage. It was a good gig, but things were fraught. Hanging around the mobile home trailers afterwards, one of the Oasis road crew, Jason Rhodes, asked REM's tour manager if he could have a pair of passes for him and his girlfriend to see REM at the MacAlpine Stadium in Huddersfield. I don't know if REM were miffed because Oasis had pulled that date due to recording commitments, but the REM tour manager said if Jason wanted to go, he should buy two tickets. Liam was up in arms about this and went for the REM tour manager who scarpered into the band's trailer. Liam's blood was up now, and he started kicking the trailer door and shouting obscene threats. In the end Ian Robertson had to restrain him from kicking the trailer door in. I'd wandered off to get our mam, Auntie Mary and our older Gallagher cousins, Willie and Alan, to bring them to the backstage area. When I returned Liam seemed to have calmed down.

'Good gig,' I said enthusiastically.

Smack. Liam's fist just pounded into the side of my face and my eyes exploded. As I pulled back he was up for more, ripping the sleeve off my jumper. That was it. I just steamed into him. We wrestled to the floor and I ripped his new Lacoste cardigan in revenge. While I was struggling with Liam on the ground our mam was going livid telling Liam to behave himself. Ian Robertson stepped aside – 'I'm not interfering with family business' – before wandering off to get a better view of our scrap. Alan White was standing open-mouthed. Eventually I let Liam up and he immediately picked up a full can of beer and threw it straight at Noel's head. Noel didn't respond and Liam was threatening to start on him. All the guys out of the American rap group Spearhead were watching.

'You guys are brothers? Man, I can't believe it, you're mad.'

Alan White whispered to me, 'You're all mad.'

'You get used to it,' I replied, as I dejectedly pulled off my ripped jumper over my bruised and scratched face. Our mam was beside herself with embarrassment, barking, 'Oi, Liam and Paul, behave yourselves – shaming me in public', and then my two Gallagher cousins who were in their mid to late 30s started on each other, threatening to punch each other's lights out, until their mother, my Auntie Mary, intervened and nipped it in the bud. It was strange seeing my cousins getting like that. It reinforced what I've always thought – we didn't get those moody tempers from our mam's side of the family. It was certainly a Gallagher thing.

When the coast was clear and Liam had cleared off, Bonehead told me that Liam had been like it all day. Apparently, earlier on, U2's Adam Clayton had gone into Oasis's trailer and helped himself to a packet of cigarettes from the band's rider. Liam's hackles rose immediately 'You've got fuckin' millions of pounds, go and get your own fuckin' cigs.' The room, as usual, fell silent and everyone kept quiet, as is the norm when Liam decides he's got too much energy to keep locked in. Beware whoever gets in his way; he's the proverbial bull in the pen.

After the gig, I headed back to my Auntie Mary's for a barbecue with my mam and cousins. I suppose it seems strange that we should see my dad's side of the family, yet not speak to our dad. The truth is that they know what he's like now, although for years he lied to them and used to pretend he was still with us even though we'd left.

Liam and Noel, meanwhile, were standing up ready to ruck at the side of the road, like two tinkers with a grudge. The reason was that Liam didn't want to wait for the police escort, because then they'd be stuck in all the concert traffic and it would take about three hours to go 20 miles. Noel wanted to do things by the book. He ended up just biting his lip and leaving Liam to rant and rave, refusing to react to his fierce taunts and constant provocation. As ever, Bonehead, Guigsy and Alan didn't join in, although Liam invited them to, ending up scowling at them and abusing them when they didn't back him against Noel. Silence is golden if you're a member of Oasis when Liam's having a bad day.

A year later and Oasis, fronted by the Brothers Grimm, were back in the country again. I went over with my mam and met up with my Auntie Kathleen and her three kids and my Auntie Bridie and her daughter. Noel had kindly paid for all the hotels. It was a really good atmosphere. The Dublin crowds are special and everyone was in a good mood. There were familiar faces everywhere. I had to laugh at all the street traders who were selling big bushy stick-on Gallagher eyebrows, and all these Dublin kids walking around with them on. Inside the Point we arrived to catch the last ten minutes of Heavy Stereo's set, my mam sitting down with my aunties and cousins. I decided to go and stand on my own at the back. I've always done this at Oasis gigs. It's like a ritual, although in the places they played in the early days, that's where the bar was.

Oasis opened with 'The Swamp Song'. Liam shouted out to the crowd in a mock Irish accent, 'Are ye mad for it?', and the resultant reply from the crowd was deafening. This was real rock and roll in the raw. Then later Noel donned his acoustic guitar and strummed the opening chords of 'Wonderwall', and the 8500 crowd just started singing en masse. Noel didn't sing one line. He played the whole song through to the end, merely accompanying the 8000 voices on his guitar. I felt a sudden shiver down my spine and a rush of emotion for the first time ever at a concert, and I felt tears streaming down my face. It was almost the first time in my life I've felt that way and I'm only admitting it now. I was crying my eyes out, because I was so happy and I don't believe it could have happened anywhere in the world except Dublin.

Why was I crying? I was born in Manchester and raised there, but Dublin and Ireland are the city and country I hold dearest to my heart. I was thinking of my mother and her childhood; having to leave the country of her birth to escape the terrible poverty trap and look for work, having to leave a country she loved as there was nothing there for her, and then everything she went through afterwards. 'Wonderwall' summed all that up. Noel says that 'Wonderwall' is about his girlfriend Meg, but what makes it a great song is that it can work on many different personal levels. To me, our mother is the Wonderwall; she was always there for us growing up and she never let us see her feeling down. No matter what any of her sons achieve in this life, we'll never be as unselfish as our mother. A month or so later at Maine Road, Noel dedicated 'Don't Look Back In Anger' to my mam, and although I felt a lump in my throat then, I'll always see 'Wonderwall' as my mam's song.

My mam loved the gig. My aunties and cousins did, too. They'd never seen Oasis live before.

The next day the headline in the *Dublin Evening Herald* read 'Gallagher Evening Glory: The world's biggest rock and roll band returns to its roots'. Aileen O'Reilly wrote:

It was a once in a lifetime experience – the Champagne Supernova of gigs – the night when the world's most idolised second generation Irish rebels played the first of two sell-out dates at the Point.

They may be unpredictable, they may be unashamed hell-raising rock and roll stars, but they've crossed the great divide and their songs connect with the rebel in every generation.

Suddenly, last night every other group ever idolised became a distant memory. The future of rock and roll was here, live and ready to be worshipped in all its Mancunian, laddish glory.

It wasn't until later, when Noel emerged alone, armed only with an acoustic guitar, that the audience really got a chance to join in.

As he began to strum the opening bars of 'Wonderwall', the crowd took over and in the most breathtaking highlight of the night, sang the song to the end under the gasoline glow of zippos while he played on, head down, bathed in a solitary spotlight, without singing a word . . .

I'd always hoped my brothers would make it to the top, and I now knew they had. The second night was also a great gig and everyone in the crowd was ecstatic, especially the ticket touts who'd been getting up to £200 a ticket. Everyone was on a high and the two nights had been like two big New Year's Eve parties.

Well, I knew it was all too good to be true. Somebody had said earlier in the day that they'd heard a rumour my father was in town. I just put this depressing bit of gossip to the back of my mind and certainly didn't pass it on to my mother to spoil her night and weekend. As it transpired our dad had in fact checked into the same hotel as Noel and Liam and the rest of the band.

I was drinking in the bar. Noel came over and said, 'Don't look now, but Dad's over there in the corner.'

Liam was up in his room, and Noel was worried about what

Liam would do when he came down and saw his dad, particularly as Liam had already been upset earlier in the day by a phone call from him via the *News of the World*. We decided it would be best if Liam were told, but I doubted that he'd be able to remain cool and collected about it. Noel said he'd go and tell him and I waited, feeling all that old anxiety building up.

What did my dad want with us? He was accompanied by a *News of the World* journalist. They said they wanted a reunion story. What the hell was that supposed to be? They wanted to stir up trouble and rub salt in old wounds in public. If my dad had wanted to know us, why didn't he stay in and look after us when we were younger? I don't even think it was guilt catching up with him; just a nice lump sum of money proffered by the *News of the World*. He's always giving crap to the papers, saying that he wants to see Liam and Noel again and be friends; be a father to them. Well, what about me? I notice I don't get a mention, but then I'm not a rich pop star. If my dad wanted so badly to see Liam and Noel or any of us, wouldn't it have been better for him to have written a heartfelt letter asking for a private meeting? At least then he wouldn't have ruined everyone's weekend and made himself look such an idiot.

After waiting what seemed like an eternity, Liam came down. Sure enough, he went for my dad, threatening him until the security stepped in. I think it was exactly what the press and my dad wanted. Looking back on it, the best way to have got at our dad would have been to nonchalantly say hello and then ignore him. He was after an emotional response and an emotional response is a sign that there's some feeling. I didn't feel anything. I just thought, What a sad old man. As the police came and things were being smoothed over with the hotel management, Noel, Liam and I suddenly found out we were still brothers. We should have been able to laugh it all off, and I must admit I was more concerned for our mam and for Liam than anything. My dad doesn't bother me in that way. He's not interested in me because I'm not rich. I had a bit of consoling to do with Liam and Noel. After things had calmed down, Liam went over to chat to Bonehead. Noel went to bed, visibly upset. I caught a taxi back to my hotel and first thing the next morning I told our mam about what dad had tried to do. My mother was angry that he had the nerve to try and cash in on Liam and Noel after all these years.

Before we left for the airport, I saw Liam and he seemed in good spirits. I wouldn't be surprised if just having the chance to shout at our dad and threaten him had removed some kind of demon from his memory.

The papers that morning were a treat: 'Liam Bops his Pop'; 'Liam Hooks Dad in Anger'. I saw what happened and Liam never laid a finger on him. I suspect if he had, he'd have put him in hospital and our dad would have sued him for assault with lots of encouragement from the papers. Liam had had a very stressful week with constant press attention and boozing which led to a slanging match with INXS frontman Michael Hutchence, an argument with Patsy, and to top it all our dad trying to goad him with a phone call and then an unwanted appearance. The *News of the World*, of course, milked the incident to death. They had even taped the phone call they'd set up earlier and allowed readers a chance to hear it by ringing in on an 0891 number. Low lives.

Our Liam had enough on his mind and doesn't find stress that easy to deal with. Our dad knew that. It was the same method he'd use to annoy blokes on the building site when we worked with him. Later in the lobby he again tried to wind Liam up, when he could see Liam was angry.

'Go and get Patsy Henshit to calm you down,' he said. 'Stop acting like a silly boy.'

Liam was threatening to break his legs while the band's security men dragged him off. Our dad was still trying to get to him: 'You couldn't break Percy Sugden's legs.'

No blows were struck, but the papers got the story they wanted. That, after all, is what mattered to them.

So Oasis have done it. Manchester is buzzing again on band nights, and imbued with that same cocky self-confidence that it had back in '87, '88 and '89. No self-respecting eighteen-year-old lad can get off with a girl unless he dresses and has his haircut like Liam Gallagher. The city is jumping, and Oasis are a talking point. No one doubts that in the next two years or so a band as big as Oasis will emerge again in this town, and everyone is keeping a sharp eye out for 'the next big thing'. There are so many local band nights on now, doing brisk business and showcasing local talent.

Some people say that Noel and Liam's heads have disappeared up their own bottoms which is why they don't live in Manchester any more, but I think it goes beyond that. Noel needed to go off and enjoy his fame and money, get his albums written and recorded and be on hand to keep an eye on the business. Being in a famous band in Manchester isn't a big deal and there's not a lot for your average millionaire to do. Somebody up here sees Mick Hucknall out of Simply Red or Barney Sumner out of New Order and it's, 'So what, he's only a musician.' It made me laugh when Liam went down to the Hacienda at Christmas in 1994 with a huge minder. Everyone was slagging him off. 'Look at that bighead. What's he got a minder for? No one's going to bother him in here, it's only Liam Gallagher.' But would they have said that if Prince or Madonna had walked into the Hacienda with a minder? In 1994, Oasis must have outsold them by about ten to one in the UK. It's just how us Mancunians are – you can't play the superstar in this town, even if you are one. Of course, Liam with his bad boy reputation might not be so safe in Manchester as he is in London, unless he's got plenty of mates with him. Liam is 24 years old and it's the first time he's ever left home, so people shouldn't be too hard on him. Everyone needs to get away from their home town at some point. London will get on his nerves eventually.

Not long ago I bumped into one of Liam's old teachers from St Bernard's primary school. She still works there and said that all these five- and six-year-old pupils know that Liam is an old boy. They put their hands up in class and ask questions like, 'Miss, Miss. Did Liam Gallagher wear a jumper like this when he was at this school?', 'Did Liam have trainers when he was seven?', 'Did Liam used to draw pictures of houses when he was five?', 'Was he any good at colouring in?' and 'Did he have a girlfriend?' It's like 'Watch out Burnage, a whole generation of kids who want to be our Liam are growing up before your eyes'. It'll be like that old science fiction film, *Village of the Damned*, where the aliens take over the kids and then take over the village, only it will be loads of Liam clones walking round abusing each other and trying to be better than each other. Lock up your daughters, lock up your Ready Brek and don't lend them anything. They're coming.

About a year ago, Liam was on Deansgate in Manchester city centre, surrounded by about fifteen girls fawning around him. It's bumper to bumper traffic on that road for most of the day and it's always busy. Two girls in an open-topped car stopped at the lights nearby. Liam knew the girl who was driving. 'Liiaaam,' she shouted to him and he immediately went over for a chat. Deansgate is narrow, with one lane of traffic each way, and her's was the first car at the lights. Those lights changed from red to green, to red again and back to green. In all, they continued chatting for about 20 minutes, so on a hot summer's day our Liam had traffic on Deansgate backed up for quarter of a mile – and not one car in that queue beeped its horn.

Star quality or what?

Encore

PEGGY GALLAGHER

My mother had eleven children and has 24 grandchildren. Paul was her first grandchild and Noel was her second. I think Paul was her favourite but she loved Noel too. She always said Liam was very cheeky and wouldn't do as he was told. When we were in Ireland she'd ask Liam to go and fetch her some turf from the shed and he wouldn't do it. He was always full of the devil and would stand outside her window pulling faces at her. She used to get mad at him and say to me she'd have to call the Garda (the police) after him to teach him some manners. Mind you, she used to spoil them when they were kids. If they couldn't get something off me, whether it was sweets or whatever, they'd always get it off their gran. They had great times in Ireland when they were kids, going down to the beach at Enniscrone with their Uncle Paddy, who'd also take them out playing football and take them fishing.

It makes me sad to think my mother had eleven of us and is living all on her own now. I try to get back to Ireland every year to see her. She's very proud of all her grandchildren, but I think she's got a special fondness for Paul, with him being the first. When he was twelve he bought her a pension book holder out of his paper round money as a little present and she's still got it. She's thrilled when she hears Oasis on the radio – she knows all the songs and was especially delighted when Noel gave her a mention on Gay Byrne's show on TV over there. It would be really nice if she could have seen them play live, but she can't even get up the stairs nowadays. I'm not sure I could live in Ireland – maybe I could get a little holiday home there one day. I'm happy to stay where I am in Manchester. This is my home and it'll always be a home for my boys whenever they need it. They know it's there for them. When Noel first left home to move in with Louise Jones, I missed him like mad, but because he's not been living at home for nearly six years now I've got used to him being away. I miss Liam an awful lot and I'll probably miss Paul most of all when he moves out.

I cried every time I saw Oasis on television early on. *The Word* was the first TV show they did, and that's when I cried the most, but I was really thrilled when Noel went on Channel 4's *Big Breakfast* and said he wrote 'Live Forever' for me. I've had some great times with my boys – they are my life, really, and are very good to me. When I read in the paper that they did this and did that, I just take it with a pinch of salt. It used to upset me at one time, the way the papers used to write about them, but I know what they're like and so do the neighbours – and they've always been smart and well-behaved, or at least while I had an eye on them. I've been to see them play a few times. I especially enjoyed Slane Castle in Ireland and I'm going to see them when they play in Cork later this year. They introduce me to all these famous people. I've met Bono out of U2 and he was a very nice man – he even kissed my hand and said I reminded him of his mother.

I was very ill recently and had to go into hospital – I thought I was on my way out. I caught pneumonia and the boys and their girlfriends looked after me very well. After I came out I stayed at Noel's house in London with my sister Kathleen and nephew Michael, who came over from Ireland to take care of me. Noel went away on holiday, but he left his chauffeur Simon and his Rolls Royce at my disposal and we had a great time sightseeing. Because of my illness, I have to take it easy now and not work any more. I've been looking after men for over 35 years, so now I want to spend more time in my garden and maybe do some travelling. I always dreamt of going to New York, so if Richard Branson is reading this . . . But what I'd really like to do is go over and see Oasis when they play in America and surprise Noel and Liam by just turning up at their concert.

I feel proud and lucky to have all my three sons grown up and healthy, and I'm very pleased for Liam and Noel and their band. I think they'll go from strength to strength and get better and better. I'm proud of Paul too, especially as he had the hardest time growing up – and it was often left to him to look after Liam while I went out to work, when he was only a little boy himself.

Paul and I were really close as he was growing up. He was an easy boy to bring up; he always did what you told him. He never got into any of the rigmaroles that the others got into. He was always on his best behaviour. At parents' night, the teacher used to say, 'Your Paul is a pleasure to teach.' It was the total opposite with Liam.

I always treated my boys the same. I tried to be as fair as possible, but it was Paul who suffered more than the others, being the eldest. He probably had to grow up quicker. I used to ask him to look after Liam and he was marvellous. I could always rely on him to be there for me. When he started to rebel, I told him I was going to throw him out. I threw him out in his underwear in the cold night once until he'd stopped being cheeky.

I think out of the three of them, Paul is the most romantic and sensitive, telling me about his girlfriends and bringing them home. He's often come back from town having bought me flowers. He's very thoughtful like that.

After Liam and Noel's success, my greatest wish is to see Paul do well with this A&R work and band management.

BROTHERS

Money doesn't always bring happiness, however. If it was left to me, I'd like to see the three of them settled down, married, bringing up a family and living just around the corner from me. I'd like to think I could see each of them every day. I suppose every mother wants that.

Peggy Gallagher, March 1996

PAUL GALLAGHER

I'm proud of my brothers and most of all proud of our mother. It's an Irish thing in a way – lads and their mothers. I think it was the playwright Sean O'Casey who said, 'If only we had two mothers and no father.' I'm proud to be a Gallagher. I admit I was never the most focused of people growing up. I had dreams like anybody else, but no goals. It was going to take an almighty kick up the backside to get me finally to do something with my life, and that's what Oasis have been – a forcefully aimed boot where the sun doesn't shine. I was a scally lad. As an Irish boy in Manchester you're culturally torn. You're not English and white or ethnic and black – you are transparent, a nothing. I spent almost half a lifetime living from hand to mouth and being a scally, doing any work I could get and trying to have as much fun as I could. But, like the words of our Noel's song, 'Cigarettes And Alcohol': 'When it comes on top, You got to make it happen.' I made it happen. I took the junk of my life as a main course, sprinkled it with my mother's love and suffering, garnished it with my brothers' fame and desires, stuck it all in this book and shut it. What's fame, anyway? Somebody once asked the late great Bob Marley how it felt to be famous. He thoughtfully stroked his chin, smiled and said, 'Well, I can't answer that, man, because I'm not famous to me.' He didn't reply, 'Being famous, I'm mad for it.' With different drugs came a different attitude.

A lot of people are jealous of my brothers. They look at Noel and Liam and think they've got it all – fame, money, power, women, nice houses, Rolls Royces, millions of fans, talent and charisma. But life is weird and what you gain on the swings you invariably lose on the roundabouts. They can't just nip down the pub any more, they don't know who their real friends are and they don't know who they can trust. All conversation and all life for them begins and ends with Oasis. I'm not even in the band but conversations including the words Oasis, Liam, Noel, fights and arguments are an everyday occurrence. My brain starts going into erase mode; someone speaks to me and I just drift off. I love my brothers' music, but all the other stuff gets tedious.

Can you imagine half an hour of any given day going by when Noel and Liam aren't thinking Oasis, band, music and stardom? Even the down-to-earth, 'we're just normal lads from Manchester' bit becomes too self-conscious. Noel and Liam are both stars and they have to live with that. It's a mind trap, and their love of music and having to prove they are better than the rest ends up cutting them off from everything else. It's the old story of King Midas who loved gold more than anything else in the world, so when he was granted a wish, it was that everything he touched turned to gold. His wife turned to gold, his children, his food. His life became polluted by his own desires, and that's the reality for my brothers. The press try to glamorise it – they want us to think that because somebody is rich and famous they are having a better time than you or I; that they are more important and happier.

Happiness is an ever-expanding concept. No matter how happy you are you could always be happier and so you strive for that, then you get unhappy when you can't achieve it. Me? I'll take a little bit. A little bit of notoriety, a little bit of money, a little bit of happiness and spread it around. I don't want it all; I don't want the whole rainbow. Just give me half a rainbow and peace of mind.

This is my full story. I've never been so honest in my life; honest about how I feel inside when it still seems choked up and mixed up at times, honest about our childhood and growing up and honest when I say I'm a big fan of my brothers' music. If I've left anything out it's because it's gossip, plain fiction or nobody's business but mine.

BROTHERS

What's the future for my brothers? Professionally speaking, they'll go all the way to the very top and be the biggest British band since the Beatles. On a personal level, Liam has never had to even rent a flat in his life, sort out bills and accounts or look after himself. Luckily he's in a financial position to afford to pay others to carry out life's little chores. On the surface you'd say that Liam has got every single thing he ever wanted out of life. Noel, he's sacrificed a hell of a lot to get to where he is now. He's got respect from the people he wanted respect from. He's wealthy and admired in all the right circles, just as he was around our little council estate in Burnage where he grew up. I hope those demons that exist inside him have finally been exorcised or contained.

Finally to me. I can see life's possibilities now that I understand what I'm capable of. A lot of things in life are bullshit, but whether you're a president or some young kid signing on for welfare, one thing in life is for sure: at one time or another you have to swallow a lot of it. I'm just determined that starting now, in the summer of 1996, it's no longer going to be my staple diet.

Rock 'n' Roll? Well, I'll always love good old-fashioned guitar music and going to gigs. I'd like to travel a bit more, read a lot more and learn to chill out. I got tired of begging for places on guest lists, so this summer when Oasis play Kneb-worth and Loch Lomond in Scotland, I'll be getting a good suntan while roaring drunk, gazing at the long blonde sands as they are gently caressed by the cool blue lips of the Caribbean ocean. I'll raise a glass as the sun is setting, turn on my ghettoblaster and pump out: 'You can wait for a lifetime to find your place in the sunshine, You might as well do the white line, 'Cos when it comes on top, You gotta make it happen.' Cheers, Noel. Cheers, Liam. *Slainte*, Mother. I'll send you a postcard and bring you back a nice present. God bless.

Paul Gallagher, July 1996

Early Oasis gigography (1991–93)

Oasis gigs 1991

1. 18th August
BOARDWALK,
MANCHESTER
Supporting Sweet Jesus

Oasis gigs 1992

2. 15th January
BOARDWALK,
MANCHESTER
Supporting Sweet Jesus

3. 19th April
DARTFORD POLYTECHNIC
STUDENTS UNION, KENT
Supporting the Ya Yas

4. 20th April
HIPPODROME,
MIDDLETON
Supporting Revenge

5. 5th May
CLUB 57, OLDHAM
Supporting the Ya Yas

6. 14th July
BOARDWALK,
MANCHESTER
Headlining

7. August
BOARDWALK,
MANCHESTER
Support band

8. 13th September
VENUE, MANCHESTER
Support band in
The City Fringe

9. 22nd November
BOARDWALK,
MANCHESTER
Supporting Molly Halfhead
and the Cherries

Oasis gigs 1993

10. 5th January
BOARDWALK,
MANCHESTER
Supporting the Essence

11. March
LA BATEAU, LIVERPOOL
Headlining

12. April
KRAZYHOUSE,
LIVERPOOL
Headlining

13. May
BOARDWALK,
MANCHESTER
Headlining

14. 31st May
KING TUT'S WAH WAH
HUT, GLASGOW
Supporting 18 Wheeler

15. July
BOARDWALK,
MANCHESTER
Headlining

16. July
MANCHESTER
UNIVERSITY
STUDENTS UNION
Supporting Dodgy

17. July
LE BATEAU, LIVERPOOL
Headlining

18. 11th September
THE DUCHESS, LEEDS
Support band

19. 14th September
CANAL CAFE BAR,
MANCHESTER
Creation Bands Night with
18 Wheeler, during
In The City

20. 7th October
MANCHESTER
UNIVERSITY STUDENTS
UNION
Supporting Liz Phair

21. 14th October
MANCHESTER
UNIVERSITY STUDENTS
UNION
Supporting the Milltown
Brothers

22. 27th October
KEELE UNIVERSITY
Supporting the BMX Bandits

23. 28th October
SHEFFIELD UNIVERSITY
Supporting the BMX Bandits

24. 1st November
THE WHEREHOUSE,
DERBY
Supporting the BMX Bandits

25. 3rd November
WULFRUN HALL,
WOLVERHAMPTON
Supporting the BMX Bandits

26. 28th November
THE LEADMILL,
SHEFFIELD
Supporting CNN

27. 1st December
THE BIRMINGHAM
INSTITUTE
Supporting St Etienne

28. 2nd December
THE PLAZA, GLASGOW
Supporting St Etienne

29. 4th December
WARWICK UNIVERSITY
Headlining

30. 8th December
WULFRUN HALL,
WOLVERHAMPTON
Supporting Verve

31. 9th December
MANCHESTER
UNIVERSITY
Supporting Verve

32. 10th December
THE CAT HOUSE,
GLASGOW
Supporting Verve

33. 11th December
THE MILL,
PRESTON
Supporting Verve

34. 14th December
THE KINGS HALL,
BRADFORD
Supporting Verve

35. 16th December
KRAZYHOUSE,
LIVERPOOL
Supporting Real People

Discography

UK

Label: Creation

7" Singles		Highest top 40 chart position
Supersonic	11 April 1994	31
Shakermaker	20 June 1994	11
Live Forever	8 August 1994	10
Cigarettes And Alcohol	10 October 1994	7
Whatever	19 December 1994	3
Some Might Say	24 March 1995	1
Roll With It	14 August 1995	2
Wonderwall	30 October 1995	2
Don't Look Back In Anger	19 February 1995	1

Albums		
Definitely Maybe	29 August 1994	1
What's the Story (Morning Glory)	2 October 1995	1

Ireland

Label: Creation

7" Singles		
Supersonic	5 April 1994	—
Shakermaker	20 June 1994	3
Live Forever	8 August 1994	17
Cigarettes And Alcohol	10 October 1994	23
Whatever	19 December 1994	5
Some Might Say	24 April 1995	3
Roll With It	14 August 1995	2
Wonderwall	30 October 1995	2

Albums

Definitely Maybe	29 August 1994	9
What's the Story (Morning Glory)	2 October 1995	1

USA

Label: Epic

US Promos

Live Forever (LP Version	August 1994
Supersonic (Edit/LP Version)	January 1995
Rock 'N' Roll Star (Edit/LP Version)	January 1995
(What's The Story) Morning Glory	October 1995
(What's The Story) Morning Glory (Edit/LP Version)	October 1995
Champagne Supernova (Edit/LP Version)	1995
Wonderwall	November 1995
Live In Chicago	1995

7" Singles		*Highest top 40 chart position*
Supersonic	11 September 1994	13
Live Forever	18 December 1994	2
Rock 'N' Roll Star	21 May 1995	36
(What's The Story) Morning Glory	17 September 1995	24
Wonderwall	5 November 1995	1
Champagne Supernova	4 February 1996	1
Don't Look Back In Anger	30 May 1996	10

Albums

Definitely Maybe	16 October 1994	1
What's the Story (Morning Glory)	1 October 1995	2

Our Noel's Song Book

Music in the best sense, does not require novelty; nay the older it is, and the more we are accustomed to it, the greater its effect.

Wolfgang Von Goethe

I have to confess I was always impressed with Noel's ability on the guitar, even when he'd be cranking up the volume on his electric and drowning out that week's episode of *Minder* on the TV and I'd be shouting at him to turn the bleeding racket down. He was moody enough to be in one of those Goth bands of the early eighties, but thankfully, and impressively, as a composer leaned more towards the Beatles than Sisters Of Mercy. It would be impossible for me to go through every available Oasis song, but here are my interpretations, together with some of Noel's, on their most popular songs.

Don't Look Back In Anger – Well, you've read this book. The song title speaks for itself. Noel's themes are always about feeling trapped by the past, wanting to break away and taste his freedom:

> Stand up by the fireplace,
> Take that look from off your face,
> You ain't ever gonna burn my heart out.

When we were younger, our mam always made us have our photographs taken in front of the fireplace. Naturally, we didn't really enjoy this ritual, and our mam used to tell us to put our faces straight and smile. She used to send the pictures over to our relatives in Ireland so they could see what a happy family we were.

Rockin' Chair – This appeared on the B-side of 'Roll With It', but is a far superior song as far as I'm concerned. In fact it's probably my personal favourite.

> I'm older than I wish to be,
> This town holds no more for me.
> All my life I've tried to find a better way,
> I don't care for your attitude,
> You put me down,
> I think you're rude.
> All my life I've tried to find a better way.

I love this song because I was put down a lot of my life and now refuse to be. I think with Noel, it's half a falling out of love song and half his response again to our strange upbringing. There's a sense of being older than your years, of resolving to lead your own life from now on.

Slide Away – This was without a doubt the best song on the *Definitely Maybe* album for me. It's a love song on a par with 'Tin Soldier' by the Small Faces. There's no doubt that this one is about his ex-girlfriend Louise and is about knowing that you're in love, but facing the inevitability of splitting up ... It seemed to just appear in the set, a major brainstorm of Noel's. It says it all about the highs and lows of being in love.

Married With Children – This again is very much Louise Jones inspired. Noel was living with her, playing his songs all day and night at home while she was out working, and when they'd argue she would hit out at what she knew would get at Noel the most. I think he's written a lot of it from her point of view; our Noel examining his conscience.

> I hate the way that you are so sarcastic and
>   you're not very bright.
> You think that everything you've done's
>   fantastic,
> Your music's shite, it keeps me up all night.

BROTHERS

Live Forever – I've always thought that this one is one of Noel's anthemic odes to liberty and our mother . . .

> Maybe I don't really want to know,
> How your garden grows,
> Cos I just want to fly.
> Lately did you ever feel the pain,
> In the morning rain,
> As it soaks you to the bone.
> Maybe I just want to fly,
> I want to live don't want to die.
> Maybe I just want to breathe,
> Maybe I just don't believe.

Our mother is an obsessive gardener; it's her pride and joy and we all used to help her in it. When our dad was living at home it was just about her only pleasure and I think Noel had always wanted our mam to feel brave enough to move us all away from him. This is one of our mam's favourite songs.

Wonderful – As ever there are many different themes inter- twined in this song. You always have to watch for the odd line in Noel's songs. They are rarely about just one subject. He knows everything in life intertwines and has a knock-on effect. Yes, 'Wonderful' is a love song and is in part about Meg Matthews, but I personally think there's an ode to our mother in there, again going back to the time when we left our father and found our freedom.

> Today is gonna be the day,
> They're gonna throw it back to you,
> By now you shoulda somehow,
> Realised what you gotta do,
> I don't believe that anybody
> feels the way I do
> about you now.

It's another great favourite of our mother's.

Talk Tonight – This is Noel's paeon to the pressures of fame, feeling rootless and alone. Noel's the one who carries all the pressure in Oasis. He's the man who has to keep delivering the songs and make sure the band stay up to scratch and don't start resting on their laurels. It's why Oasis have still got their best to come. Noel needs and wants to keep impressing people and as long as a songwriter and group do that, they'll stay at the top for a very long time.

Fade Away – I know Noel's particularly proud of these lyrics. With a few stolen riffs from an old Wham song, this is about how all the dreams you have as a child fade away so quickly when you're faced with the brutality of the real world. Again it's Noel experiencing that 'life as trap' syndrome, wanting to be free. When you're a kid you always want to be a spaceman when you grow up, and you believe that it is quite possible. What happens to that belief; is it unrealistic? No kid ever said 'I want to pack boxes in a warehouse'.

D'yer Wanna Be A Spaceman? – 'Fade Away' part one. Memories of childhood and hanging around with mates, day-dreaming and escaping from the tensions of life at home and at school.

Noel's songs are full of references to drugs and the scally dream of breaking out of the trap in your mind. It's a sense of 'sieze the day' – if you want to make something of yourself do it now. Freedom is the big issue; freeing yourself from the restraints others put on you – restraints imposed because of your class and ethnic background or any part of your make up. Turn every disadvantage into an advantage. I've known him all my life, but as a songwriter he rarely fails to impress me. There's a lot going on in that noggin of his. Rest assured, it'll be a good while before that well runs dry.